NEW HEAVEN?
NEW EARTH?

An Encounter with Pentecostalism

NEW HEAVEN?
NEW EARTH?

An Encounter with Pentecostalism

Simon Tugwell OP, George Every,
John Orme Mills OP and Peter Hocken

Preface by
Professor Walter Hollenweger

TEMPLEGATE PUBLISHERS
Springfield, Illinois

First published by
Darton Longman and Todd Ltd.
89 Lillie Road
London SW6 1UD
England

Published in
the United States of America in 1977 by
TEMPLEGATE PUBLISHERS
302 East Adams Street, P.O. Box 963
Springfield, Illinois 62705

ISBN 87243-072-3

Contents

Preface
"Towards a Charismatic Theology"

PROFESSOR WALTER HOLLENWEGER
Professor of Mission in the University of Birmingham

A GENUINE DIALOGUE with the Pentecostal movement will lead the traditional churches not to imitate the Pentecostal movement, but to make a *critical* examination of their own tradition. A dialogue with the traditional churches should not lead the Pentecostal movement simply to become assimilated to them, it should lead the Pentecostals to look critically at the original task of the Pentecostal movement in the setting of Christianity as a whole.

With these words I concluded my *The Pentecostals* some years ago[1]. I expected the Anglican neo-Pentecostals to tackle the task of a 'charismatic theology'. By and large – with some notable exceptions – they took up one of two positions. Either they did exactly what I hoped would not happen: namely, they imitated the Pentecostal movement in spite of the recommendation by Donald Gee[2], a notable teacher of the classical British Pentecostals, *not* simply to imitate classical Pentecostalism on a higher social level. Or else they said: Pentecostalism has made us better Anglicans. We believe and teach and celebrate everything traditional Anglicanism stands for. There is no need for a critical review of our theological position. Neo-Pentecostalism does not change any of our melodies, but it changes the rhythm and sometimes the key. Neo-Pentecostalism does not change our theology, but it makes it more fervent Neo-Pentecostalism does not change our churches, but it lights them up. It does not change our ministry, but it makes it more credible. It does not change our ecumenical commitment, but it makes it more alive.

Similar things happened within the Lutheran, Reformed and other Protestant traditions. When Pentecostalism reached the Roman Catholic church I felt new hope. But to my dismay most of the Catholic neo-Pentecostals followed the Protestant and Anglican example – of course in the Catholic mood. However, some Catholics understood that 'charismatic theology' does not merely mean to introduce a chapter on 'charismata' in an otherwise unchanged theological system. The authors of this book belong to those few who did understand that 'charismatic theology' is more than an addition, a new mood, a new key, or brighter light.

Although *New Heaven? New Earth?* has been written by four British Catholic theologians, it is nevertheless a thoroughly ecumenical book. Indication of their ecumenical approach is that they start with the *reality* of Pentecostal liturgy and spirituality (here and in the Third World) and not with Pentecostal *concepts*. They take as the text for their theological investigation the creative *liturgy* of the Pentecostals and not their *liturgiology*, their 'primal screaming' as a break-through into communication and not their theories on communication, the ways in which their *lived reality* transcends the characteristically Protestant and Evangelical *propositions*. They judge Pentecostalism not simply on its own evidence but on what it is likely to contribute in the long run for the whole of God's people.

And what it contributes in the first place is confusion, although that should not astonish us. The first Christians brought confusion to the synagogue. The first missionary, the apostle Peter, brought confusion to the apostolic committee in Jerusalem when he went to the heathen officer Cornelius and discovered that the Gospel was bigger than he and his fellow apostles had thought [3]. Saint Thomas contributed confusion when he used the insights and tools of Aristotle in Christian theology. So did the Franciscan and Irish saints and last, but not least, the reformers. The reception of the Kimbanguist churches [4], the important and growing Aladura [5] and other charismatic African independent churches, into the World Council of Churches in Canterbury (1969) and Nairobi (1975) will not only strengthen the charismatic understanding of ecumenism in World Council circles but will also confuse them. 'Ecumenism, it needs to be said, leads from clarity into confusion – in particular from the unreal clarity that characterises every self-sufficient and self-explanatory system into .. apparent confusion ... a form of chaos over which the Spirit of God broods and out of which the Spirit of God is forming the richness of the new creation' [6]. In this ecumenical and charismatic confusion the 'primordial words' might be uttered which are understood without the need for 'clearer' and

10

cheaper explanations. Unfortunately our 'theological poets' are all too often silenced when their words are strait-jacketed into false clarity[7]. So far the traditional churches have made the committee room the principal locus for the re-ordering of Christian ritual and ecumenical relationship, as if the Trinity were organised like an English committee. As long as this is the case we shall be forced to look to churches in the Third World and to prayer and action groups amongst us in order to observe the natural processes at work whereby living worship ritual comes into being and ecumenical grass-root fellowship pushes ecumenical thinking forward.

Challenging indeed, one is tempted to say. One might go on to ask: What is 'false clarity' and what is 'true clarity'? What is 'destructive confusion' and what is 'creative confusion'? If it is true - as the authors imply – that speaking in tongues, prophecy and apocalyptic world views are not intrinsically Christian but in fact fundamentally human - one might ask further: When and under what conditions does an apocalyptic vision turn into a tyrannical time-table or a meaningless speculation? When on the other hand does it become a life-sustaining glorious hope? When and under what conditions does prophecy become the religious small-talk of the self-sufficient, self-centred religious sect or even the cause of our and others' enslavement? When on the other hand does it become the eye-opener that makes us aware of aspects, dimensions, colours, thoughts, even feelings and fragrances, which were always there, but of which we were unaware? When and under what conditions is 'speaking in tongues' just another stuffy ritual which appears precisely on time, just like the Nine O'Clock News? [8] When on the other hand does it become the break-through into communication with God, the universe, humanity, myself, the *ecclesia catholica* at large?

These are the kind of questions I expected a charismatic theology to take seriously, a theology which starts consciously with the 'confusion' of an ecumenical-catholic-pentecostal spirituality. In this volume I found four authors who were prepared to wrestle with these questions. They are Roman Catholic, I am Reformed. They are British, I am Swiss. But their questions are my questions (and incidentally many of their answers are also answers which make sense to me, but that is not important). Could it be that these questions are a kind of provisional clarity, a kind of provisional 'statement' towards a charismatic theology? And incidentally

11

towards a new understanding of charismatic ecumenism?

For, it seems to me, the spirituality of our ecumenism and the ecumenicity (or catholicity) of our spirituality will be the acid test for all that we do in the church. In a review of Simon Tugwell's *Did You Receive the Spirit?*, a black pastor in a little-known American Pentecostal church expressed this as follows: In the preface Tugwell says, 'If there is anything in the book that turns out to be contrary to the mind of the church, I pray that it may be blotted out from the minds of all who read it'. To this the black pastor, Herbert Daughtry, asks: 'I wonder which church Tugwell means? Coptic? Baptist? Pentecostal?' [9]

I cannot answer for Simon Tugwell nor for the other authors of this book. But I know which church I mean, which I believe to be indestructible. It is that church which is still in the making, that church which is ahead of us. What forms that coming church will take is difficult to say. But I do not believe that it is possible to turn back again to the denominationalism and sectarianism of the past. Too much has happened in the charismatic and ecumenical field. I do not know whether we will ever achieve that ecumenical-catholic-pentecostal all-embracing charismatic theology. Present theological tools might be inadequate to bring into focus that reality which could perhaps emerge. That would be a challenge for theologians to think bigger and deeper, to ask wider and more ecumenical questions, to look for better tools. This book is an invitation to search for such tools.

[1] W. J. Hollenweger *The Pentecostals*, London 1972, p. 508.

[2] Donald Gee 'To Our New Pentecostal Friends', *Pentecost*, no. 58 (1962), p. 17

[3] Discussed in detail in W. J. Hollenweger *Evangelism Today*, Belfast (Christian Journals Ltd.), 1976.

[4] The most up-to-date research on Kimbanguism in W. Ustorf *Afrikanische Initiative. Das aktive Leiden des Propheten Simon Kimbangu* (Studies in the Intercultural History of Christianity, Vol. 5), Berne and Frankfurt (Lang), 1975. Cf. also W. J. Hollenweger *Pentecost Between Black and White*, Belfast (Christian Journals Ltd.), 1975

[5] Cf. J. D. Y. Peel *Aladura: A Religious Movement among the Yorubas*, London OUP, 1968.

[6] Peter Hocken in this volume, p. 50.

[7] Simon Tugwell in this volume, p. 147.

[8] Cf. again Donald Gee 'How to Lead a Meeting; the Breaking of Bread Service', *Study Hour* 5/2, 15.2 1964, pp. 27-29. W. J. Hollenweger 'The Social and Ecumenical Significance of Pentecostal Liturgy', *Studia Liturgica* 8/4 (1971-72), pp. 207-215 and 'Conversion: L'homme devient homme' in *Chemins de la conversion*. Rapports, échanges et points de vue de la XLVe semaine de missiologie de Louvain 1975 (Museum Lessianum, section missiologique no. 60), Brussels (Desclee de Brouwer), 1975, pp. 78-101.

[9] Herbert Daughtry in *International Review of Mission*, 63/252, Oct. 1974, pp. 580-583.

The Significance and Potential of Pentecostalism

PETER HOCKEN

CONTENTS

Introduction

PENTECOSTALISM IS A major topic of contemporary Christian interest; the church press abounds with accounts of 'charismatic happenings' and with admonitions to the Churches to face the challenge of Pentecostalism. In a period of runaway inflation with the publishing world particularly vulnerable, the market for pentecostal literature is one area of sure and undoubted expansion.

This represents a remarkable shift from the days when other Christians regarded Pentecostals as sectarian fanatics, whose existence and multiplication was simply to be regretted. From being objects of suspicion, Pentecostals have become subjects of respectable interest, not merely to students of the esoteric but at all levels of Christian conversation.

The principal cause of this change is the increasing penetration of the traditional Churches[1] by the pentecostal movement or charismatic renewal[2]. The unexpected outbreak of pentecostal groups in the Roman Catholic Church has played an important part in making Pentecostalism more respectable – a possible irony of the Spirit – for this has made more problematic the ready classification of Pentecostalism as a form of Evangelicalism, whether legitimate or deviant. The co-existence and interpenetration of extempore prayer in a pentecostal style with liturgical forms of worship and a sacramental emphasis has drawn the attention and interest, not only of Catholic Christians, but also of those among the ecumenically-committed who have not hitherto shown much sympathy with the Evangelical cause. The spread of Pentecostalism beyond the Evangelical world[3] marks a check to this polarisation

17

between ecumenicals and Evangelicals, for the neo-Pentecostal outside Evangelical circles is typically open and sympathetic to the ecumenical movement and naturally understands his pentecostal flowering as itself an ecumenical occurrence.

These factors are particularly operative in the Anglo-Saxon world – both with the spread of the charismatic movement and in general attitudes to Pentecostalism among white Christians. When we extend our horizons beyond Europe and North America, we find another and perhaps more significant reason for taking seriously the whole pentecostal explosion. For in an age when the traditional Churches have accepted, at least in theory, the right of Third World Churches to be truly indigenous and free from all forms of ecclesiastical colonialism, Pentecostal-type Churches and sects are amongst the most successful, in terms both of numerical expansion and of cultural adaptation[4]. As the centre of gravity of the Christian world moves south, and we pass from the age of Amsterdam and Evanston to that of Bangkok and Nairobi, the pentecostal voice is more centre-stage and less an interesting but fringe development.

The accelerating flow of pentecostal printed matter has consisted almost entirely of the testimonial, the didactic and the apologetic[5]; there has been much less serious theology[6]. Pentecostals readily explain their own success and impact in terms of the power of the Holy Spirit and the rediscovery of the 'Full Gospel'[7] and tend to regard studies of a more analytic kind as profane intrusions on the unadulterated work of God.

Whilst Christian theologians have been slow to take Pentecostalism seriously, the subject has attracted the attention of the behavioural sciences, the sociologists[8] even more than the psychologists[9]. Indeed theologians unsympathetic to enthusiastic heart-religion are likely to treat the studies of the behavioural scientists as sufficient explanation for these extravagances of the human spirit. The sociological writing ranges from general theory concerning the rise and fall of sects to studies of particular sectarian groups; whilst the former show the similarities between pentecostal groups and other sects, the latter are more likely to pick out differences within the pentecostal world, e.g. between black and white Churches, between first and second generation immigrants, between classical and neo-pentecostals[10]. However, whilst the theologian needs to acknowledge the necessity of such studies, he cannot remain satisfied with their explanations, however competent

18

and comprehensive, unless he is to abdicate his own discipline and faith.

This essay is written, not against the behavioural scientists, but as complementary to their studies in the distinct discipline of Christian theology. This theology takes account both of the divine and of the human, that is, of primary and secondary causes. The theologian attempts to understand what is happening in terms of the acts of God and of the acts of men. It is characteristic of the Catholic tradition to maintain that the efficacious Word of God necessarily produces created effects, and that what is created is material for human understanding. Theology studies these data precisely as the work of God in man as perceived by the light of faith.

The theologian concerned with Pentecostalism is then concerned to affirm the legitimacy and importance of his contribution in the face of two quite opposite attitudes: the Pentecostal who is apt to regard attribution to God as all-sufficient, and the humanist who would only admit the findings of empirical science. Such a Christian theology is an essential ingredient in any assessment of the religious significance of the whole pentecostal movement.

The distinctive features of Pentecostalism

ANY THEOLOGICAL ANALYSIS of the pentecostal phenomenon must attempt to identify the characteristics that distinguish the Pentecostals from other Christians.

Such an attempt must, I believe, examine the strengths of Pentecostalism before noting its weaknesses, because only its positive features reveal its significance and potential. This section quite deliberately ignores the seamy side of Pentecostalism, prescinding from its banalities and its blind spots, though these will receive some attention subsequently, as factors within the complex world of Pentecostalism threatening the realisation of its potential.

This task of identifying distinctive features cannot be done from books alone; a study of pentecostal literature in search of the distinctively Pentecostal will yield such items as Baptism in the Spirit, and the gifts of the Spirit (especially tongues, prophecy and healing), the collection of which may then be regarded as 'the essence of Pentecostalism'. This essay follows a different method:

19

the distinctive features here selected have been chosen as a result of participation, not merely observation, in Pentecostal services; the authors quoted are generally adduced as written evidence in support of my experience and judgment; the real test of what is here affirmed must be its correspondence with what Pentecostals of all shades do, not simply with what they think they do. Naturally what I have come to regard as distinctive features are seen and interpreted through Roman Catholic spectacles; that is not a drawback, but it does need complementing by similar observations from other Christian traditions.

The Rediscovery of charismata pneumatika. Pentecostals who simply point to God as the explanation for pentecostal achievement will often add reference to 'baptism in the Spirit' and the nine Gifts of the Holy Ghost.[11] This is indeed to take a first step on the road of theological explanation, but if the grounds for distinguishing these nine are not indicated, then the theological reflection has hardly begun.

Among the activities described as *charismata* in the New Testament, there can be no doubt that Pentecostals regard the nine listed in 1 Cor. 12: 8 – 10 as of particular significance in the recovery of the apostolic pattern of ministry in the power of the Spirit. Whilst many classical Pentecostals simply state that there are nine Gifts of the Holy Ghost[12] most neo-Pentecostals seek to relate these nine to other lists of *charismata* found in the New Testament, e.g. in Rom. 12: 6 – 8 and 1 Peter 4: 10 – 11.[13]

Whilst the classical Pentecostals generally emphasise 'Baptism in the Spirit',[14] the neo-Pentecostals often give greater attention to the nine Corinthian charismata, partly because of difficulties with classical Pentecostal teaching on 'Baptism in the Spirit' and partly because they identify the recovery of these gifts as the distinctive feature of the pentecostal movement.[15]

The greater theological concern of many neo-Pentecostals, together with their need to explain themselves within their own traditions, has led to numerous attempts to classify charismata, a task rarely attempted by classical Pentecostals. So authors use such terms as charismatic gifts, extraordinary gifts and supernatural gifts; few use the Pauline phrase 'spiritual gifts' still favoured by most classical Pentecostals.[16]

This neo-Pentecostal terminology reflects the tension between, on the one hand, the conviction that the nine Corinthian charismata are of particular significance, and on the other hand a desire to relate these to other New Testament charismata and to avoid all accusations of focusing on the extraordinary and sensational.

None of the proposed alternatives are satisfactory. The most commonly used, that of 'charismatic gifts'[17] is tautologous (the idea of a non-charismatic gift is a contradiction in terms) and focuses on the manner of reception (the *quo*) rather than on the nature of what is received (the *quod*).

The phrases 'extraordinary gifts' and 'supernatural gifts' are found in a few Roman Catholic authors[18] and clearly arise from a concern to locate these charismata within a received theological framework. 'Extraordinary gifts' suggests that the decisive criteria are either rarity (extraordinary in occurrence) or visual impact (extraordinary as phenomena);[19] not surprisingly this phrase has little appeal within the pentecostal movement, the whole thrust of which is to present these gifts as part of ordinary Christian life. 'Supernatural gifts' may suggest the lack of a natural basis for these activities and can imply that other New Testament gifts are not equally the work of grace.[20]

Some authors deal with this label problem by varying their terminology and avoiding technical terms, thereby attaching less theological weight to the particular phrases used.[21]

Why are neo-Pentecostal writers somewhat reluctant to use the language of spiritual gifts, of *charismata pneumatika*, found in 1 Corinthians?[22]

Two factors are certainly relevant: the meaning of *spirit* in received Christian usage and the range of meanings given to *pneuma* in St. Paul. In Western Christian usage, *spirit* has hardly been a central concept; in St. Paul *pneuma* is a basic term though with various levels of meaning.[23]

E. Schweizer writes of *pneuma*:

> For Paul the Spirit of God is not an odd power which works magically; the Spirit reveals to the believer God's saving work in Christ and makes possible his understanding and responsible acceptance thereof. For this reason the *pneuma*, though always God's Spirit and never evaporating into the *pneuma* given individually to man, is also the innermost ego of the one who no longer lives by his own being but by God's being for him.[24]

21

This passage endorses what others have called 'the apportioned Spirit'[25]; but it is very doubtful whether all anthropological usages of *pneuma* in Paul can be subsumed within this category.[26] Indeed, it may be that the widespread tendency to interpret *to pneuma mou* in 1 Cor. 14: 14 in terms of the apportioned Spirit of God follows from the assumption that glossolalia is essentially an ecstatic form of utterance.[27]

The listing of a distinct category of charismata in 1 Corinthians 12: 8 – 10 is, it would seem, more the work of the Corinthians that of Paul himself;[28] the Christians in Corinth have written to the Apostle with questions about 'spiritual gifts' (cf. 1 Cor. 7: 1 & 12: 1) and the most that can be claimed is that Paul accepted their terminology in his reply. So he can urge them to 'earnestly desire the spiritual gifts' (1 Cor. 14: 1).[29] But this classification, which reflects interests foreign to Paul's basic concerns, is not used elsewhere in the Pauline writings;[30] in fact nowhere else besides 1 Corinthians 12 – 14 does Paul make any classification within the sphere of charismata. So, for example, the list in Romans 12: 6 – 8 includes one charisma listed in 1 Corinthians as 'spiritual', viz. prophecy, along with other gifts not so described, viz. service, exhortation, the giving of aid.

The reappearance in the 20th century Pentecostal movement of the whole range of charismata described in 1 Corinthians 12 as *pneumatika* suggests that there are objective grounds for distinguishing these from other New Testament charismata, and that Paul's lack of interest in this distinction may be due to the familiarity of the first Christians with the full range of gifts, pneumatic and other.

I am suggesting then that what distinguishes the charismata described in 1 Corinthians as *pneumatika* is the particular level or zone of the human that they activate and engage.[31] What is new in Pentecostalism is not the occurrence of particular pneumatic phenomena nor the initial opening-up of the pneumatic dimension in individual Christians;[32] rather is it the organisation, embodiment and expectation of all these gifts within the life of Christian communities, i.e. the articulation and organisation in corporate Church life of what has over the centuries been known only spasmodically in isolated instances.

This restoration of *charismata pneumatika* as part of normal Church life can be understood theologically as the reactivation in Christian community of levels and capacities of the human spirit that have long lain dormant in Christian life. The unfamiliarity of these pneumatic activities reveals to Western Christians the extent' to which their religion has become a cerebral affair, engaging the mind more than the heart. However,the rediscovery-view of spiritual gifts is a white Western perspective; for many Christians in the Third World, the exercise of these capacities in Christian life is a Christianisation, a penetration by the Holy Spirit of God, of faculties already active in worship and human communication. Thus David Barrett in his analysis of contemporary religious movements in Africa notes that the Christian message as it got through to Africans was very different from the gospel the missionaries thought they were proclaiming, and he identifies the differences in terms of the pneumatic:

> These grievances became articulated in certain biblical themes differing from tribe to tribe but centering around the desire to manage church affairs free from foreign control, the desire to shake off white political domination, and emphasis on *pneuma* (spirit), and the desire to experience biblical release from sickness, witchcraft and sorcery: in short, the desire to control their own destinies by exercising the biblical power promised to the people of God and derived from *pneuma*.[33]

This emphasis on the human spirit is alien to Pentecostals only if it is presented as a demythologising of the Holy Spirit, that is to say, if one is in effect saying: 'It isn't really the Holy Spirit, it is only the human spirit.' A theology of the Spirit faithful to the New Testament will rather see that every breath of God's Spirit is life-giving to man, and that it is only the coming of God's Spirit that truly reveals the full potential of man, the humanity of Jesus Christ. Such an approach shows more clearly than theologies of the Spirit based on constant miraculous interventions *ab externo* how the exercise of *charismata pneumatika* is no indication of Christian maturity[34] and how the phenomena alone are no sure guarantee of the Holy Spirit.[35]

Seeing such phenomena as activities of the pneumatic in man means that the levels activated by glossolalia are the same in Christian prayer as in devil worship, but the meaning and effects in the two instances are diametrically opposed. It is the same level in man, that in one case is being opened to the creative work of the Holy Spirit of God as in the other is being enslaved to the powers of evil.[36]

The possibility of abuse is no more a ground for anxiety about these phenomena *in se* than it is in any other areas of human activity, e.g. of the human reason.

Identifying the basic rediscovery of Pentecostalism in this way takes the weight off the disputed question of 'Baptism in the Spirit'; the pentecostal contribution is the functioning of the pneumatic under the influence of the Holy Spirit (and its interaction with the rest of Christian life), whereas spirit-baptism only concerns the entrance into this dimension. The objections to a rigid categorisation within the Christian life, dividing off those filled with the Spirit from the converted not yet filled, are basically psychological; that is to say, that the levels or layers of the human are not so mutually exclusive as such a theory presupposes, nor is there only one road into the depths of man.

It is then insufficiently precise to say that Pentecostalism involves the rediscovery of charismata in general. Nonetheless the rediscovery of *charismata pneumatika*, at least for Western Christians,[37] does seem to generate an awareness of all Christian life as gift and so promote a recognition of endowments already operative as also being charismata.

Receiving God's Word. The spiritual gift of prophecy illustrates the gift-character of the Word of God, not just as given once and for all, but as constantly uttered and renewed; by its regular exercise Pentecostalism shows that Christians are not simply hearers but are also speakers of the Word. Pentecostals believe prophecy to be the utterance under the influence of the Holy Spirit of a word of God addressed to a particular contemporary situation.[38] J. Rodman Williams writes:

> In prophecy God speaks, It is as simple, and profound, and startling as that! What happens in the fellowship is that the Word may suddenly be spoken by anyone present, and so, variously, a 'Thus says the Lord' breaks forth in the fellowship ... in prophecy God uses what He finds, and through frail human instruments the Spirit speaks the Word of the Lord.[39]

Pentecostals are not the first group of Christians to believe in and practise prophecy in the post-apostolic era,[40] nor are they the first to believe in the inner illumination of all believers by the Holy Spirit. But prophecy adds to inner illumination the element of public proclamation (so calling for an element of public discernment) and it is this that Pentecostals have extended beyond a narrow circle of inspired leaders to all 'Spirit-filled' believers.[41]

The Pentecostal practice of prophecy can here confront other Christians, both Catholic and Protestant, with what they officially declare the ministry of preaching to be. The teaching of Vatican II suggests that preaching, particularly the liturgical homily, partakes of the character of the Word of God, and is not simply a human adumbration of that Word.[42] Stronger statements can be found in Protestant sources.[43] Prophecy often shocks visitors to Pentecostal Churches because ordinary human beings claim to receive a Word from God – so whilst in theory the Pentecostal belief that prophecy is for all generations adds little to received theologies of the Word and of its ministry, in practice their prophecy challenges other Christians to believe that they can receive a Word from God to speak in the name and strength of Jesus Christ.

Relating prophecy to preaching as common yet distinct instances of man empowered to speak God's Word shows how spiritual gifts need to be situated in ordinary Christian life, avoiding the danger of treating charismata as freak phenomena unconnected with day-by-day Christian living and worship.

Pentecostal practice here has important consequences for the theology of revelation e.g. promoting a comparison between, on the one hand, the relationship between biblical inspiration and Pentecostal prophecy, and, on the other hand, the relationship between Scripture and tradition, as taught by Vatican II and understood in contemporary Catholic theology.[44]

Common to both instances are:

– the attribution of a clear priority and a 'once and for all' character to the biblical Word

– the interpretation and application of the 'once and for all' biblical Word in an ongoing Christian ministry that shares in the authority of the Word, who is Jesus Christ.[45]

– the impossibility of a total separation between the contrasting elements, the original and the ongoing, there being a sense in which both Christian prophecy and Christian tradition precede and find embodiment in the written Word.[46]

All these activities are both human and divine, the Spirit of God

25

working in, among and through men; both Christian prophecy and Christian tradition are open to some degree of abuse, with the possibility of their expressing human cussedness and immobility, personal pride and arrogance, as well as the saving Word and Gospel of the Lord.[47]

So whilst classical Pentecostals have little time for the notion of tradition, their practice and beliefs concerning prophecy imply a high degree of continuity between the apostolic Church and subsequent generations, with a view of Christian cooperation in the one completed work of Jesus Christ that is closer to the Catholic than to the Protestant tradition.[48] A greater appreciation of the Pentecostals could then help to widen the theological debate on Scripture and tradition, by extension to the spheres of worship and preaching, of prophetic use of the Scriptures and of experience in discernment. In this they have something in common with the Orthodox, who would also criticise Western Catholics for limiting the theology of tradition to the context of doctrine, theology and Church government.[48a]

Body and Spirit. Pentecostals also share with the Orthodox, though in quite a different manner, an acceptance of the body in worship, so that Pentecostal services commonly accord a greater place to bodily activity and movement than received forms of Catholic and Protestant worship. The most obvious examples of bodily involvement are hand-clapping,[49] upstretched arms in prayer and the imposition of hands in ministry to others. Observers may feel that these gestures are easily copied and fail to see that Pentecostal practice has overcome at rather deeper levels the body-soul dichotomy that is our common Western inheritance.

It is significant that speaking in tongues, the charism that is often experienced by Pentecostals as the gate-way into the exercise of other spiritual gifts,[50] is very much a bodily activity.[51] There is something earthy about spiritual gifts! Pentecostal congregations are often aware of the spiritual benefits of really vigorous singing. Most importantly, the art of discernment comes to include an element of diagnosing the spiritual through the physical; the senses are taken up into the process of 'picking up what is there'.[52]

Thus Pentecostal imposition of hands may well include a diagnosis of what is happening in the people being prayed for, e.g. how they are responding to the prayer, what increases and what

26

diminishes tension. Likewise Pentecostal ministration often includes advice (or command) to do something bodily: to stretch hands in the air, reaching out to God in supplication; to breathe deeply, inhaling the breath of God into the lungs and heart; to perform bodily gestures facilitating a release of the Spirit; to make noises in an attempt to trigger off glossolalia.

It is in this 'body-ministry' that a difference between what Pentecostals do and what they say they do is particularly apparent. Their theory is all in terms of the work of God and says little about the contribution of the believer; basic dispositions, especially faith, will be emphasised, but the physical details of ministration rarely feature in their testimonies.[53]

Healing and Salvation. The close interaction of body and spirit in Pentecostal practice can be seen clearly in the prominence of healing in their preaching and ministry. The characteristic Pentecostal message is that Jesus saves the whole person; as Francis MacNutt says:

> ... Jesus was typically Hebrew in his view of man: he did not divide man into body and soul, but he saw him as a whole person. He came to save persons, not just souls. He came to help the suffering in whatever way they were suffering. Sickness of the body was part of that kingdom of Satan he had come to destroy.[54]

This connection between physical healing and then spiritual salvation has been a constant feature in the history of Pentecostalism, despite controversies about the universal healing Will of God and about the ministries of healing evangelists.[55] Classical Pentecostals, at least in the Western world, do tend to envisage healing and saving as distinct blessings of the Lord, though the former is seen as a sign of the power of God for the latter. Third World Christians, less affected by Western dichotomies between body and mind, between physical and spiritual, are less likely to see these blessings as so distinct and to stress bodily healing in a way that is dangerously divorced from the salvation of the whole man.[56]

A development among neo-Pentecostals that may hasten a more holistic approach to healing is the ministry of 'inner healing',[57] which is the extension to the psychological realm of Pentecostal 'divine healing':[58]

> The basic idea of inner healing is simply this: that Jesus, who is the same yesterday, today, and forever, can take the memories of our past and
> 1 *Heal* them from the wounds that still remain and affect our present lives;
> 2 *Fill with his love* all these places in us that have been empty for so long, once they have been healed and drained of the poison of past hurts and resentment.[59]

This development, viewed with some unease by classical Pentecostals because its biblical basis is less obvious,[60] has been most marked in the Catholic tradition as a consequence of the widespread concern to revitalise the sacrament of penance.[61] This psychological extension of the healing ministry leads to a greater awareness of healing as process, not simply as event (classical Pentecostals sometimes seem to think in terms of instantaneous cure or no cure[62]), and to less sharp opposition between supernatural healings and natural processes of healing and recuperation.[63]

The neo-Pentecostals have also introduced a community dimension into the healing ministry with the rise, particularly in North America, of charismatic communities covenanting together in a common life.[64] These households and clusters of households can help all engaged in healing ministries to realise the importance of a setting of love and acceptance for the process of personal healing[65]; they can point to a remedy for the largely unacknowledged problem of healing evangelists leaving a trail of disillusioned sick as well as of exultant healed.

These developments among neo-Pentecostals widen the concept of healing so that in effect all the liberating and transforming works of God's Spirit can be comprehended as forms of healing. MacNutt is heading in this direction when he details four basic kinds of healing:

> there are three basic kinds of sickness, each requiring a different kind of prayer:
> 1 Sickness of our spirit, caused by our own personal sin.
> 2 Emotional sickness and problems (e.g. anxiety) caused by the emotional hurts of our past.

3 Physical sickness in our bodies, caused by disease or accidents.
In addition, any of the above – sin, emotional problems or
physical sickness – can be caused by demonic oppression, a
different cause that requires a different prayer approach.[66]

This schema is still individualistic in formulation and does not
effectively integrate MacNutt's own concern to overcome the
dichotomy between personal healing and social justice.[67] The
growth of socially cohesive pentecostal communities (whether
covenanting communities or grass-roots popular movements,[68]
makes possible a radical social critique, based on the power of the
Holy Spirit to heal sick societies as well as diseased persons.
Elsewhere in this book John Orme Mills draws attention to the role
of apocalyptic imagery in generating expectations of social
transformation;[69] as is seen by John the visionary of Patmos, the
leaves of the tree of life are for the healing of the nations.[70]
   Such an approach contests the simplistic theory of sociologist
Werner Stark about religion and politics:

> If reform is a distinct possibility, a political party rather than a
> religious sect will appear on the scene; if reform is, or is judged, a
> virtual impossibility, a religious sect rather than a political party
> will appear.[71]

Such an analysis, which at the personal level is similar to saying
'Only the medically incurable ask for religious healing, the rest send
for the doctor', pays insufficient attention to the relationship
between the immediately practical and the ultimate vision; it lacks
any typology or sacramental theology.[72] All deliverances now are
partial realisations and foretastes of the final deliverance; all healing
now is a visible pledge of the final resurrection.[73]

   This expectation of corporate healing is not to be reduced to the
social improvement that results from personal religious conversion
and a change to more purposeful moral life.[74] Though this social rise
may appear to demonstrate a concern for social justice, it can remain a private by-product of evangelisation unrelated to the biblical
images of corporate salvation and deliverance. Where this happens,
the healing power of the Gospel is blunted and high personal expectations coexist with acquiescence in the social status quo and

29

minimal expectations of social reform.

There is potential in the Pentecostal movement to bring together the theological concept of the Church as sacrament of salvation[75] and the psychiatric concept of therapeutic community[76] in an exercise of spiritual gifts of healing (*charismata iamatōn en tō autō pneumati*) for the whole body of Christ.

Creative Liturgy. Health and creativity go together. So it is not so odd to select creativity in liturgy as a distinctive contribution of the Pentecostals, even though they equate liturgy with lifeless ritual and typically reject printed orders of service.[77] Sociologists of religion have been quick to point out the highly ritualistic character of Pentecostal worship, and it is perhaps because Pentecostals have been simply worshipping God with body and spirit (rather than trying to produce liturgies with which to worship) that their experience has important lessons for liturgical renewal.

In his study of sectarian religion, Werner Stark observes:

> even in informal services there soon tends to develop a core of set forms . . . As the sect worships Sunday after Sunday, its members notice that certain arrangements are more satisfying than others, and it is no wonder that they are selected for retention and repetition, or at least for frequent re-enactment.[78]

Moreover the form taken by sectarian ritual is likely to be in conscious protest against the patterns of ritual in the established Churches. These features can be verified in some Pentecostal Churches, particularly for example among immigrant groups[79] Malcolm Calley, an anthropologist, in his study of West Indian Pentecostals in Britain not only sees the order and form of their services in ritual terms, but also such activities as the establishment of a new congregation, fasting and the approach to the understanding of Scripture.[80]

Calley's study shows that Pentecostal worship is more ritualist than that of other Christian bodies which have protested against formalism in the name of the freedom of the Spirit. This direct consequence of Pentecostal use of the body has, together with their biblical fundamentalism, led some assemblies to resurrect long-neglected rites and practices mentioned in the Bible, e.g. the washing of feet, anointing with oil, corporate fasting with prayer in preparation for major Church decisions, dancing before the Lord.[81]

The particular genius of the Pentecostals lies in achieving forms of worship combining undoubted leadership with real scope for congregational initiative, both individual and corporate. It is only to the occasional visitor unfamiliar with their worship that the whole event seems chaotic and unstructured.

Besides the possibility of individual interventions from the floor (e.g. in ejaculatory shouts, in prophecy, in a tongue, with an interpretation)[82] Pentecostals often sing and pray together in a spontaneous manner. Corporate singing in tongues allows for an over-all harmony to be formed out of the spontaneous song of each contributor. This form of prayer can be a vivid illustration of the unity of the Body of Christ, within which each member plays his distinctive part and so contributes to the rich harmony of the whole, and is often the feature in pentecostal worship that makes most impact on the first-time visitor. Another and less melodious form of congregational spontaneity, sometimes called 'a word of prayer'[83] involves all praying aloud without conscious attempt to harmonise, when the unity is more in the consciousness of all addressing themselves to the same task. All these experiences can reveal a richer notion of 'active participation'[84] than is generally found in the ordered forms of the traditional Churches, both Catholic and Protestant, for whom vocal participation is largely restricted to saying or singing what is prescribed at the moment appointed.

Within the Pentecostal movement such forms of spontaneity have been developing within an over-all structure orally transmitted.[85] Not anything can be done at any time.[86]

Giving such scope to all worshippers does not deprive the leaders of their role; they are those who exercise particular forms of ministry, rather than those who decide what will happen and when. Openness to the pneumatic makes discernment imperative; the Pentecostal pastor, presiding at worship, ideally discerns what is happening more than he determines what will happen.[87]

This Pentecostal experience contains important lessons for preparation of worship. Despite different attitudes towards fixed and free forms of worship among Catholic and Protestant Christians, their forms of preparation are very similar – a manner of preparation that is basically academic and studied. The less liturgical traditions differ from the more liturgical only in having more that is prepared for each occasion!

Unplanned pentecostal worship is not however unprepared. But the preparation is of a different kind – the preparation of a person for a task rather than of a script for publication.[88]

One Pentecostal contribution is the reminder that the only appropriate preparation for worship is worship, that the only true liturgical creativity is the creativity of man at worship. Without necessarily copying pentecostal forms of worship, other Christians can learn from them the basic unity between spiritual growth and creative ability in prayer and worship. Learning this will expose the barrenness of much liturgical experimentation[89] and the futility of any search for a relevant liturgy that is not one with the search for God. Until this happens, Christians will confuse renewal with the production of a new printed rite[90] and students of ritual will have to look to secular rituals or the worship of independent Churches to observe the processes whereby living social ritual arises and suffers change.

Outward Signs and Inner Reality. The pentecostal acceptance of the body in prayer and worship has important consequences for the *sign* element in Christian life. Though Pentecostals stress the importance of experience of the Spirit, this is not simply an appeal to the private experience of individual believers; rather they expect experience of the Spirit to be accompanied by signs visible to others.[91] Hence an integral element in the classical Pentecostal teaching on 'baptism in the Spirit' is insistence on visible manifestation in outward signs, particularly in glossolalia, often in this context called 'the initial evidence'.[92] Likewise they expect the preaching of the Word to be confirmed by such visible signs, as indicated in Mark's final verse:

> they went forth and preached everywhere, while the Lord worked with them and confirmed the message by the signs that attended it[93]

Simon Tugwell, OP makes an interesting comparison between the Catholic understanding of sacraments as efficacious signs and the classical Pentecostal understanding of tongues as the initial evidence of spirit-baptism.[94] This line of thought shows the need for a bringing together in closer interaction of outward signs and inner reality. Catholic theology, which has long made this distinction between *sacramentum* and *res sacramenti*,[95] has perhaps succumbed to a degree of rationalisation in the face of apparently unimpressive results (the influence of infant baptism is clearly strong) so that the sacramental signs have come to be seen in some isolation from the grace they are held to confer. As a result, Catholics have been led to affirm at one and the same time the efficacity of the sacraments as visible signs of inward grace and the invisibility of the grace conferred! In this process, an important component in the notion of visible sign has been lost, namely that its efficacy is part of its visibility. Without this holding together of efficacy and visibility, signs are reduced to little more than educational aids and handy mementoes.

Though classical Pentecostals do not use the language of sacramentality and indeed do not theorise about signs, their integrated view of body and spirit is shown in a practice in which the visible manifests the invisible as the body manifests the soul. The idea of a totally invisible spiritual reality in man would make discernment impossible, and is ultimately as absurd as a totally invisible man. Man and grace are inseparably both visible and hidden – or better, both visible and becoming visible.[96]

Discernment, which must mean discernment by others in the Christian community, guarantees an element of objectivity. A recognition of the dialectic between subjective claims and objective discernment can help to end the somewhat sterile opposition between the Evangelical appeal to personal experience and the Catholic suspicion of any claims to subjective experience. Indeed the almost total agnosticism of some modern Catholics about personal experience of God is quite untraditional.[97]

The truth enshrined in distinctions between the outward and the inward, between sign and reality, is the complexity of the human; there are many levels of life in man, and activities at any one level have repercussions and implications for other levels. A sacramental theology recognises that everything means more than appears on the surface, an idea that links with the heightened sense of expectation that characterises the Pentecostals.

The Pentecostal attention to the body is more in danger of yielding to the opposite temptation, namely of eliminating the gap between sign and reality: 'All that is there is what you immediately see to be there; all that has happened is what you immediately see to have happened.' Such forms of reduction eliminate man's symbolic

33

capacity and ignore the complex interaction of the various levels of the human.[98]

The Pentecostals have succeeded in integrating the quest for total sanctification with the concern for worldwide evangelisation. Some Catholic difficulty with unfamiliar charismata stems from some centuries of considering the 'extraordinary' only in the context of sanctification;[99] similarly, the sacramental notion of efficacious signs has conceived efficacy in terms of personal sanctification (of believers) unrelated to mission and evangelisation. It is clear that the New Testament understanding of *sign*, the meaning of *semeion*, applies both to the Christian and to the non-believer.[100] Such an understanding is in fact implicit in the teaching of Vatican II on the Church as sacrament,[101] though this missionary dimension has hardly as yet begun to influence the popular conception of sacramental efficacy.

Experience, Discernment and Doctrine. Bringing together outward signs and inner reality alters the relationship between experience and doctrine. So we must examine the common affirmation that Pentecost (in Pentecostal parlance) is an experience rather than a doctrine. This premise is prominent in explanations of how the Pentecostal movement can involve Christians from very varied doctrinal backgrounds, for, it is claimed, they are all having the same experience of the Spirit. Thence it is but a short step to the neat theorem 'Experience unites, but doctrine divides'.

Whilst there is truth in the view that Pentecostalism is based on an experience of the Spirit rather than on a doctrine of the Spirit, a complete dichotomy between experience and doctrine is virtually impossible in practice and any tendency in that direction ultimately devalues the significance of the experience. Any account of the relationship between experience and doctrine must allow for a two-way movement: doctrine following experience as its interpretation and doctrine conditioning, even making possible, subsequent experience.[102] However it is not easy to determine whether people have had a *similar* experience (it is impossible to have the *same* experience); attempts to describe experience involve an element of objectification, which cannot avoid theoretical presuppositions, and with religious experience therefore express a theology and doctrine in the description.[103]

34

As already indicated,[104] Pentecostals do not simply exalt subjective experience over the objective doctrine. What is distinctive in Pentecostalism is that objective counter-balance to subjective experience is not primarily doctrine but visible signs. Rather than claiming that all Pentecostals have had a similar experience, it is more accurate to say that they recognise in each other equally visible (and corporately approved) signs of the Spirit's presence[105].

The subsidiary place accorded to doctrine in Pentecostal life is not so much its subordination to experience as its being secondary to discernment. Whereas for the traditional Churches, the first objective test is that of doctrine, i.e. subscription to/correspondence with official credal formulae, for the classical Pentecostals the primary objective test is often that of discernment, within which of course there are doctrinal elements. The divinity of Jesus Christ enters into any Pentecostal judgment of the rightness of things, but it is an element within the discernment of spirits. The first question a classical Pentecostal will ask is not likely to be whether a person's theology is orthodox, but whether his heart is right; and the condition of hearts is material for discernment.

It is this distinctive ordering of experience, discernment and doctrine that gives the best in Pentecostalism that characteristic quality of spiritual pragmatism that can so astonish other Christians.[106] This has been evident in the rapidity with which many classical Pentecostals have revised their judgment about Catholics in the light of the spread of the charismatic movement in the Roman Catholic Church. Whilst there are Pentecostals who reject the possibility of 'Spirit-filled' Catholics,[107] the experience of Catholics in the charismatic movement has been one of rich welcome from their classical Pentecostal brethren. As a Pentecostal pastor told me: 'We hadn't thought this was possible for Roman Catholics. But the Lord has done it. Praise His wonderful Name!' They still cannot explain. But they cannot deny what they see.[108]

This does not represent the abandonment of objective criteria, but the application of a different order of criteria in which the discernment of spirits is the over-all task. Doctrinal orthodoxy becomes a part of something bigger, namely the determination of what God is doing here and now. This can only be done in the context of prayer and worship, the practice of which is threatened and thwarted by doctrinal heterodoxy.[109]

35

The challenge to Pentecostal self-understanding

This account of the distinctive features of the Pentecostal movement differs markedly from the typical Pentecostal understanding.

Classical Pentecostals and most Protestant neo-Pentecostals commonly identify the movement in terms of the action of God, giving the fullness of the Spirit and the ministry-gifts of the Holy Ghost; this is often described in terms of 'the Full Gospel' and the recovery of the real New Testament patterns of ministry and church order. W. T. H. Richards is representative in saying:

> A truly Pentecostal church is a New Testament church. It follows the same pattern, preaches the same truths, enjoys the same power. Pentecostals maintain that all that was preached and experienced in the early Church is for the Church today and that God never intended that there should be any difference.[110]

This characteristic appeal to the visible signs of God's action is testimony rather than theology. It is a claim or series of claims made in faith and appealing to visible signs in support.[111] Tongues and healing are often given prominence in these claims.[112]

The supernatural character of these phenomena is taken to be self-evident. The work of the Holy Spirit is then understood in terms of miraculous intervention, so promoting an 'all or nothing' view of authenticity. Similar phenomena found in non-Christian religions will then be simply dismissed as forms of satanic counterfeit.[113]

In such assumptions we can see the influence of the Protestant background out of which the Pentecostal movement has developed. The only distinctive features which interest Pentecostals are those advanced as visible evidence of the divine, and these are understood in terms of a theology of nature and grace, of sin and redemption, taken over from the milieux of origin.[114]

That classical Pentecostals commonly interpret Pentecostalism in evangelical Protestant terms is also evident from its ready characterisation as a revival movement. The Pentecostal movement is seen as the greatest and most important in a sequence of spiritual revivals, a view that accords with the common claim that it heralds the Second Coming of Jesus.[115]

Besides locating the source of more powerful revival in the gifts of the Spirit, Pentecostals often note another respect in which they differ from their predecessors, here again tending to oppose divine and created causality;

> The Pentecostal Movement does not owe its origin to any outstanding personality or religious leader, but was a spontaneous revival appearing almost simultaneously in various parts of the world. [116]

These features apart, the average Pentecostal account of Christian history is remarkably similar to the typical conservative Evangelical presentation in successive stages of pristine purity, wholesale apostasy and Gospel revival. [117]

The classical Pentecostals in their conscious understanding and use of the Bible are predominantly fundamentalists, particularly in the white Western world. [118] But in other and more intuitive ways they use Scripture with a creativity similar to much biblical handling of earlier passages of Scripture; so a contrast can sometimes be noted between non-fundamentalist forms of Scriptural usage, e.g. the adaptation and reinterpretation of biblical parables and images in Pentecostal prophecy, and the fundamentalist attitudes found in sermons and pamphlets.

This tension illustrates an underlying theme throughout this essay, namely, the ways in which Pentecostalism as living reality transcends the characteristically Protestant and Evangelical framework out of which it has grown and within which it is still understood by most of its adherents. What we may call the problem of Pentecostal wine in conservative Evangelical bottles has been present throughout the history of this movement, but it has been made more explicit by its spread to the Roman Catholic Church. [119]

Professor Hollenweger, writing of the literature on Pentecostalism, has noted this challenge:

> Catholics have rightly seen that the Pentecostals are – in contrast to their self-interpretation – not a typically Protestant church. [120]

That Pentecostalism is incompatible with Catholic theology can only be maintained by accepting this Protestant account. In fact, the more Pentecostalism is described and defined in doctrinal and theological terms, the less will it be distinguished from Evangelical Protestantism [121] and the more difficulties it will raise for those in other Christian traditions.

However, the writings of Catholics caught up in the Pentecostal movement show that it is possible to exercise spiritual gifts and to develop elements of Pentecostal practice without subscribing to the theological understanding that classical Pentecostals have taken over from their Protestant origins. [122]

Classical Pentecostals both exaggerate and minimise their own significance. They exaggerate when they simply proclaim their own fullness in exclusivist terms and deny to others the operation of God's Spirit; this renders their claims to significance akin to being big fish in a small pool. They minimise when they are unaware of the significance they have for forms of Christian life unknown to themselves, e.g. for traditional liturgies, for monastic life, for the role of the Church in heaven, for Christian social involvement.

The greater openness of the Catholic tradition towards nature and creation can ground a different and more flexible understanding of Pentecostalism's potential. It will be more aware that the coming of the Holy Spirit marks the birth of the new creation and the renewal of the face of the earth, so revealing the cosmic scope of the work of redemption. It will envisage the possibility of a 'Pentecostal humanism' in which the coming of God's Spirit in visible signs fashions the new man, revealing the true divinely-given potential of the human spirit. [123] It will provide a sounder basis for discernment in that authenticity will be seen less in terms of 100 per cent or 0 per cent, either wholly God or wholly man, wholly God or wholly the devil, but more in terms of God's Holy Spirit or evil spirits [124] working in and through the human spirit (these alternatives producing clearly opposite results). God works in and through man, and the phenomena we encounter are therefore mixed. This enables a more tolerant attitude to be adopted towards the immature and the bizarre, neither of which have to be rejected a priori as inauthentic.

What contribution is this proposing for Catholic theology? I am not simply concerned to affirm the mutual compatibility of Catholic faith and Pentecostal praxis. Nor am I suggesting that Catholics have a ready-made theology of nature and grace, of creation and redemption, that can be neatly inserted as a replacement for present Pentecostal theory. What I do believe is that a Catholic starting-point reveals exciting possibilities in exposing the limitations and distortions that arise from a defective theological self-understanding. The distinctive features of Pentecostalism examined above [125] are intended to show how a different theological approach can reveal perhaps unsuspected potential and how features of Pentecostal life can introduce a new dimension into the wider ecumenical debate, e.g. on Scripture and tradition, on world and sacrament, on objective doctrine and subjective experience. [126]

Some Catholic presentations, no doubt influenced by apologetic concerns, are too complacent in their explanations of the compatibility of Pentecostalism and Catholicism; these, e.g. some statements on 'Baptism in the Spirit'[127] are often at the level of Pentecostal terminology, which inevitably reflects a theology, and in too uncritical an affirmation of compatibility fail to appreciate the size of the theological task demanded by the whole pentecostal experience. The theological work is only just starting and it may be many years before it reaches maturity! [128]

One challenge to the classical Pentecostals lies in this sphere of theology, despite their general suspicion of or lack of interest in this aspect of Christian life. For what is challenged is their self-understanding; and the challenge consists in their life and practice being bigger and better than their theory.

The quality of spiritual pragmatism already noted[129] gives hope that the Pentecostals will prove less intractable and more flexible than their theological forebears. For the challenge is not to abandon what is most distinctive of themselves, but to let go what is not adequate to their real distinctiveness.

But if this hope is to be fulfilled and the gap between praxis and theology, between heart and head, is to be bridged, then Pentecostal suspicion of theology must be taken with the utmost seriousness. Pentecostals see in the activities of theologians, historians and critics a compromising of the full Gospel, and the substitution of human subtlety for divine wisdom.

The fear that theology saps rather than feeds faith is not illusory. Pentecostals can only be expected to acknowledge a role for theology when they see the Christian mind truly at the service of God's Spirit and power. They confront theologians with the demand for renewal of the mind[130] and insist that this can only follow, not precede, the renewal of the heart. [131] Understanding the works of God is itself the gift of God:

Now we have received not the spirit of the world, but the Spirit which is from God, that we might understand the gifts bestowed on us by God. [132]

39

This argument of St. Paul is one more congenial to Pentecostals than to professional theologians, namely, that the work of Christian theology can only be done from 'within', however that 'within' is subsequently explained.[133] We can only speak of that which we know, and we can only speak in faith of that which we know in faith:

> The unspiritual man does not receive the gifts of the Spirit of God, for they are folly to him, and he is not able to understand them because they are spiritually discerned.[134]

The Complexity of Pentecostalism

Any assessment of the Pentecostal movement must recognise its complexity – a complexity far greater than Pentecostals commonly realise. Professor Hollenweger, one of whose major achievements is to have documented in detail the great variety in Pentecostal practice and belief, mentions the reaction of classical Pentecostals to his study.

> Pentecostals were astonished – and partly also a little embarrassed – at the many varieties of Pentecostal belief and practice. They had previously been in the habit of regarding the kind of Pentecostalism prevailing in their own church and their own country as the normal kind, the 'official' pattern.[135]

So we find many assumptions of Pentecostal uniformity (widespread among neo-Pentecostals as well as in the Pentecostal Churches), e.g. that all filled with the Spirit have had the identical experience, that they all understand this experience in the same way and use identical terminology to do so, that this experience makes all recipients fully one in the Spirit, that all such Spirit-filled people pray in a similar style, using the same language, singing the same songs and adopting the same postures.

Probably the most important causes of pentecostal variety are socio-cultural, particularly the differences between white Pentecostalism on the one hand and black and brown varieties on the other hand.[136] Since a high percentage of Pentecostal-charismatic literature is of white provenance (much in English is from the United States), the excessively uniform picture of Pentecostalism often found is painted in white Western terms, generally ignoring the negro Churches in our own midst as well as the Pentecostal movement in the Third World. Not only does this narrow view excise a major element in the potential of Pentecostalism, but it ignores those parts of the Pentecostal world in which the differences between classical Pentecostalism and classical Protestantism are most marked.[137] Indeed, Third World Pentecostalism, along with other forms of indigenous Christian independency,[138] shows up the Western character of the Reformation controversies.

Many of the features selected as distinctively Pentecostal are more prominent and widespread in black than in white Pentecostalism. Indeed, in the Third World, some of these features are found in groups not generally classified as Pentecostal, e.g. in many African independent Churches. This categorisation reflects the basically doctrinal criteria used to determine what groups are and are not Pentecostal.[139] The limitations of such criteria then become apparent when applied to Third World Churches that do not understand themselves in these terms.[140]

The exercise of such spiritual gifts as prophecy and healing are perhaps more prominent in black than in white Pentecostalism. So the sociologist Bryan Wilson can write:

> In Brazil and elsewhere in Latin America the appeal of Pentecostalism, which in America and Europe we should regard as a conversionist movement, may have much less to do with the specific elements which have been significant in its spread in Protestant societies, and more to do with those thaumaturgical aspects which are part of its inheritance.[141]

In African independent Churches the practice of healing has more distinctively Pentecostal a flavour with those groups that link the ministry of divine healing with filling by the Holy Spirit.[142]

The exercise of prophecy is prominent in Third World Pentecostalism and is not restricted to those movements classified by Barrett as prophetic,[143] a classification that is based on the prophetic character of the founder and subsequent leaders and that ignores the practice of prophecy in ordinary worship. Hollenweger writes of the independent African Pentecostal pastor:

41

He is ultimately a prophet. And adherents of such a prophet believe that he has eyes in his feet, which stay awake when he sleeps. He prophesies, and like his fellow prophets of the Old Testament has experienced a call in a vision. By taking over this double function[144] from Zulu tradition, the Zionist prophet, travelling through the country, has an advantage, in spite of his limited schooling, over the head of an Ethiopian church, who sits in Johannesburg and types letters.[145]

In the sphere of worship, Third World Pentecostals naturally incorporate a greater element of bodily movement, whether of processions, dances or forms of physical ministration, than is generally found in white Christian circles.[146] Here Pentecostalism with its openness to the non-cerebral and to bodily forms of expression has a capacity to express the native genius of non-European cultures denied to a naked religion of the Word. Though in theory Catholicism with its heritage of ritual and sense of the symbolic ought to have a greater capacity for cultural adaptation, this seems unlikely to be realised until the Catholic authorities come to terms with the need for liturgical creativity and acquire greater flexibility in relating given liturgical structure to free composition.

Variations in the distinctively Pentecostal occur not only between cultures and races, but also from Church to Church and from congregation to congregation. Whilst some Pentecostal assemblies will provide plentiful evidence of these distinctive features, in others there may only be residual traces of earlier pentecostal vigour. Preachers may then lament the decline from past standards:

> In many areas of the world the movement is still a force to be reckoned with, and its evangelistic fervour is a wonder to many. Yet today in certain sections there are ominous signs of deterioration, and a decline in spiritual power is abundantly evident.[147]

. The spiritual in man admits of degrees of development; spiritual gifts, for example, are not simply powers that people either have or do not have, but are capacities and endowments that may be partially or more fully developed. Classical Pentecostals who have practised prophecy for many years sometimes manifest a richness of imagery and a deeper penetrative power than is found among the more stereotyped prophecies often heard in neo-Pentecostal circles. This

42

is not simply a matter of authenticity, as is usually thought, but a question of maturity and spiritual development.[148]

Styles of prayer also vary more than is commonly supposed.[149] Language may be 16th century Authorised Version or 20th century American; even the pentecostal jargon, not the most attractive feature of the movement, varies subtly from place to place, as accents from city to city. Gestures and postures likewise spread, interact and develop; it is even possible to trace customs to the influence of particular itinerant preachers.

Thus far the complexity considered is largely that of classical Pentecostalism; but attention must be paid to neo-Pentecostalism or what Professor Hollenweger has called 'Pentecost outside "Pentecost"',[150] and to the differences between the Pentecostal Churches and the Pentecostal movement within the historic Churches. Clearly this break-out into the Churches or this out-break within the Churches[151] increases the complexity of an already complex phenomenon and is a major factor in developing awareness of its importance.[152]

Historical accounts of pentecostal origins agree in locating this out-break in the 'Van Nuys revival' centred around the person of Dennis Bennett, an Episcopalian priest in California, who in late 1959 was baptized in the Holy Spirit and spoke in tongues.[153] As is not unusual in the history of this movement, subsequent evidence indicated that this was not the first such occurrence outside the Pentecostal Churches but was that which made the headlines and so helped to uncover similar experiences in other places and communions.[154]

There is, I suggest, in the Van Nuys event a symbolic importance; for it introduces new elements that later become of increasing significance: that pentecostal groupings arise in a tradition that is episcopal, that is sacramental and that is liturgical.

That we are concerned with the rise of pentecostal groupings and not simply with the occurrence of pentecostal experience is important. Pentecostalism is more than the outbreak of glossolalia. Because spiritual gifts are primarily for the benefit of others and for the upbuilding of the Church,[155] they require a setting for their exercise and hence some social embodiment of those so gifted.

With Churches that are episcopal, sacramental and liturgical, there enters a stronger denominational commitment and a notion of membership that is primarily of a Church and only secondarily of a

43

congregation. This leads to a different pattern of loyalties – a commitment to the neo-Pentecostal group and a firm adhesion to the denomination– and to a different pattern of relationship between the group and the denomination. Whereas Churches with a congregational form of government generally have to decide for or against pentecostal revival in each congregation, Churches with an episcopal structure (whether or not their executive officers are called bishops) are more readily able to take their time, to speak when they wish, or to keep turning a blind eye. Pluriformity is easier to allow at a diocesan than at a parochial or congregational level.

That pentecostal groupings have arisen in sacramental traditions may have been unexpected, but it is not simply a tension or co-existence between contrasting styles of piety and worship. It is the Pentecostals in these traditions (first the Anglican, later the Lutheran and the Catholic) that have a particular problem defining the difference between themselves and other members of their own Churches. For those Christians who determine faith primarily by appeal to experience, it may be possible to accept the classical Pentecostal division of believers into the 'filled' and the not yet 'filled'.[156] But for those who believe that the Holy Spirit is given in the sacraments of initiation,[157] there is difficulty in marking out any category of baptised person as qualitatively different and distinctively endowed. Hence arise problems of a theological nature about baptism in the Holy Spirit, being 'Spirit-filled' and the meaning of the term 'charismatic'.

Pentecostal irruption in a liturgical tradition also poses with greater intensity the relationship between pentecostal-type prayer meetings and regular liturgical worship. Whilst these can interact in different ways, both in the influence of liturgical tradition on the form and content of prayer meetings[158] and in pentecostal impact on liturgical worship, to some extent they inevitably stand over and against each other, confronting their participants with the fixed – free, structure – spirit dialectic in a way that cannot be relaxed without abandoning either the pentecostal or the denominational.

All these consequences of the spread of Pentecostalism to the Anglicans[159] are more marked with its penetration of the Roman Catholic Church in the late 1960s.[160] Catholics with their very strong sense of denominational identity are less ready to treat confessional unity as unimportant compared with the communion experienced with brother Pentecostals. They are far more likely to develop a double loyalty, taking seriously both pentecostal fellowship and denominational unity – without thereby putting them on an equal footing.[161]

The more this double loyalty is experienced (and it is experienced before it is formulated and analysed) the greater is the tendency towards denominational organisation within the charismatic movement,[162] the greater is the concern to persuade fellow Church members (especially Church leaders) of the compatibility of both loyalties and the greater is the 'missionary' thrust in their direction. Indeed, such tendencies in the Catholic charismatic movement seem to have had the effect, at least in the United States, of helping some Protestant neo-Pentecostals to relate more creatively to their own traditions, theological, liturgical and spiritual.[163]

Nor is it surprising that those in episcopal, sacramental and liturgical traditions, especially the Catholic, categorise the charismatic movement more in terms of renewal than of revival. For the language of renewal accords better with Catholic beliefs about Christian initiation and with Catholic ecclesiology affirming the continuity in God's dealings with man, as well as having an established place in modern Catholic life.

Whereas revivals are seen simply as movements of God touching individuals, with perhaps scant respect for denominational affiliation, renewal movements are inherently more Church-centred (open indeed to being more centred on Church than on God!) and have a social dimension, being embodiments of shared ideals and currents of thought. The charismatic renewal does however differ from most other Catholic renewal movements with which it is sometimes compared[164] by being primarily aimed at the renewal of lives rather than at a renewal of ideas.[165]

Whereas revivals aim to draw others within their orbit, renewal movements aim to disappear into a renewed Church.[166] These distinct notions of revival and renewal thus ground different ecclesiologies (e.g. as to the relationship between continuity and discontinuity in the dealings of God with man)[167] and different eschatologies (renewal movements are not so readily seen as harbingers of the Parousia).

Besides its familiarity with renewal movements, the Roman Catholic Church with its traditional network of confraternities, sodalities and religious congregations already contains a high degree of structural pluriformity[168] which does much to explain the speed

45

with which Catholic authorities have given a qualified acceptance to charismatic renewal.[169] Indeed, the worldwide network of religious houses, enjoying considerable independence from episcopal control, has provided a natural channel for the rapid spread of pentecostal renewal and a series of spacious meeting-places for prayer-meetings.

The spread of Pentecostalism to the Roman Catholic Church therefore strengthens this tendency for neo-Pentecostals to experience a dialectical tension between the pentecostal and the traditional. Unfortunately this tension has not been detailed in any auto-biographical witness, although it is evidenced by two quite distinct types of neo-Pentecostal literature – the testimonial witness, which stresses the newness and importance of the pentecostal experience, and the apologetic defence, which emphasises the compatibility with tradition and the fully orthodox character of charismatic renewal.

By way of conclusion to this section on the complexity of Pentecostalism, I offer some reflections on my own experience of 'double loyalty' both because I believe it will echo the experience of others (perhaps prompting other and more ample testimonies) and because it raises important points for any assessment of the movement's ecumenical potential.

When first I participated in a (largely Catholic) prayer group, within which spiritual gifts were exercised, I was not aware of developing any new corporate loyalty beyond that group. But some months later through contact with a Pentecostal Church a 'pentecostal loyalty' began to develop. Worshipping with classical Pentecostals has become for me an experience quite distinct from sharing in Anglican and Free Church services. For in some way that is easier to recognise than to describe I identify with the Pentecostals in their distinctiveness, even though I do not understand this in their terms.[170]

This identification is not simply an acceptance of the importance of spiritual gifts. At its heart it includes standing for a dimension of Christian life for which Pentecostals stand, but it is essentially more than sympathising with a range of ideas. It includes identification with Church groups as embodiments of such ideas and expectations and as conveyors of a corpus of spiritual wisdom and praxis. It is this identification that makes me in a real sense a Pentecostal.

However, at another level I am as different from these classical Pentecostals as chalk from cheese; their language is different, their

46

style is different, their explanations and emphases are different. I experience simultaneously an *identity* and an *otherness*. So I know them and they know me within worship and witness, but outside this doxological framework conversation is sparse and not felt to be that necessary. It is the obverse of a long-familiar experience – of being being able to converse with other Christians but feeling alien as soon as worship commenced.

The resulting inter-action between the Catholic and the pentecostal is itself complex; it is primarily something happening within and only secondarily what is articulated and studied.[171] It includes various recognisable elements:

– a consciousness of some Pentecostal assemblies as places of particular blessing and inspiration

– finding there a corpus of praxis which inseparably from apposite New Testament passages is a basic source for teaching on the pneumatic (so I learn more about prophecy from how Pentecostals prophesy than from what they say about prophecy, more about healing from how they pray for healing than from what they say about healing)[172]; my pentecostal loyalty therefore includes a looking to Pentecostal sources for guidance in particular spheres of spiritual activity

– an awareness that this pentecostal discovery happens to me as a member of the Roman Catholic Church; I find hitherto neglected or unknown elements in the Catholic tradition that now acquire meaning and relevance, and I am given a new impulse to delve into the spiritual riches of my own tradition; what I then find reinforces my sense of the simultaneous identity and otherness of Pentecostalism

– an experience at each stage of the need for discernment to test all that I see the Pentecostals do and hear them say[173]

– a change in my own way of praying, ministering and living that is not simply an imitation of the classical Pentecostals

– an awareness that growth in the Spirit must challenge all arease and spheres of Christian life and commitment, and that this double loyalty poses many questions that do not arise within the horizons of the classical Pentecostals[174]

– a spotting of ways in which classical Pentecostals act in closer conformity to Catholic theology than to their own theory, e.g. in the active attitude regularly encouraged in those to whom they minister.[175]

47

What effect does this new loyalty have on my prior and more fundamental Catholic loyalty? Following the dialectic of duality, it both deepens and alienates:—

– I find strands of Catholic tradition with which I identify more strongly than before; this includes an enlivening of what is most central in the Catholic tradition, e.g. the trinitarian pattern of Christian life and worship, the centrality of liturgy, the complementarity of Word and sacraments, the Church as the Body of Christ and the communion of saints[176]

– I find aspects of contemporary Catholicism of which I am now more critical, though in a spirit of hope rather than of cynical disillusionment; so I am led to question how essentially Catholic and Christian are various practices, attitudes and mentalities certainly Catholic *de facto*.

These impressions point to a tension, inevitable as long as schisms last, between Catholic as *de facto* one tradition (or cluster of traditions) and Catholic as the fullness of the Body of Christ.[177]

This double loyalty is not to the Roman Catholic Church and to the Catholic charismatic renewal, but to the Roman Catholic Church and the worldwide Pentecostal movement (which has its origins and its lengthiest experience in the Pentecostal Churches). This double loyalty is, I believe, implicit in Catholic charismatic renewal.[178]

Ecumenical Potential and Significance

It does not require great powers of perception to see that Pentecostalism has ecumenical significance. Any movement that brings together AOGs[179] and RCs in brotherhood and common worship has potential! But neither does an observer have to search hard to find divisive tendencies among Pentecostals – whether these are within their own ranks[180] or are instances of Pentecostals conceiving their unity and identity as *anti* – others, e.g. opposing their liveliness to everyone else's presumed deadness, opposing Spirit-given pentecostal unity to an apparently man-made unity of the official ecumenical movement and the World Council of Churches.[181]

Any assessment of the ecumenical potential and significance of Pentecostalism must take into account not only the unity and diversity within the movement but also the coexistence within it of power-fully unitive and powerfully divisive forces.

Whilst Pentecostalism had an ecumenical component in its original dynamic,[182] its expulsion or exodus from the Churches that gave it birth can be seen in retrospect to have a providential character. For secession and isolation enabled them to pursue their genius and develop a complete corporate life in fidelity to their basic inspiration;[183] only because of this has pentecostal *otherness* developed so that seventy years later it can confront its elder brethren both as brother and as other. Its ecumenical potential becomes apparent at the point when it begins to penetrate the older traditions without simply luring their members out into Pentecostal assemblies or into groupings that sit light to their traditions of origin. The ecumenical potential is latent in this combination of identity and otherness.

The emergence of this new ecumenical thrust has much to say to all involved in other forms of ecumenical encounter, both the enthusiastic and the weary. This is central to the ecumenical poten-tial of Pentecostalism, and I pick out three points in illustration:

Ecumenism as the confusion of the Spirit. To some readers mention of 'double loyalty' will confirm their worst fears – that ecumenism breeds indifferentism and chaotic confusion, inevitably fostering dis-loyalty to one's own Church tradition. To others the concept will provoke comparisons with other ecumenical encounters in which 'duality' is experienced.[184]

That such concepts as 'double loyalty' and 'dual membership'[185] have received scant theological notice can be attributed to the failure of theologians to pay sufficient attention to contemporary ecumenical experience[186] and, to a lesser degree, to the reticence of those experiencing 'duality' in whatever form to articulate this experience.[187]

That the Pentecostal movement is clearly a very different kind of entity, sociologically and theologically, from the Roman Catholic Church makes plain what is also though less obviously true of other forms of dual allegiance, viz. that the objects of such dual reference are not equal. The Pentecostal experience can here help to dispel a false ecumenical democracy in which taking each other's traditions with equal seriousness is mistakenly extended to regarding the par-ties in dialogue as the same species of Christian entity.[188]

49

Ecumenism, it needs to be said, leads from clarity into confusion – in particular from the unreal clarity that characterises every self-sufficient and self-explanatory system into the apparent confusion of a pluriform world of overlapping and incomplete systems, a form of chaos over which the Spirit of God broods and out of which the Spirit of God is forming the richness of the new creation. Even the first faltering steps in ecumenical dialogue and collaboration begin this confusion and open the way to various experiences of 'duality'.[189]

Ecumenism means that no Church can adequately define itself by exclusion, and that each tradition needs to keep re-defining itself by increasing inclusion.[190] This 'confusion of the Spirit' is the very opposite of indifferentism, the essence of which is that traditions and denominations do not matter; on the contrary, ecumenism means that all traditions matter, old and new. Dual or multiple allegiance is not a diminution in attachment to one's own Church, but the acquisition of additional loyalties that enrich and deepen the original attachment.[191]

These points also mean that attention must be paid to the distinctive experience of neo-Pentecostals in each Church tradition, not making the experience of Catholic Pentecostals the norm for others. Different traditions will manifest varied patterns of double loyalty, and many of the differences betweeen Catholic and Protestant neo-Pentecostals (e.g. between renewal and revival) themselves need to interact for a richer ecumenical synthesis. Nor should the charismatic movement be taken as the only or even as the most privileged model for ecumenism and double loyalty.

The unexpected, risk and schism. The ecumenical potential of Pentecostalism is one of God's surprises. What seemed at first sight to be the cause of new divisions becomes a force for healing and a source of new hope for jaded ecumenists. This experience can correct naive assumptions that in this ecumenical age schism is a thing of the past and that the road to organic reunion will be a smooth and painless process – with its ups and downs maybe, but nonetheless a calm crossing achieved without serious risk to the passengers. Indeed, the Pentecostal movement can remind us that the greatest impulses to unity necessarily have a surprise element; for their potential is directly proportionate to their capacity to introduce that other dimension – that is at once both strange and familiar, strange because largely lost and familiar because its need was never wholly forgotten.

So with God yesterday's schism can be the source for today's ecumenism, and today's schism can be the source for tomorrow's ecumenism.[192] It may well be that the numerous schisms in Africa in recent times will face all Churches in Africa with the need for a truly indigenous Christianity and so be the prelude to a richer coming together in the years ahead.[193]

Indifferentism and sectarian self-sufficiency are, psychologically speaking, much easier options than the costliness of multiplying loyalties and apparent ambiguity. The temptation is to relax the tension by abandoning one of the loyalties; the various ways in which this can occur are the major obstacles which could thwart the ecumenical potential of the Pentecostal movement:

– by apostasy from Church of origin to join a Pentecostal assembly or free charismatic community, denouncing the tradition left as unregenerate and unspiritual
– by classical Pentecostals denying the spiritual authenticity and pentecostal character of neo-Pentecostals
– by asserting the irrelevance of all traditions and denominations (whether Pentecostal or older) in affirming the complete spiritual unity of all the 'Spirit-filled'
– by neo-Pentecostals living in a 'charismatic enclave' within their Churches and not allowing their pentecostal inspiration to interact with all spheres of life (in their Churches and in the world)
– by affirming that only ecclesiastical communion is real, reducing all else to the level of emotions and feelings and so regarding experienced communion across Church boundaries as spiritually irrelevant
– by Churches attempting to expel the 'alien' element, by rejection of practices and features associated with Pentecostalism
– by absorption of the pentecostal experience whilst excluding double loyalty, so by a form of denominational imperialism taking 'it' over and saying it's really ours and there in our tradition all the time (so e.g. denial of any tension between the Catholic and the pentecostal tends to produce a tame version of Catholic charismatic renewal purified of pentecostal 'otherness')
– by the reduction of the pentecostal contribution to a phase undergone before recovery of normal denominational balance (e.g.

51

when the role of spiritual gifts in ministry is ignored and the pentecostal element is reduced to a private experience).

Those Pentecostal enthusiasts who regard the unifying work of the Holy Spirit as instantaneous and painless are not only under-estimating the ecumenical potential of this movement but also neglecting the unity between Son and Spirit, that it is through the Cross that the Body of Christ is built up.[194]

Theology in ecumenical dialogue. The Pentecostal movement offers a different model for ecumenical progress from that generally prevailing in the ecumenical movement, particularly as to the role of theology. Instead of theologians and Church leaders communicating their ecumenical theology to the rest (a method almost certain to produce a grass-roots back-lash), the Pentecostal movement does not arise from re-thinking but springs from personal spiritual renewal and sharing in worship and ministry.[195] Such a movement responds not simply to intellectual needs and to crises in theology, but speaks to the anguish of human hearts and meets deeper needs of the human spirit.[196]

Whilst to some, such spiritual renewal simply suggests the barrenness of contemporary theology and its irrelevance to the work of the Spirit, this paper is written in the conviction that all spiritual renewal, including that experienced within the Pentecostal movement, itself raises new questions and necessitates a theological re-think. It does not eliminate theology from the ecumenical task but changes its role and presents a different model for theological renewal.[197] It requires of theology a two-way interaction between theological sources and contemporary reality – a reflection on Scripture (and Christian tradition) in the present situation and a reflection on the present situation in the light of Scripture (and Christian tradition); these are complementary processes that converge and that cannot be wholly separated in practice.[198]

This is a plea for a servant theology – a theology that is at the service of the Lord who is recognised as the agent of all salvation and a theology that acknowledges what the theologian does not know and what he cannot know. Such a servant theology can only arise from lives nourished by prayer – prayer that increases respect for the mystery of God and the utter unpredictability of His Spirit.

It is not the task of theology to plan the future on behalf of the Church; much less is it the task of theology to pronounce on what is or is not possible for God to do! It can never be the task of theology to cast doubt on the spiritual authenticity of the experience of Christians.[199] What is the responsibility of theologians is to examine the presuppositions of descriptions and explanations – to uncover the theology that is implicit in all accounts of Christian life and experience. It is the service of theology to free Christians from the limitations arising from defective interpretation of their experience.

This model points to an ecumenical theology seeking to understand the ways in which God is uniting people and to examine the language in which experiences of unity are described.

Postscript

It will be clear that Pentecostalism makes the Trinity more central to Christian life and Trinitarian theology more central in Christian thinking. It is true that Western Christianity has been consistently stronger on all that is more associated with the Second Person of the Trinity (e.g. with the Word, the Bible, the formulated, order, structure, consistency, reason) than with the Third (e.g. inspiration, intuition, impulse, unpredictability, mystery, the limitations of order and structure). However, the argument of this essay as to the significance of Pentecostalism will be misunderstood if too sharp a division is made between the Word and the Spirit.

In this world, what is not embodied is not operative. Hence, whilst Pentecostalism does represent a recovery of features more associated with the Spirit than with the Word, it only does so – and could only do so – in an embodied form in Pentecostal Churches and groupings. The body of Pentecostalism is however less rich in limbs and organisms than the older traditions in Christendom and so its significance is directly related to the degree to which its inspiration and genius can revivify this richer tradition and re-energise its creativity. It is not without point that Ezekiel's vision of the valley of dry bones[200] keeps recurring in Pentecostal visions of the Christian future.[201] Without denying what is alive in the older Churches, we can see in the Pentecostal movement an important, though not the only, force for the breathing of new life into the bones and sinews that we have inherited.

[1] To my knowledge, there is no major Christian denomination untouched by the pentecostal movement; besides those Churches known to have a vigorous charismatic wing, the Orthodox and the Quakers are also affected.

[2] In this essay 'classical pentecostal' refers to those Churches (and their members) claiming, not always in their titles, to be Pentecostal; 'neo-Pentecostal' refers to groups and persons within the traditional Churches, and 'Pentecostal' generally refers to both together. The phrase 'charismatic renewal' has become more common usage than 'Pentecostal movement' among neo-Pentecostals. This use of the term 'charismatic' has been challenged by Père Y. Congar; cf. *The Holy Spirit and Power* (ed. K. McDonnell), New York, 1975, pp. 62-64. My own reflections on this terminology are give in 'Pentecostals on Paper', I, *The Clergy Review*, November 1974, pp. 755-758.

[3] This latest stage in the pentecostal movement is studied later in this essay, pp. 43-48

[4] Cf. e.g. the sections on Brazil and South Africa in W. J. Hollenweger *The Pentecostals* (London, 1972); C. Lalive d'Epinay *Haven of the Masses* (London, 1969); *Pentecost and Politics* (S. C. M. publication).

[5] Cf. P. Hocken, art. cit., *The Clergy Review*, November 1974, pp. 750-755.

[6] The need for theological reflection is being increasingly felt and is evidenced by the Fountain Trust's recent launching of *Theological Renewal* (a thrice-yearly supplement to *Renewal* magazine) and by the document *Theological and Pastoral Orientations on the Catholic Charismatic Renewal* (Ann Arbor, 1974), subsequently referred to as 'the Malines document'.

[7] Cf. e.g. the popular Pentecostal history of S. Durasoff *Bright Wind of the Spirit* (London, 1972).

[8] Cf. e.g. C. Lalive d'Epinay *Haven of the Masses*; M. Calley *God's People* (London, 1965); B. R. Wilson *Magic and the Millenium* (London, 1975), Chapters 4-6; J. H. Fichter *The Catholic Cult of the Paraclete* (New York, 1975); J. Moore 'The Catholic Pentecostal Movement' in *A Sociological Yearbook of Religion*, Vol. 6 (ed. M. Hill; London. 1973), pp. 73-90.

[9] Cf. J. P. Kildahl *The Psychology of Speaking in Tongues* (London, 1972). Psychological studies relating to Pentecostalism have mostly concentrated on tongues for a survey see K. McDonnell *Tongues and the Churches* (New York, 1976).

[10] Cf. on the first two points M. J. C. Calley, op. cit., passim.

[11] 'Baptism in the Spirit' in classical Pentecostal belief is the experienced event of being filled with the Holy Spirit as the apostles were 'filled' on the day of Pentecost (Acts 2:4). This 'spirit-baptism' is quite distinct from and subsequent to the experience of basic conversion to Jesus Christ, and distinct from though not necessarily subsequent to 'water-baptism'. It normally has as its outward sign a breaking into tongues by the one 'baptised' (cf. Acts 10: 44-47). Cf. W. J. Hollenweger *The Pentecostals*, pp. 330-341; J. D. G. Dunn *Baptism in the Holy Spirit*, London 1970 and 'Spirit-Baptism and Pentecostalism', *Scottish Journal of Theology*, Vol. 23, 1970, pp. 397-407; A. Bittlinger 'Baptised in Water and in Spirit: Aspects of Christian Initiation' in *The Baptism of the Holy Spirit as an Ecumenical Problem*, Notre Dame 1972, pp. 12-26; S. Tugwell 'Reflections on the Pentecostal Doctrine of 'Baptism

in the Holy Spirit', *The Heythrop Journal*, Vol. XIII 1972, pp. 268-281, 402-414. The nine 'Gifts of the Holy Ghost' are: a word of wisdom, a word of knowledge, faith, gifts of healing, operations of works of power, prophecy, discernment of spirits, different kinds of tongues, interpretation of tongues (1 Cor. 12: 8-10). I here translate all the words from the Greek, rather than give the standard short form found in most Pentecostal literature and Declarations of Faith, e.g. of the Elim Pentecostal Churches, quoted by W. J. Hollenweger, op. cit., p. 519.

[12] Some accept that there can be more than nine e.g. 'I believe there are more than nine Gifts of the Holy Spirit' (D. Double *Life in a new dimension*, St. Austell, 1974, p. 12).

[13] Some also refer to Mark 16: 17-18 and Eph. 4: 11.

[14] Speaking in tongues is stressed as the initial evidence of 'spirit-baptism' by most Pentecostal Churches and their Declarations of Faith often give a special place to healing (cf. Appendix to W. J. Hollenweger *The Pentecostals*, pp. 513-522).

[15] Cf. e.g. J. Rodman Williams *The Pentecostal Reality* (Plainfield, 1972).

[16] Popular pentecostal usage is of spiritual gifts, 'Gifts of the (Holy) Spirit' or simply 'the gifts'.

[17] Cf. Thomas A. Smail *Reflected Glory* (London, 1975), passim; E. Sullivan 'Can the Pentecostal Movement renew the Churches?' (British Council of Churches, London, 1972 and *Study Encounter*, no. 35), esp. p. 2; the report of the Catholic and Pentecostal dialogue, Rome 1973, point 10 (*One in Christ*, 1974, p. 116); R. Martin 'Baptism in the Holy Spirit: Pastoral Implications' in *The Holy Spirit and Power* (ed K. McDonnell), p. 99; D. Gelpi *Pentecostalism* (Paramus, 1971), p. 224.

[18] The 'ordinary-extraordinary' language is used by D. Gelpi in *Pentecostal Piety* (New York, 1972), though he does raise doubts about its adequacy (cf. p. 32). E. D. O'Connor uses the language of 'extraordinary' and 'preternatural', though not as technical terms, in *The Pentecostal Movement in the Catholic Church* (Notre Dame, 1971), pp. 284-285. The phrase 'extraordinary gifts' was used in the 18th and 19th century debate about what was permanent in the Church and what died out with the Apostles: cf. C. Gordon Strachan *The Pentecostal Theology of Edward Irving* (London, 1973) and *The Letters of John Wesley*, ed. J. Telford, Vol. IV (London, 1931), pp. 39-41, 327.

[19] Both aspects are present in the concept of 'extraordinary graces' as found in Catholic manuals of ascetical theology. Whilst R. Garrigou-Lagrange starts on this subject by equating such graces with the *gratiae gratis datae* of St. Thomas Aquinas (graces given to persons for the benefit of others), he quickly proceeds to what he really means by the extraordinary: 'To these charisms are generally linked the extraordinary favours which sometimes accompany infused contemplation, that is, private revelations, supernatural words, visions.' (*The Three Ages of the Interior Life*, Vol. 2, St. Louis, 1948, p. 577).

[20] The Malines document comments on the supernatural character of these gifts, pp. 50-51.

[21] The phrases prophetic gifts' and 'word gifts' are examples of such descriptive usage. Cf. respectively the Malines document, pp. 34, 37, 50 and

K. McDonnell 'The Holy Spirit and Christian Initiation' in *The Holy Spirit and Power*, pp. 64-65.

[22] 'Gifts of the Holy Spirit' is of course more than a straight translation of *charismata pneumatika;* it is also a theological interpretation, though with support from the references to the Spirit in 1 Cor. 12: 7-11.

[23] 'The two words which Paul uses more than any other to describe the believer's experience of God are "Spirit" and "grace" ', (James D. G. Dunn *Jesus and the Spirit*, London, 1975, p. 201).

[24] *Theological Wordbook of the New Testament*, (ed. G. Kittel), Vol. VI, p.436.

[25] R. Jewett holds that in 1 Corinthians, apart from 2: 11 'the human spirit . . . is always the apportioned divine spirit given to Christians in the eschatological period. Paul speaks of this apportioned spirit as if it entered man's possession to the extent that it could be called his own and that it could be the subject of actions.' (*Paul's Anthropological Terms*, Leiden 1971, p. 194).

[26] R. Bultmann *Theology of the New Testament*, Vol. 1, (London, 1952), pp. 203-210 in effect accepts only a limited application of the apportioned Spirit interpretation; C. K. Barrett rejects its application to 1 Cor. 14: 14 (*The First Epistle to the Corinthians*, London 1968. p. 320).

[27] Description of glossolalia as ecstatic is misleading and unhelpful unless it is made clear what is meant by ecstacy. Dunn regards the tongues at Pentecost and in Corinth as ecstatic in a strong sense (op. cit., pp. 148-152, 242-243) but then argues that Paul 'knows and values a form of glossolalia which is not so "abandoned" as the Corinthian glossolalia – a glossolalia which can be readily controlled . . ; a glossolalia, which is a speaking of actual words; a glossolalia that is to say, which was ecstatic only in the technical sense of being automatic speech in which the conscious mind played no part, but not ecstatic in the more common sense of "produced or accompanied by exalted states of feeling, rapture, frenzy".' (op, cit., p. 243). But why might Paul have not known a variety of experiences of tongues within the one Church of Corinth?

[28] Contra Dunn, who makes *pneumatika* synonymous with *charismata* in 1 Corinthians 12-14 (*Jesus and the Spirit*, p. 208), I take this as an instance of what Jewett writes of when he says: 'Pauline usage reveals considerable sensitivity to the anthropological terms being used by his conversation partners. There is a measurable tendency to borrow these terms and to redefine them in light of Pauline theology to fit the needs of particular controversies.' (*Paul's Anthropological Terms*, p. 10).

[29] The Greek in 1 Cor. 14: 1 only mentions *pneumatika* without the word *charismata*, but translators commonly insert *gifts* – no doubt in the light of verse 1b 'especially that you may prophesy' and 12: 31a 'But earnestly desire the higher gifts' (*Zeloute de ta charismata ta kreittona*).

[30] The term *charisma pneumatikon* does occur in Romans 1: 11.

[31] No doubt this level or zone corresponds to some extent with what we now call the 'psychic' or the 'extra-sensory' but it would be misleading simply to equate the pneumatic and the psychic.

[32] Various studies have drawn attention to the occurrence of 'Pentecostal phenomena' over the centuries. Cf, e.g. Vinson Synan 'The Role of the Holy

Spirit and the Gifts of the Spirit in the Mystical Tradition', *One in Christ*, 1974, pp. 193-202; Simon Tugwell *Did You Receive the Spirit?* (London, 1972).

[33] *Schism and Renewal in Africa* (Nairobi, 1968), p. 269.

[34] Cf. 1 Corinthians 1: 11; 3: 1-3; 11: 17-19; 14: 20.

[35] This concern is found in Matthew's Gospel. 'For false Christs and false prophets will arise and show great signs and wonders, so as to lead astray, if possible, even the elect.' (24: 24). Cf. G.T. Montague *The Spirit and his Gifts*, New York 1974, pp. 38-41

[36] This is implied by the words of Jesus about the house swept clean of unclean spirits (Matt: 12: 43-45).

[37] The initial opening-up of this dimension does seem to require a yielding to something greater, with an experiencing of receiving; for converts already familiar with the pneumatic (e.g. Simon Magus?) a different pattern seems likely.

[38] Professor Hollenweger is critical of the typical Pentecostal restriction of prophecy to 'edificatory exhortation': 'Wherever the Pentecostal movement has taken on organizational forms, spontaneous prophecy which goes beyond exhortation for edification has necessarily been rejected as "Satan deceiving and misdirecting simple souls".' (*The Pentecostals*, p. 345.)

[39] *The Era of the Spirit* (Plainfield, 1971), p. 27.

[40] Cf. the essay by G. Every 'Prophecy in the Christian Era', passim.

[41] A distinction must be made between the office of prophet (given only to a few) and the gift of prophecy (which can be desired by all). Cf. Arnold Bittlinger *Gifts and Ministries*, London 1974, p. 65.

[42] Cf. *Constitution on the Sacred Liturgy*, paras. 51-52 and *Dogmatic Constitution on Divine Revelation*, para. 9.

[43] Cf. Karl Barth *Church Dogmatics*, Vol. 1, Part 2, pp. 743-758.

[44] Cf. *Dogmatic Constitution on Divine Revelation*, Ch. II 'The Transmission of Divine Revelation', paras. 7-10.

[45] There is an analogy here with the relationship between the 'once and for all' sacrifice of Jesus Christ and the sharing of the Church in that one sacrifice through the sacrificial act of the Eucharist.

[46] On the element of interpretation of Scripture in the exercise of prophecy see G. Every 'Prophecy in the Christian Era', especially pp. 163-4, 190-3, 199.

[47] This touches on the question of infallibility. Here it is sufficient to note the extremely restrictive terms in which Vatican I defined papal and ecclesial infallibility.

[48] Pentecostal belief about other spiritual gifts also implies this continuity, but prophecy is instanced here in the context of receiving the Word.

[48a] Cf. G. Every *Misunderstandings between East and West* London, 1965, pp. 67-68.

[49] Hand-clapping for the first Catholic Pentecostals was not a copying of classical Pentecostal' practice, but the introduction into worship of an element from secular (student) celebration.

[50] Morton Kelsey speaks of glossolalia as a '*rite d'entree* to the deeper levels of the psyche' (*Tongue Speaking*, London, 1964, p. 231).

[51] This has been stressed in the teaching of Simon Tugwell, OP.

[52] This spiritual sensitivity fits in with the biblical language of spiritual sight and spiritual hearing. Cf. also note 96.

[53] At the level of popular description this combination can represent a healthy spiritual focus; it is less commendable at the level of theological reflection.

[54] *Healing* (Notre Dame, 1974), pp. 62-63.

[55] W. J. Hollenweger *The Pentecostals*, pp. 353-367 treats of these disputes, the doctrinal aspect concerning the widespread view: 'Anyone who believes is healed; anyone who is not healed has not believed aright.' (op, cit., p. 357).

[56] Cf. J. O. Mills VI p. 102 and note 62, p. 115; Kofi Appiah-Kubi 'The Church's Healing Ministry in Africa', *The Ecumenical Review*, July 1975, pp. 230-239.

[57] Also referred to as 'the healing of memories' and 'the healing of emotions'. Cf. F. MacNutt *Healing*, p. 163; D. & M. Linn *Healing of Memories* (New York, 1974).

[58] Pentecostals typically dislike the term 'faith healing', with its emphasis on man, and term their practice 'divine healing', so stressing the action of God.

[59] F. MacNutt *Healing*, p. 181.

[60] This does not mean that psychological healings are unknown in the ministry of classical Pentecostals, but that such a categorisation and approach is not a part of their tradition.

[61] Cf. M. Scanlan *The Power in Penance* (Notre Dame, 1972); F. MacNutt *Healing*, pp. 285-290; D. Gelpi *Pentecostal Piety* (New York, 1972), pp. 3-58. The Catholic rediscovery of the ministry of healing is also much concerned with, though far from confined to, the renewal of the sacrament of anointing of the sick.

[62] A. Linford, a classical Pentecostal, gives as the marks of gifts of healing: spontaneousness; usually immediate and complete; chiefly wrought on unbelievers; may be exercised by any believer; external power. (*A Course of Study on Spiritual Gifts* (Nottingham, no date), pp. 62-63).

[63] The approach to healing of Christian faith harnessing the life-giving forces in God's creation has been led by Agnes Sanford, an American Episcopalian, author of numerous popular books, in particular *The Healing Light* (1949) and *Healing Gifts of the Spirit* (1966).

[64] Among the best known of these communities are the Word of God community, Ann Arbor, Michigan, and the Church of the Redeemer, Houston, Texas. Cf. G. Every 'Prophecy in the Christian Era'. pp. 193-4 and note 118. On Houston cf. M. Harper *A New Way of Living* (London, 1973) and, for origins, W. G. Pulkingham *Gathered for Power* (London 1973). Cardinal Suenens relates this dimension of charismatic renewal to other contemporary experiences of community formation in *A New Pentecost?* , Ch. VIII 'The Holy Spirit and New Communities', London, 1975, pp. 136-158.

[65] MacNutt has some perceptive comments about contrasting approaches in the healing ministry, between an emphasis on power and an emphasis on love, reflecting differing conceptions of God. Cf. *Healing*, pp. 151-153.

[66] *Healing*, p. 162.

[67] Cf. MacNutt's comments on his Latin American experience, *Healing*, pp. 25-30.

[68] E.g. the *Brazil para Cristo* movement led by Manoel de Mello: cf. *Pentecost and Politics* (S. C. M.) pp. 17-18; W. J. Hollenweger *The Pentecostals*, pp. 100-101.

[69] *New Heaven? New Earth?*, V and VI.

[70] Apoc. 22:2.

[71] *The Sociology of Religion*, Vol, 2. p. 53.

[72] Only an understanding of man that recognises levels of human life that are both distinct and inter-related can cope with the fact that spiritual health is related to other levels of health but is neither identical with nor wholly dependent on them. A sacramental view holds together all these levels in the context of an eschatological vision of the New Adam in the New Jerusalem. Cf. passage referred to in note 98.

[73] Belief in an imminent Parousia, anticipated by many Pentecostals is not essential to our recognition of the importance of the Pentecostal revival of 'end-time' consciousness. Insistence on literal imminence is a crude telescoping of the symbolic, whereby the future is made actual and anticipated in the present, and apocalyptic imagery is reduced to a form of scientific code.

[74] The latter is the focus of Peter Wagner's defence of Latin American Pentecostals against charges of indifference to social justice: *Look Out! The Pentecostals are Coming* (London, 1973), pp. 137-148.

[75] The Church is 'the universal sacrament of salvation' (Vatican II, *De Ecclesia*, para. 48).

[76] Cf. M. Wilson *Health is for People* (London, 1975), pp. 51-55; J. Mathers 'Therapeutic Communities', *Community Schools Gazette*, Vol. 68, no. 2, pp. 80-87; D. Clark *Social Therapy in Psychiatry* (London, 1974); M. Jones *Social Psychiatry in Practice* (London, 1952).

[77] Professor Hollenweger has drawn attention to the tendency for white Pentecostal Churches to move in the direction of written orders of service, 'The Social and Ecumenical Significance of Pentecostal Liturgy', *Studia Liturgica*, 8, no. 4, 1971-72, pp. 211-212. Kevin Ranaghan mentions such printed forms being used in services of baptism among classical Pentecostals, 'Conversion and Baptism: Personal Experience and Ritual Celebration in Pentecostal Churches', *Studia Liturgica, 10*, no. 1 1974, p. 73, note 7.

[78] The Sociology of Religion, Vol. 2, p. 310.

[79] I am not intending to imply that Pentecostals are all sectarian. On this point cf. W. J. Hollenweger *The Pentecostals*, pp. 502-505.

[80] *God's People*, pp. 5, 48 (note 1), 61.

[81] On dancing see W. J. Hollenweger 'Danced Documentaries: The Theological and Political Significance of Pentecostal Dancing', *Worship and Dance* (ed. J. G. Davies), University of Birmingham, 1975, pp. 76-82.

[82] It is a test of the liveliness of a Pentecostal assembly not just whether such interventions occur but whether they are encouraged and accepted from outside the ranks of the leaders and 'nuclear members'.

[83] Jim Cavnar describes his astonishment at first encountering this form of corporate prayer: "Once we were all comfortably settled Ray said, 'Well, let's begin with a word of prayer'. What a shock to us when suddenly everyone in the room simultaneously burst into loud and enthusiastic prayer." (*Participating in Prayer Meetings*, Ann Arbor, 1974, p. 10).

[84] Vatican II's Constitution on the Liturgy states: 'Mother Church earnestly desires that all the faithful be led to that full, conscious, and active participation in liturgical celebrations which is demanded by the very nature of the liturgy.' para. 14, Cf. also paras. 21, 27, 30 and 50.

[85] 'The Pentecostals thus demonstrate that the alternative to a written liturgy is not chaos, but a flexible oral tradition, which allows for variation within the framework of the whole liturgical structure, similar to the possibilities of variation in a jam session of jazz musicians.' (W. J. Hollenweger 'Liturgies, Pentecostal', *A Dictionary of Liturgy and Worship*, ed. J. G. Davies, London 1972, p. 241).

[86] '. . . if someone sings a song of praise in the *Kyrie* part, or gives a prophecy in the invocation part, he will be corrected either by the pastor, or by an elder, or if he persists, by the immediate and spontaneous singing of the whole congregation' (W. J. Hollenweger art. cit. in note 85, p. 241).

[87] 'Their own preachers do not dance either; their duty is not to dance, but to interpret the dances." (W. J. Hollenweger 'The Social and Ecumenical Significance of Pentecostal Liturgy', *Studia Liturgica*, 8, no. 4 1971-72, p. 210).

[88] Such a change in preparation for ministry and preaching is described in the testimonies of some priests in *The Lord is My Shepherd* (ed. G. Kosicki), Ann Arbor, 1973.

[89] As will the barrenness of much opposition to liturgical creativity.

[90] This is neither to reject altogether the need for liturgical legislation nor to deny a proper function for liturgical commissions. But it is to see the renewal of liturgy as a creative process necessarily involving all persons in the Christian community at whatever level.

[91] 'Discussing the ecclesial significance of the altar service a leading American Pentecostal minister has said that in the early days of the denominational period a crisis experience was not considered valid unless it happened in the context of the congregation. Later it became common to think that the experience was real if there were just two people praying together. More recently there has been a swing back at least to insist that private experience is incomplete until it is publicly acknowledged in the congregation.' (K. Ranaghan 'Conversion and Baptism; Personal Experience and Ritual Celebration in Pentecostal Churches', *Studia Liturgica*, 10, no. 1, 1974, p. 72.

[92] Cf. the Declarations of Faith printed in W. J. Hollenweger *The Pentecostals*, pp. 517, 520.

[93] Mark 16:20.

[94] Cf. 'The Speech-Giving Spirit' pp. 152 below.

[95] Cf. e.g. B. Leeming *Principles of Sacramental Theology* (London, 1956), pp. 251-263.

[96] If in sound theological fashion we approach the visibility of grace from

God's standpoint, we will say that to God all things are visible and from him nothing is hidden (Ps. 139; Mt. 6: 4,18) and that the sanctification of believers increases their likeness to God and their capacity to see the works of God.

[97] From the New Testament onwards (e.g. Eph. 1:17; Col. 1:10; John, 17:3) Christian tradition affirms that the Christian is called to a knowledge of God, a quest that is presupposed in the writings of Christian mystics. So, e.g., 'All rational beings, angels and men, possess two faculties, the power of knowing and the power of loving. To the first, to the intellect, God who made them is forever unknowable, but to the second to love, he is completely knowable, and that by every separate individual.' (The Cloud of Unknowing, Ch. 4, Penguin edn., p.55)

[98] Cf. p. 29 above and note 72.

[99] Cf. note 19 above.

[100] This applies to the distinctive Johannine sense of semeion as well as to that in the Synoptics and Acts.

[101] Cf. De Ecclesia, paras. 1, 8, 48.

[102] At the origins of Pentecostalism, with Charles Parham in Topeka, Kansas, U.S.A., belief in glossolalia as the sign of the Spirit preceded its occurrence (cf. H. V. Synan The Holiness-Pentecostal Movement in the United States, pp. 100-102; J. T. Nichol The Pentecostals Plainfield 1966, pp. 26-29); something similar had happened with the Irvingite movement in the 19th century (cf. C. G. Strachan The Pentecostal Theology of Edward Irving, pp. 61-69).

[103] It is of course possible to say that experiences have the same forms of expression phenomenologically speaking.

[104] In the section 'Outward Sings and Inner Reality', pp. 32-34 above.

[105] So, for example, the exercise of spiritual gifts, a sense of the presence of God, and of the particularity of his love ('He loves me!'),a freedom in prayer with a new predominance of praise and thanksgiving, a thirst for prayer and for the Word.

[106] At their worst, doctrinal fundamentalism can make Pentecostals as rigid as any; but I have argued that this rigidity is not central to what is most distinctive in Pentecostalism.

[107] e.g. W. T. H. Richards Pentecost is Dynamite (London, 1972), pp. 77-80 and The Charismatic Movement in the Historic Churches (London, 1972).

[108] This conversation took place in Birmingham in 1975 at a church where the attitude towards Catholics has changed markedly over the past three years.

[109] Professor Hollenweger has drawn attention to the highly pragmatic way in which the apostles and elders at Jerusalem accepted the conversion of the Gentiles (chapter on 'Conversion' in Evangelism Today, Belfast 1976).

[110] Pentecost is Dynamite, p. 52.

[111] Pentecostals make appeal to New Testament texts emphasising testimony to visible events, e.g. Matt. 11: 4-5; II John: 1; Acts 2:33.

[112] These are of course two of the most visible of the spiritual gifts, particularly when as with classical Pentecostals healing refers almost entirely to physical cure and amelioration.

[113] E.g. D. Watson *One in the Spirit* (London, 1973), p. 96.

[114] Cf. H. V. Synan *The Holiness – Pentecostal Movement in the United States*, pp. 217-218.

[115] Cf. W. J. Hollenweger *The Pentecostals*, pp. 415-421.

[116] Donald Gee *Wind and Flame* (London, 1967), p. 3.

[117] Cf. P. Hocken 'Pentecostals on Paper', I, *The Clergy Review*, November 1974, pp. 762-767.

[118] For the white Western character of biblical fundamentalism cf. G. Every 'Prophecy in the Christian Era', pp. 187-9 below.

[119] The same problem arises from the spread of the Pentecostal movement to the Orthodox and to various Anglican Churches, but it is being posed on a wider scale in the Roman Catholic Church.

[120] *New Wine in Old Wineskins* (Gloucester, 1973), p. 48.

[121] The real distinctiveness of Pentecostalism is only barely indicated in official Declarations of Faith. Nichol notes of the Statement of Truth drawn up by the Pentecostal Fellowship of North America: 'Except for Article Five, this entire formulation was taken from the Statement of Faith that was drawn up in 1943 by the National Association of Evangelicals.' *The Pentecostals*, pp. 4-5).

[122] I am arguing here that Catholics can have a different theological understanding, not that all do. Donald Gelpi, SJ is one Catholic writer who has insistently warned against the danger of Catholic Pentecostals accepting a Protestant theology along with new life in the Spirit. Cf. *Pentecostal Piety*, pp 61-80, and 'Ecumenical Problems and Possibilities' in *The Holy Spirit and Power* (ed. K. McDonnell), pp. 173-186. I find Gelpi's writings unduly negative, with more about the problems than about the possibilities.

[123] Cf. the chapter 'His Lifegiving Body' in Thomas Smail's *Reflected Glory* (London, 1975) in which he speaks of a 'charismatic humanism' (p. 122) proclaiming 'the rising of the total man in the power of the Spirit'. Smail's book is important for grounding this hope in a pneumatic Christology.

[124] The possibility of neutral spirits need not be excluded.

[125] Cf. pp. 19-36.

[126] Much light has been thrown on these controverted areas between Catholic and Protestant by the theological tradition of the Orthodox Churches. The Pentecostal injection sometimes reinforces, sometimes challenges the Orthodox contribution.

[127] As e.g. S. Carrillo 'The Baptism in the Holy Spirit' in T. Flynn *The Charismatic Renewal and the Irish Experience* (London, 1974), pp. 167-188.

[128] This is more a statement of how theology grapples with the data of contemporary Christian experience than a criticism of particular attempts to do this.

[129] Cf. p. 35 above.

[130] Cf. Rom 12.2 and J. O. Mills, pp. 99-100.

[131] As love necessarily leaps ahead of understanding, and brings about its own form of knowledge, so will opening of the heart to God's Love lead on to renewal of the mind.

[132] 1 Cor. 2:12.

[133] Catholics will tend to be rather more flexible than Evangelicals as to

the criteria for being 'within'.
[135] 1 Cor. 2:14.
[135] *The Pentecostals*, p. 499.
[136] The predominantly oral and non-literary nature of Pentecostal communication does not promote accurate knowledge of those neither met nor seen – this applies particularly to racial and cultural differences.
[137] Some authors describing Latin American Pentecostalism with sympathy, e.g. R. Wagner, *Look Out! The Pentecostals are Coming* and J. T. Nichol *The Pentecostals*, Ch. 10. conceive it in white terms with a resulting emphasis on quantitative expansion. Contrast these with Hollenweger's *The Pentecostals*, esp. Chs. 6-8.
[138] Cf. *African Independent Church Movements* (ed. V. E. W. Hayward), London, 1963.
[139] Cf. comments on Nicholas Bhengu in W. J. Hollenweger *The Pentecostals*, esp. pp. 132-133.
[140] The Aladura Churches of West Africa do not fulfil Hollenweger's criteria for inclusion in his study (cf. criteria given on p. xix) but Bryan Wilson writes of them: 'The movement was affected by the pentecostalism being disseminated in Nigeria by the Apostolic Church missionaries from Britain, and perhaps by other pentecostalist bodies, but the central idea of gaining spiritual power was certainly indigenous.' (*Magic and the Millennium*, London 1975, p. 164). Cf. also op. cit., pp. 174-178.
[141] *Magic and the Millennium*, p. 121. Wilson's fascinating study, admirable in attention to detail and in the balance of his judgments, by its very categorisation of religious responses, especially that of the thaumaturgical on pp. 53-60, does tend to force sects into one category thereby falsifying the role of elements not really fitting that category, e.g. 'Once sectarian proselytizing missions had been established, the indigenous thaumaturgical preoccupation acquired reinforcement, for even in conversionist sects thaumaturgical elements often persist – in glossalalia, faith-healing, and prophesying' (op. cit., p.. 147).
[142] Cf. W. J. Hollenweger *The Pentecostals*, Ch. 12, esp p. 157.
[143] *Schism and Renewal in Africa*, p. 47.
[144] i. e. of king and of medicine man.
[145] *The Pentecostals*, p. 158. Cf. too B. Wilson *Magic and the Millennium*, pp. 143-147.
[146] Cf. W. J. Hollenweger, art. cit., *Worship and Dance*, cf. note 81 above.
[147] W. T. H. Richards *Pentecost is Dynamite*, p. 68.
[148] Cf. quotation from D. Double *Life in a new dimension* (St. Austell, 1974) in G. Every art. cit., p. 191 below.
[149] As always in life, anxiety and the burden of freedom produce a pressure to imitate and hence to standardise. The Holy Spirit produces variety in harmony (cf.1 Cor. 12:4-6 with the juxtaposition of *varieties* and *same*).
[150] *The Pentecostals*, p. 3.
[151] Both forms of description are appropriate. Some neo-Pentecostals have only discovered after the event that others have experienced the same phenomena (cf. C. Urquhart *When the Spirit comes*, London 1974), whilst

others have been influenced by classical Pentecostals; several authors here refer to the influence of the Full Gospel Businessman's Fellowship International (cf. J. T. Nichol *The Pentecostals*, p. 241; E. D. O'Connor *The Pentecostal Movement in the Catholic Church*, Notre Dame 1971, p. 24).

[152] Even before this outbreak, as early as 1953, Lesslie Newbigin urged upon Catholics and Protestants the need for a positive approach to Christians of a pentecostal type, which he saw as a third bloc (his use of the term 'pentecostal' is wider than that adopted in this essay). Cf. *The Household of God*, Chapter IV.

[153] Cf. D. Bennett *Nine O'Clock in the Morning* (Plainfield, 1970); M. Harper *As at the Beginning* (London, 1965), pp. 60-70; M. T. Kelsey *Tongue speaking* (London, 1964), pp. 98-104;

[154] Apart from the early instance of Alexander Boddy, who always remained an Anglican (cf. W. J. Hollenweger *The Pentecostals*, pp. 184-185), other precursors of Bennett can be traced (cf. J. T. Nichol *The Pentecostals*, p. 240).

[155] Cf. 1 Cor. 12:7 and 14:12.

[156] There are other grounds on which objection is made to this Pentecostal classification e.g. that it separates the Spirit from Christ (T. A. Smail *Reflected Glory*, pp. 44-50), that it is divisive and elitist (D. Bridge and D. Phypers *Spiritual Gifts and the Church*, London 1973, pp. 131-139).

[157] I.e. in baptism, confirmation and eucharist.

[158] Cf. K. Ranaghan 'Liturgy and Charisms' in *The Holy Spirit and Power* (ed. K. McDonnell), pp. 139-171.

[159] For its origins in Britain and in the Church of England see M. Harper *As at the Beginning*, pp. 80-89, but cf. also note 154.

[160] The most detailed account of the origins of the movement among Catholics is in E. D. O'Connor *The Pentecostal Movement in the Catholic Church*, pp. 39-107.

[161] I have deliberately chosen the descriptive term 'loyalty' rather than the theologically weightier term 'membership'. The latter would in any case be misleading and inaccurate in this context, suggesting a more total and structured adhesion than is involved in the new forms of belonging and attachment described by the term 'loyalty'... Stephen Clark has a somewhat careless account of this double loyalty: 'Those of us who are involved in the Catholic charismatic renewal find ourselves members of two Christian bodies: the largest Christian church in the world and a very dynamic movement involving people from all the churches.' (*Where are we headed?*, Notre Dame 1973, pp. 49-50)

[162] The charismatic movement within the Roman Catholic Church has become the most organised section of the pentecostal world, with its own national committees, conferences, publishing houses, communication centres and prayer-group directories.

[163] The first International Conferences on the Holy Spirit among both Lutherans and Presbyterians took place in 1972. Ralph Martin lists denominational charismatic organisations and contacts in the U.S.A. in *The Holy Spirit and Power* (ed. K. McDonnell), p. 105, note 2.

[164] Stephen Clark has made such comparisons, particularly with the

liturgical movement, in *As the Spirit leads Us* (ed. K. & D. Ranaghan), Paramus 1971, pp.17-37, *Building Christian Communities* (Notre Dame, 1972) and *Where are we headed?* (Notre Dame, 1973), p. 19.

[165] Such comparisons also show further differences between the charismatic and other renewal movements, e.g. what is meant by participation, the role of structures within a movement, its ecumenical spread. Cf. P. Hocken 'Catholic Pentecostalism: Some Key Questions' *The Heythrop Journal*, Vol. XV, 1974, pp. 280-282.

[166] '. . . the ambition of the Charismatic Renewal is to eliminate itself as soon as possible, much as, on another level, the biblical or liturgical movements have ceased to be identifiable groups and disappeared into the life of the Church. The purpose is to disappear when the goal is reached' (L, J. Cardinal Suenens *A New Pentecost?* p. 113).

[167] Cf. J. O. Mills, III, pp. 83-5; IV, pp. 88-9: V pp. 94; VI, pp. 105-6.

[168] Other Christians may not always realise how the extensive system of religious orders has preserved in the Roman Catholic Church a greater variety than public image and often official statements would suggest.

[169] Besides the statements of some episcopal conferences (e.g. U.S.A., Canada), see the words of Paul VI to the International Conference held in Rome at Pentecost 1975 *(New Covenant,* July 1975).

[170] That is, I identify with Pentecostals as indicated on pp. 19-36 above, differing from their self-understanding as stated on pp. 36-40.

[171] This is deliberately worded to evoke a comparison with Aquinas' teaching on the New Law: 'principaliter lex nova est lex indita, secundaria autem est lex scripta' *(Summa Theologiae,* 1a 2ae, q. 106. a. 1).

[172] Francis MacNutt's book *Healing* illustrates such a pragmatic form of learning, in which more attention is paid to experience and what is done than to general theories.

[173] This discernment, which needs to take place within a Church tradition, involves scrutiny of the Scriptures and Christian tradition (spiritual as well as doctrinal) in addition to a testing of the fruits.

[174] e.g. the treatments of apocalyptic, tongues and prophecy by the other three contributors to this book.

[175] Sometimes more so than the ministry-styles of Catholic neo-Pentecostals.

[176] I have tried to show this in my book *You He Made Alive* (London, 1974).

[177] It is basic to Roman Catholic understanding that the visible Church in communion with the See of Rome is not simply one among a number of embodiments of the mystery of Christ on earth, but Vatican II has broken the simple equation between the Mystical Body of Christ, and the Roman Catholic Church (cf. *De Ecclesia,* para. 8, especially the phrase *Haec Ecclesia. in hoc mundo ut societas constituta et ordinata, subsistit in Ecclesia catholica).*

[178] Not all Catholics involved in charismatic renewal understand their experience in this way; they are more likely to do so, the more contact they have had with other Pentecostals, particularly those from the Pentecostal Churches. But the literature on sale at gatherings within Catholic charismatic renewal does indicate loyalties, and it regularly includes

material from non-Catholic Pentecostal sources.

[179] AOG is often used as an abbreviation for Assemblies of God.

[180] Whilst the period up to the 1920s was the main phase of pentecostal fission (cf. H. V. Synan *The Holiness- Pentecostal Movement in the United States,* pp. 141-163; J. T. Nichol *The Pentecostals,* pp. 81-93), the movement continues to have a relatively high rate of schism (cf. H. V. Synan, op. cit., pp. 195-196; C. Lalive d'Epinay, *Haven of the Masses,* pp. 84-95; B. Wilson (on West African sects) *Magic and the Millennium,* pp. 160-167).

[181] The man who has done most to banish negative attitudes among Pentecostals is surely David du Plessis, who in 1949 was the first classical Pentecostal to approach the W.C.C. and subsequently the only Pentecostal observer at the Second Vatican Council. Cf. W. J. Hollenweger *The Pentecostals,* p. 7; M. Harper *As at the Beginning,* pp. 51-59.

[182] Cf. W. J. Hollenweger *The Pentecostals,* pp. 505-507.

[183] The same can be claimed for many of the secessions involved in the rise of African Independent Churches. These are applications of a theology of God as the One who can bring good out of evil.

[184] E.g. in Inter-Church marriages (cf. *One in Christ,* 1968, pp. 130-136; 1969, pp. 64-105; *Beyond Tolerance,* London 1975), and in Areas of Ecumenical Experiment in Great Britain (cf. R. M. C. Jeffery *Ecumenical Experiments: a Handbook,* B.C.C., 1971; D. Blatherwick *Adventures in Unity,* B.C.C., 1974; *Guidelines for Local Ecumenical Projects,* Consultative Committee for Local Ecumenical Projects in England, 1975). For similar questions arising in a different context cf. J. Nijenhuis 'The Possibility of Plural Ecclesial Membership and General-Christian Membership in the Netherlands', *Journal of Ecumenical Studies,* Vol. 11, 1974, pp. 748-749.

[185] Whilst 'double loyalty' is a less precise concept than 'dual membership', the latter also admits of a range of possible meanings as diverse as the concepts of membership found across the ecumenical spectrum. Sympathetic Catholic commentators have found less difficulty with the language of duality in the context of Inter-Church marriages, including the possibility of forms of dual membership for the children of such marriages, than with its application to Areas of Ecumenical Experiment and ecumenical congregations (cf. works listed in note 184). Whereas in the former, membership is being used in an ontological sense, in the latter it is far more canonical being concerned with voting rights, inclusion on membership registers and representation on denominational bodies. Cf. P.Hocken 'Roman Catholics and Ecumenical Experimentation', *One in Christ,* 1974, pp. 256-266.

[186] Whilst I have much sympathy with Professor John Macquarrie's ecumenical reflections in *Christian Unity and Christian Diversity* (London, 1975), it is still – despite the author's emphasis on 'practical ecumenism as the first and foundational step towards the goal of unity-in-diversity and diversity-in-unity' (p. 26) – a theologians' ecumenism. The ecumenical events mentioned are confined to theological agreements and Church union schemes.

[187] In Great Britain the Association of Inter-Church Families has done much to bring forms of this experience to the attention of Church leaders

and ecumenical commissions. Further information available from 23 Drury Lane, Lincoln.

[188] It is, I believe, this basic disparity between the Christian bodies described as Churches that grounds the possibility of dual and multiple allegiance. The Roman Catholic Church, which alone is organisationally one Church at the international level (in contrast to a communion or federation of autonomous national or regional Churches) would then for Catholics have some form of primacy over other and subsequent loyalties.

[189] It should be clear, e.g. from notes 184 and 185, that there are many and varied experiences of 'duality' and that we should expect ecumenical advance to produce yet further new forms and variations.

[190] Just as schisms are prepared by dissentient groups within a Church, so in reverse reunion may be preceded by the development of loyalties which begin outside one's tradition but lead towards one loyalty to Jesus Christ within one reunited Church.

[191] It is important not to understand this in quantitative terms, e.g. as a split in one's affections. Such a quantitative approach overlooks the mysterious character of the Church in which the core is the Christ confessed by each Church.

[192] A theology of schism is surely an integral part, though not the conclusion, of a theology of ecumenism.

[193] African Independent Churches are in general now eager to join Councils of Churches and gain ecumenical recognition. Cf. D. B. Barrett *Schism and Renewal in Africa*, pp. 199-203. Three such independent Churches were admitted to full membership of the World Council of Churches at the Nairobi Assembly in 1975 (the Kimbanguist Church from Zaire was already a member) and one other to associate membership.

[194] For an account of the Holy Spirit and the Cross see T. A. Smail *Reflected Glory*, pp. 104-118.

[195] Cf. W. J. Hollenweger *The Pentecostals*, pp. 4-9 in regard to the rise of the Pentecostal, movement within the traditional Churches of the U.S.A.

[196] This is probably the point on which a pro-Pentecostal apologetic should centre.

[197] Cf. T. A. Smail 'Theology of Renewal and the Renewal of Theology'. *Theological Renewal*, No. 1, pp. 2-4.

[198] James Dunn writing of the widespread modern occurrence of glossolalia writes: 'The importance of such manifestations in religious history for our understanding of the event of Pentecost was rightly stressed by K. L. Schmidt.' (*Jesus and the Spirit*, p. 150). There is nothing essentially different about utilising the contemporary experience of glossolalia and prophecy to understand apposite New Testament texts from interpreting passages on prayer from the experience of prayer.

[199] This is the task of discernment, within which there is a doctrinal component.

[200] Ezekiel 37:1-14.

[201] Classical Pentecostals have sometimes defended neo-Pentecostals remaining within their Churches of upbringing by saying: God is not only the One who creates out of nothing, but is he who raises from the dead!

67

New Heaven? New Earth?

JOHN ORME MILLS OP

CONTENTS

I. PENTECOSTAL AND APOCALYPTIC

GOD, IN THE VERY last great vision recorded in the book of Revelation, tells the seer John that he is renewing the whole universe. 'Look!' he says. 'I am making all things new.'

Man is scared of the new. More exactly, although we are all constantly chasing novelty there is much in our make-up which will resist anything novel that touches the deepest part of ourselves. By human reckoning there is little space for the future to break into our lives, little space for what is new and revolutionary to enter and change us, because the great majority of our consciously held religious attitudes – the attitudes that control our way of looking at the world and shape our moral values – were moulded in the sheltered milieu of our early childhood, when most of us were well out of hearing of the earth's prophets, poets and protesters. So those prophets, poets and protesters contest among themselves for our hearts and minds with the odds heavily against them all.

And has the going ever been so hard for them as in this present society, with its uncanny capacity for absorbing and co-opting even its most uncompromising opponents? This is the society which turned Picasso into a millionaire and his most savage paintings into good financial investments; a society whose moderately well-heeled, well-intentioned hawkers of ideas – its intelligentsia and media men – have in hardly half a decade detached 'theology of liberation' from its roots in the anguish of the poor and detached the so-called counter culture from its roots in serious social criticism and have converted both into anybody's and everybody's playthings. Can nothing escape such a society's neutralising, trivialising force? Not even the gospel message, which claims to be ever set over against the world, to be ever new?

Today a growing number of Christians are aiming to enrich their lives by becoming, through the sharing of prayer together more open to the working of the Holy Spirit, so prominent in the pages of the New Testament. And some of these Christians are ending up badly disappointed. There is no one reason for this. The real source of trouble in a prayer group is rarely, though, that the people in it are being too bold in their aim. No, a much more common reason why things go wrong is that the people in it have never been bold enough! The almost exclusive emphasis found in some groups on acquisition of charisms and on immediate fulfilment, accompanied as this invariably is by absence of emphasis on that future dimension – that 'lively expectation' – which was so marked a feature of the primitive church, means that from the start such groups unwittingly are dominated not so much by the values of New Testament Christianity as by the values of our present-day consumer society, outward appearances notwithstanding.

Now, what made the Pentecostal revival in the United States at the beginning of this century important, what set it against the world and much contemporary religious practice as if it were something startlingly new, something that could transform men's lives, was not (to take the most obvious example) that people 'spoke in tongues'. After all, if considered apart from its Christian context speaking in tongues is not a particularly interesting or unusual phenomenon, let alone something to astonish or disconcert the Christian world.

No, what was arresting about those first twentieth-century Pentecostals was their conviction (a conviction tongue-speaking and the other gifts they believed they had been given irrefutably confirmed, in their opinion) that the new pouring-out of God's Holy Spirit on them had empowered them to share fully the life of the church of the apostles, the 'church of Pentecost'. And – so alive was their vision of the New Testament church – this meant that they experienced a fresh, urgent sense of expectation which they could identify with that known by the first generation of Christians. The charismatic manifestations emerging among them – tongues, healing, exorcism, prophecy – they interpreted as signs that they were living in the 'last times'; the scriptures were being fulfilled: here was the 'latter rain' spoken of by Joel and James, portending the coming of the Lord in glory at the world's end. Is it surprising, then, that they had such confidence, such hope? Were they not *already* seeing around them indications that all things were being made new, as told in the book of Revelation?

Maybe it was John the Divine himself who first used the word *apocalypsis*, which opens the Greek text of his book and eventually was turned into its title, in order to describe a book of visions of the end of time.[1] We can certainly say he uses the word in a special way: for him *revelation* describes both the process of unveiling the ultimate issues of history and those ultimate truths unveiled. And ever since the third century Christians have called similar Christian or Jewish writings 'apocalypses'. Not until 1,600 years later did biblical scholars, looking for a collective term which would describe not only the literary genre but also the realm of ideas from which this literature came, coin the word 'apocalyptic'.

This now much misused word is one I cannot do without in the following pages, but do not be misled because 'apocalyptic' recurs in these pages even more frequently than the word 'Pentecostal'. Although here there is only room to explore ways towards answering two interrelated questions which sound fairly narrow and abstruse, these two questions in fact raise issues both central to the Christian faith and, I believe, of central importance to all who would reflect on the significance of Pentecostalism. This is the first of them: what reason have we to think that an encounter by members of the main Christian churches with 'classical' Pentecostalism could help to bring about *a renewed and revitalized awareness of the apocalyptic element in the Christian tradition?* Secondly, what meaning (if any) could this 'apocalyptic element' possibly have for the Christian of today?

II. ABANDONED EXPECTATIONS

COME, LORD, COME QUICKLY!' a man prayed. 'Yes, Lord, quickly!'
'Quickly, Lord!' These were the voices of others praying with him.
But what exactly were that group praying for? The warm bright
glow that seemed to descend into the centre of their circle regularly
at ten to nine every Monday evening? Was that all? Perhaps that
was all, for a year later that group was divided, bickering and
desolate. It is a very different sort of coming that the Lord is promis-
ing when he says at the end of the book of Revelation, John's
Apocalypse, 'Surely I am coming soon.' Not a comfortable glow but
something much more worthwhile to pray for: a judgment. A judgment to end all judgments.

Apocalyptic ideas centre round that notion of a 'last judgment', a
notion older than any apocalyptic but the one which the Jewish
apocalyptists were fired to push into the very middle of the picture
... and, in doing so, transformed. And, all things considered, what
an amazingly enduring hold the prospect of that Last Great Day had
on the Christian imagination! Easter followed Easter, the years
stretched into decades, the decades into centuries, and where were
the signs that John had been right when he had said 'The time is
near?' Instead, Christianity had grown into a state religion and most
Christians, far from being members of a persecuted minority waiting
hopefully for its Deliverer and for the revolutionary transformation
of the world order he would bring, were owners of a big stake in the
world order already established. Devout Christian emperors identified their own rule with Christ's kingdom. Christians went on saying in their creeds that Christ 'will come again in glory to judge the
living and the dead', but the Jewish thought-world in which expectation of a final cosmic judgment by God had emerged had vanished

74

when the Church was still very young; 'eternal life' had come to be thought of primarily in Greek terms, in terms of immortality of the soul rather than resurrection of the body. Surely, then, it would not have been surprising if in actual fact even long before the middle ages began 'the judgment' had come to be seen as something private, something virtually identifiable with each individual's moment of death, and Christ's return as something very remote and secondary? This is true of a growing number of people. Yet throughout the middle ages expectation of Christ's great and terrible coming did still capture the minds of multitudes of men, although it was a coming looked forward to less in hope than in fear. Among the rootless poor in particular millenarianism (the belief, based on Rev. 20:4-6, that at the end of time the blessed would be raised to rule what was often a very earthy paradise) was far from dead. From the eleventh century to the seventeenth it inspired a number of popular revolutionary movements, and the wild and heterodox Christian Sibylline oracles which excited so many of the leaders of these movements were possibly the most influential writings known to medieval Europe after the Bible and the works of the Church Fathers.[2] But not only on the fringes of society but also at its centre at least some of the content of the credal affirmations of Christ's coming in glory survived even into modern times, although torn from its roots in a past thought-world, simply because the imagery of Jewish apocalyptic (its angelology and demonology, its pictures of heaven and hell,), which had been taken over by the Christian church with few modifications, lived on long after the historical thrust of apocalyptic had been almost forgotten. For that imagery gave expression only too well to man's deepest hopes and fears, his joy and anguish. Its prominence in the Bible also helped to preserve it, and so did Christian apocalypses outside the Bible like the *Apocalypse of Paul*,[3] whose descriptions of hell's torments entered popular tradition and penetrated formative minds like Dante's. Some of that imagery is with us still. Shunned by many modern Christians, it does not crop up merely in the occult paperback but sprouts, disguised, in places less expected – as, for instance, in the teachings of the Aetherius Society.[4]

Now, the Aetherius Society's bizarre brand of flying saucery exemplifies the fact that it is never possible totally to separate all the imagery from the basic ideas it conveyed. And indeed, even today, even in the world outside the Christian community, there thrive in often heavily secularised guises – the doom boom, the jump to the moon, anarchism and the demo, the novels of Patrick White and Tolkien – enunciations or actings-out of fragmented apocalyptic fantasies which are more than mere repetitions of archetypal imagery, for they convey hints of some of those abiding elements of the apocalyptic message I shall be trying to pick out shortly. This is why there seems to be 'something religious' about them. But fragments they merely are. Whereas in, say, the New Testament writings apocalyptic is an integral part of a total picture of the universe, these present-day fragments of apocalyptic are atomised. They are, then, at the edge of man's world, not the centre. They do not hold his world together for him. Not normally, at any rate. So they do not confront him with a call to total personal commitment.

Ironically, it was a millenarian, Newton,[5] who, by giving Western man a picture of a virtually self-sufficient universe theoretically infinite in time and space, a universe in which we could stand up and say 'All the future is ours and ours alone', did more than almost anybody else to make it difficult in the long run for even the great majority of plain church-goers to find room in the centre of their conscious world for apocalyptic (or, more specifically, for ways of comprehending reality deeply rooted in apocalyptic). It was not, however, until the 1870s that 'informed opinion' in England became decisively secularised,[6] and much later still before the great intellectual and social upheavals of the last three centuries began to have significant impact on popular religious thought and feeling among members of the major denominations of the English-speaking world. Even in the early 1950s, in some Roman Catholic schools in certain of the the more remote bits of the United States, children were not merely being warned of the imminence of the day of judgment but were actually being given a date for it by zealous persons who had read things into the Fatima prophecies of 1917 which we can safely say were never there. But by the middle of this century, although over half of all the people in the English-speaking world calling themselves Christians still clung to some notion of 'life after death',[7] what quite a number of these people were now looking forward to – when they gave the matter any thought at all – was something very private and not specifically Christian. For these men and women heaven had, it would almost seem, dwindled to the size of a sitting room in suburbia, a room just large enough for a happy reunion of loved ones. Some of the central tenets of the Christian

76

faith (especially those concerning resurrection, judgment, heaven and hell), which had their most primitive formulations in a culture where apocalyptic was very much alive, had quietly dropped out of the personal belief systems of throngs of practising Christians, leaving only their ghosts behind. To find Christians for whom the age-old expectation was still a live part of their faith increasingly one had to look in the direction of the sects . . . groups who had insulated themselves from the onslaught of modern thought, modern technology.

But if, in the lives of most modern Christians, only the ghost of these central tenets of faith survive, who can lay ghosts of such a kind? They haunt not only plain church-goers but all the uncommitted millions as well! For these seemingly untenable tenets of faith have had an immeasurable influence in the shaping of the mind of Western man and they are still a part of his world, even if now a part commonly unrelated to the other parts, a part banished to life's margins or into the darkness of the unconscious [8] to endure like components of a shattered space-ship rolling interminably in orbit. They come into modern man's world as the 'fragmented apocalyptic' I have already spoken about, which it is only too easy to think we can live with comfortably and safely because it does not hang together to form an integrated world-picture which demands to be accepted by us as a picture of our own 'real' world, and so makes no demands on faith. At any time we feel we can, as it were, slap the book shut and say 'Ah well, it is only a story'.

In contrast, at the core of the Christian claim is an insistence that the 'story of Jesus' is *not* 'only a story'. Christians tell their contemporaries that the doings and sayings of a man who lived out his earthly life a couple of thousand years ago have a unique bearing on their own lives. But that is not all. To convey what they mean by that claim Christians must confront their contemporaries with the New Testament writers, who interpreted the significance of that man's life for all humanity (past, present and to come) in terms of the world-picture of their own time, of their own culture – the world-picture shared by him whom they were writing about. An apocalyptic picture. 'Apocalyptic was the mother of all Christians theology'[9].

Of course, some of the imagery and most of the cosmology [10] in this apocalyptic were solely part-and-parcel of the culture and lost their original significance when the culture disappeared. But some elements in it are of lasting importance not only because the basic Christian message cannot be detached from them without being badly distorted but also because they are in Western man's very bones. Even when other Christian concepts had crumbled it was still hard for him not to see himself or his people or the whole of mankind as moving towards some ultimate fulfilment. Until about the time of World War Two he still had an instinctive sense of being in a time-stream, of having a destiny.[11] He might have long abandoned all thought of a divine judgment but not of an 'end-time' (*eschaton* in Greek – hence the term 'eschatology', the part of theology concerned with the final destiny both of the individual and the cosmos). And this eschatological concept of time was rooted deeply in biblical apocalyptic. One of the major social consequences of modern technology has been an undermining of this sense of destiny, but its eradication has led to a growing feeling of meaninglessness: the substitutes do not satisfy the deepest human yearnings. A succession of pleasant kicks – what compensation is that for loss of a feeling of direction? In one of England's newest new towns the young spray their own slogans across the signs on the new highway.

It is, maybe, not wholly coincidental that serious questioning of the values of technological society and recovery of an awareness of the importance of the apocalyptic dimension in the New Testament message began round about the same time. For the ghosts of the Last Things confront man still – that is clear – and in trying to exterminate them he has come near to exterminating himself. As at least some of the madness and violence of our century bears witness, 'fragmented apocalyptic' can be very dangerous. If we are to survive and grow we shall have to salvage our abandoned expectations even if the old language that clothed them will no longer do; we shall have to reintegrate into the centre of our lives the complex of meanings behind those outlandish credal statements . But how? Some of the preparatory back-room work has already begun. In the last century there was a growing tendency, particularly among educated protestants, to see Jesus basically as an ethical teacher. And then, in 1892, a young man, Johannes Weiss, wrote Jesus's idea of the Kingdom of God appears to be inextricably involved with a number of eschatological-apocalyptic views ... The Kingdom of God as Jesus thought of it is never something subjective, inward or spiritual'.[12] A few years later Albert Schweitzer developed still further this apocalyptic interpretation of Jesus and the apostolic church. The 'rediscovery of apocalyptic' has in fact, been at the heart of theological debate in this century, particularly in Germany but now to an increasing extent in the English-speaking world as well.

However, before suggesting why this debate has been largely ignored or misunderstood by the man-in-the-pew I must first say what I see to be the permanent salient features of apocalyptic which I believe to be of such abiding importance in Christianity and the life of Western man. And I have no chance of doing that convincingly without also saying something about the world in which apocalyptic came to its full maturity: the stormy world into which Jesus was born.

III 'BE HOPEFUL, YE RIGHTEOUS ... '

HOW HARD IT is for us to put ourselves in the place of the Israelites and get an inkling of how powerfully their covenant with God, with Yahweh 'who had led them out of the land of Egypt', shaped their whole way of understanding the world, their 'universe of meaning ', giving them that capacity to scan the past and describe the present in terms of past symbols which is to be seen in its most developed form in Jewish apocalyptic writing. [13] If the covenant conditions were known and kept, then the effect of God ought to be discernible: the very *completeness* of this world view, rooted in a radical belief in the supremacy of Yahweh, contained within itself the seeds of crisis. For when could the righteous suffer without bringing about doubt in the effectiveness of God?

During the five centuries between the return of the Israelites from exile in Babylon and the birth of Jesus the tensions grew. Time and again it looked as if the promises which had been given to Israel through the prophets were being realised in the post-exilic theocracy. [14] Time and again those hopes were crushed by fresh onslaughts of seemingly invincible heathen conquerors, by the secularising force of Greek ideas (so influential among the mighty of the land), by the widening gap between rich and poor and the increasingly oppressive power of the very rich. [15] Pious men wrestled with the problem of the suffering of the just against a background of violence and disaster, [16] and eventually a significant minority of people had come to believe that the situation was so desperate that salvation could – and would – only arrive *through God's direct intervention and his overturning of the entire existing order.* Their certainty of God's justice and loving-kindness and of the truth of the promises he had given through his prophets was the ground of their hope: all authen-

80

tic apocalyptic expectation is rooted in this conviction that God's transcendence and God's immanence are two sides of the same coin, that the God who is 'high above the heavens' will not see his people perish but will come and save them himself. This expectation was not, for these Jews, mere wishful thinking – a desire for a pleasant life. Rather, the drive towards it came 'from Job and the prophets, from *the thirst after righteousness'.*[17]

Already, first of all in Ezekiel 38-39 and then in post-exilic prophecy – particularly in Zechariah, Joel and Isaiah 24-27 – the ingredients of apocalyptic were present. Here already were pictured the terrible onslaught of Israel's enemies, now discerned as the naked forces of evil, and their destruction by God in battle; the arising of the saviour-figure; hints of what was later to be the concept of resurrection; and a universalizing of the ancient concept of the Day of the Lord, so that it became the day when God will pass final judgment on the whole earth. In the book of Daniel, the first and the greatest Jewish apocalyptic book, which was written in the shadow of the Great Persecution by the Greek Seleucid rulers and Judas Maccabeus's desperate fight to overthrow them these ingredients were integrated and clarified. Influences originating outside Israel did play a part in this process, but a minor one.[18] The fundamentals of apocalyptic had their origins in the history of God's chosen people. It has, in fact, been argued that what is novel and distinctive about this apocalyptic is not its ideas, but its literary form: for instance, that its basic object is to help to make the universe's final mystery comprehensible by the presentation of a man's life in the light of the end-time.[19] Even if this is all it is – a literary form – nevertheless it is a distinctively *Jewish* literary form, in the sense that the age-old Jewish aversion to abstractions is very much in evidence in it. It does not present the conflicts in this world and the movements in heaven and the relations between them as realities discernible only to our intellect. Like all future apocalyptic, it appeals to all the resources of our imagination. It addresses the whole of our being. It would be wrong, though, to think of apocalyptic as 'merely' a literary form, for the form cannot be divorced from the content and over the centuries each helped to shape the other. Simply by the way the authors placed in relation to each other and to their overall schemes of thought those basic ideas first voiced by the prophets, those basic ideas were altered. And clearly in what they were doing the apocalyptists were not responding just to private

81

whims but to deeply-felt longings within Israel.[20]

Who, then, were the authors of these writings that made the marrow crackle in men's bones? Of the individuals, we know virtually nothing. Behind the books, in the shadows, there appear to be standing clusters of people rather than individuals: many of these books can be seen as collections of what was first intended to be the 'secret wisdom' of a particular group of believers.[21] But this is likely to call up in our minds pictures of groups rather like the present-day prayer group mentioned at the beginning of section II – groups practising a passive, purely personal piety. Although their books may be 'a literature of the oppressed who saw no hope for the nation simply in terms of politics or on the plane of human history'.[22] that does not mean those people thought they were fighting a 'purely spiritual' battle.[23] In ancient Israel it was never possible to draw a line between 'religion' and 'politics', and the Zealots – Israel's freedom fighters – were to find in apocalyptic both inspiration and powerful propaganda. The writers themselves, however, saw *all political events as part of a greater struggle being fought out in the whole wide universe,* as we can discern in the way the books are written.

What we find in them (and, if you are looking for a handy example, read Daniel 7-12) are descriptions of the destiny of man, earth and heaven composed of accounts of visions interwoven with cosmological schemes and schematised pictures of universal history. The accounts of visions are themselves composed of complexes of cosmic and mythological motifs taken not only from the prophetic writings but also from the most archaic more-than-half-forgotten traditions of ancient Israel and drawn on by the apocalyptists (consciously or unconsciously) to construct world pictures that quite often seem to have been inspired in the first place by authentic ecstatic experiences.[24] To try us still more, even when – as in Daniel 11 – these authors are speaking of specific historical persons they are never alluded to directly but clothed in pseudonyms, and so become masked actors, larger than life. Ptolemy I Soter is always 'the king of the south'. For all these writers were convinced that they were living in 'the last days', and from this viewpoint the particular and the individual has a cosmic as well as a historical significance. Continuously the apocalyptists are leading our eyes to and fro between the immediate foreground and the great horizon. Pseudonymity even extends to the authorship. Each book addresses primarily the men of the generation when it was put together, urgently trying, while time lasts, to batter consciences or reassure the faithful remnant. But it is ascribed to a seer of the remote past, for the beginnings of time were seen to foreshadow the end-time now at hand: 'As were the days of Noah, so will be the coming of the son of man.' (Mat.24:37). So Noah or Enoch or Moses or Ezra, for instance, possessor of the 'secret' of history now disclosed as history races to its termination, is depicted as predicting all that is to come. The early readers or hearers, to whom the symbols and allusions which seem so obscure to us clearly spoke very powerfully, would have seen themselves without great difficulty as participants in the huge cosmic drama being unfolded before them, all part of God's mighty plan. Their very situation would have made understanding easier.

But can it matter whether we, 2000 years later, understand this literature or not? Curiously, for some of the people alive today who are fighting seemingly hopeless battles against obnoxious regimes or policies that question is not an obvious one: they can respond to facets of this literature in a way even scholars cannot. As one of them said to me, '*Then* the book of Revelation made sense to us'. It is not very likely that you or I will have that man's experience, however. Our battles with evil will be less dramatic, if no less dangerous. Luckily, what we are interested in is not this ancient literature itself but those things in it which became part of the 'common consciousness' of the world in which Christianity was born.

The first and most important of these is the notion of a *break* in history, the advent of a totally new age to replace this age 'of sadness and infirmities' (cf 4 Ezra [2Esdras in the Apocrypha] 4:26-37). The divine intervention is seen as the ultimate triumph of justice:

Be hopeful, ye righteous; for suddenly shall the sinner perish before you,
And you shall have lordship over them according to your desires.
(1 Enoch 96:1).

Almost identical with the notion of 'break' is the idea of a 'critical turning-point' which is conveyed here – a basic apocalyptical concept that in scripture can be traced back to Dan. 7:27. Tables will be suddenly turned

Now, for people who could only make sense of God's purpose and man's destiny in these terms there was bound to be less and less room for the greys of worldly compromise and reformism:

everything was black or white. Human beings were either 'children of light' or 'children of darkness'. Dualism as a concept may have originated outside Palestine, but it would not have entered so deeply into the consciousness of these people if it had not conformed to and articulated some way they already possessed of making sense of the world. And if it had not been for their dualistic way of understanding the human condition it is unlikely they would have adopted the dualistic notion of 'two ages' imported, we suspect, originally from Iran – the notion of a 'present age', dominated by the wicked, set against an 'age to come'. Here is an *ethical* dualism not contradictory to belief in the supremacy of Yahweh but rooted in it! The novelty is an understanding of the world and its history that has been called 'antagonistic';[25] apocalyptic theology is through and through 'a theology of conflict', a tightly-woven tapestry of antitheses. It is this that makes it so different from so much of the religion of antiquity. But all that I am saying would only be of academic interest if it were not for the fact that especially in times of crisis and cultural despair people whose understanding of the world has come to be dualistic – who interpret it in terms of conflict – are likely to have a strong sense of the *imminence* of that age to come.[26]

For a long time, however, the 'new age' was seen as this world renewed. The Lord says to the archangel Michael: 'Destroy all wrong off the face of the earth' (1 Enoch 10:15 – written a few years after Daniel). An apocalyptist writing even during the boyhood of Jesus says:

Our blood shall be avenged before the Lord.
And then His kingdom will appear *throughout all His creation,*
And then Satan shall be no more,
And sorrow shall depart with him.
(Assumption of Moses 9:7-10. 1).

Despair of all earthly blessedness only predominates among Jewish apocalyptic authors after the destruction of Jerusalem. Then one of them writes 4 Ezra, and another tells us

The youth of the world is past,
And the strength of the creation already exhausted . . .
And the pitcher is near to the cistern,
And the ship to the port:

And the course of the journey to the city,
And life to its consummation.
(2 Baruch 85:10).

But even for this author there is some continuity with earthly life: man is not a disembodied spirit when he confronts his Maker (cf. 2 Baruch 49:2-51:3). With the emergence of the apocalyptic conception of the end-time and judgment not only did the idea of a saviour-figure, a messiah, become more central but so did the idea of resurrection, which acquired an increasingly universal significance. All mankind, of every generation, is subject to the judgment of him who holds all ages in his hands . . . and it is the *whole* of man which is subject to that judgment – meaning, for Jews, body as well as soul (for the body was seen as an essential aspect of personality).[27] Asserting the truth of resurrection is a way of yet again affirming God's righteousness, of affirming the certainty of God's promise that the usurped creation will be restored, that he 'will make the last things as the first' (Epistle of Barnabas 6:13) and his children will possess 'all the glory of Adam' (Qumran Manual of Discipline col. IV). In affirming faith in man's subjection to God the resurrection hope also affirms that man is not forever subject to the 'powers of this world'.

The *hope* of the kind we find in Jewish apocalyptic is in fact the second of its salient features which have had an enduring influence on men's minds, at least in the West. It is hope rooted in the new vision of history as *wholly* in the control of God – the vision perceived by men standing, so they believed, close to the end of 'this present age' and so able to glimpse the outline of the whole of God's mighty plan. The degree to which these men were conscious of the 'things to come' was unprecedented. For them the future was not an indefinite featureless extension of the present or a cyclic repetition of the past; never before in history had it loomed up as something so distinct, so different, capturing people's imaginations and changing their attitudes to the world around them. Man's future is *not* just a product of the interactions of this world's 'powers'; his destiny is *not* controlled by what those 'powers' determine to be 'the facts of the situation': this is a recurring message of apocalyptic. Today the message is still implicitly repeated every time any of us recite with a Christian interpretation the psalmist's words

The Lord says to my lord
"Sit at my right hand,
till I make your enemies your footstool."
(110 [109] :1)

and in so doing recall what has been said to be 'the heart of primitive
Christian apocalyptic, according to the Revelation and the Synop-
tists alike'.[28]

Jewish apocalyptic's stress on *the cosmic* is its third enduring salient
feature. Many of the creators of these writings were led by their vision of history to see all things as predestined by God, because
foreknown by him, but their doctrine of predestination was not quite
like the ones taught by St Augustine and Calvin. For the apocalyptist the battle between light and darkness was not primarily a battle
between 'elected' men and 'damned', but (as I have already hinted)
primarily a cosmic battle. By saying all things were predestined they
were asserting that dominion does not ultimately belong to the
'powers' that seemed to control the universe ... 'powers' which
might assume the form of Roman emperors or astrologer's stars.
The themes of cosmology and judgment were interwoven in their
thinking:

And the whole order of the stars shall be concealed from sinners
And the thoughts of those on earth shall err concerning them ...
Yea, they shall err and take them to be gods.
(1 Enoch 80:7[29]).

Everything was seen *as a whole:* no line was drawn between cosmic
action and moral action. (Is it, then, strange that the gospel writers
tell us that while Jesus hung on the cross 'there was darkness over all
the land' [Mark 15:33 par.] ?) The present historical conflict was
seen either as a reflection of or else a participation in a great cosmic
conflict. So the author of Ephesians was voicing the deep conviction
of many a fellow-Jew, non-Christian as well as Christian, when he
said 'We are not contending against flesh and blood, but ... against
the spiritual hosts of wickedness in the heavenly places' (6:12).
And into a land seething with these ideas came Jesus.

IV HE WHO IS TO COME

'AND JOHN, CALLING to him two of his disciples, sent them to the Lord, saying, "Are you he who is to come?" ' (Luke 7:19 par.).

Jesus replies to John the Baptist's question –the earliest question about Christ – by pointing out that things Isaiah prophesied would be signs of the incoming of the messianic age were actually appearing among them.[30] All Jesus says and all his miracles repeat in one form or another his basic message, 'The time is fulfilled and the kingdom of God is at hand' (Mark 1:15). And he commands his disciples to proclaim the coming of the Kingdom in the same way – namely, not only in word but also in deed: he appoints them 'to preach *and* to have authority to cast out demons' (Mk 3:14f). Every healing, every exorcism, in fact everything said or done by Jesus or 'in his name' announces the reign of God and God's supremacy over the 'powers' of this world.

Here we can discern all three of the salient features of apocalyptic I described in section III, all of them very familiar to Jesus's world. But if 'apocalyptic was the mother of all Christian theology',[31] this certainly does not mean that Jesus's proclamation is merely an extension of apocalyptic. He had a different understanding of the way holiness is to be attained. We may recognize in his proclamation the liberating aspect of Jewish apocalyptic I have spoken about, but not its equation of righteousness with meticulous observance of the rabbinic interpretation of the letter of the Law (notice what Jesus says in Mark 7:8).[32] He asserts that there are no limits to the transforming power of the incoming Kingdom over *any* part of the order of this world, however 'sacred' or 'despicable' by men's standards. For the apocalyptists the victory of God can only be interpreted as the salvation of the 'righteous'. But what is

87

'righteousness'? Jesus asserts again and again in his words and actions the distinctiveness of God's righteousness compared with human righteousness, and also its universality.[33] Further, there is, in his own prayer life and in his teaching on worship, an eschatological emphasis that daringly goes beyond anything found in the Jewish apocalyptical sects,[34] and in his forewarnings there is an even greater element of urgency than in any Jewish apocalyptic literature: the Kingdom is so close not a moment is to be lost (cf. Luke 17:22 ff); his mission preludes the eschatological 'times of distress' (cf. Mat. 10:34 ff). Indeed, what above all is distinctive about Jesus's message is his insistence that acceptance of the Kingdom is somehow associated with acceptance of *him*.[35] Jesus believes *himself* to be the bringer of salvation, the bringer-in of the end-time: 'Whoever receives *me* , receives not me but him who sent me' (Mk. 9:37). And he brings this salvation in a way that is wholly unexpected, in a way very alien to contemporary Jewish hopes. His way of bringing in salvation is a way of suffering (cf. Mk 8:29-32).

Even so, though he is very much more than just a brilliant new apocalyptist, and some of the things he says and does clash with some current apocalyptic presuppositions and expectations, this does not alter the fact that his mission is deeply rooted in apocalyptic. Furthermore, when any of us reflect on even the mightiest manifestations of God's saving love we do not bring to these things a mind like a blank sheet of paper. Our reflections take shape within our own particular mental framework, a framework of logic and symbol. New knowledge may alter the framework, but not replace it. And this is as true of the reflections of Peter and Paul, and James and John, as it is of yours and mine. The suggestion that Jesus's resurrection to glory – the mystery at the heart of Christianity – is merely some sort of projection of the faith of the disciples simply does not hold water,[36] but it is equally hard to think that those disciples would have grasped the enigma of this extraordinary man Jesus, and especially of the meaning and outcome of his death, if apocalyptic expectation had not been part of their thought-world. By such means does God make himself known to men!

The notion of *break,* which I said in section III was the most important of the distinguishing features of apocalyptic, important not least because it transformed the meaning of a wide range of concepts (such as the concepts of resurrection, of messiah, and of that upheaval which would mark the establishment of the Kingdom), recurs

88

throughout the accounts we have of Jesus's ministry, expressed in a fairly wide variety of manners. It is present, for example, in the idea of a radical reversal, a 'critical turning-point', which underlies Jesus's assurance to his followers that although to all outward appearances they are a weak minority hopelessly outnumbered in a hostile world, nevertheless as a group they will survive and the situation will be transfigured, as it is the Father's desire to 'give them the Kingdom' (Lk 12:32).[37] However, this basic feature – break – and also the two subordinate salient features of apocalyptic which I have mentioned (namely, hope unfettered by the claims of the 'powers' of this world and perception of the cosmic significance of events) all have their ultimate expression in the Easter event and the disciples' response to it.

Apocalyptic itself being averse to abstractions, the disciples, that first Easter did not think consciously in abstract terms such as 'break'. That is obvious enough. They thought in concrete images – the notion of the eschatological son of man's accession to the heavenly throne, the expectation of a general resurrection, and Jesus's teachings about the Kingdom. What is not quite so obvious is that although the Easter event became accessible to human understanding through apocalyptic, it also *altered the content of apocalyptic*. The thinking of that little circle of men and women was apocalyptical, but it was already different from Jewish apocalyptic not only because Jesus had revealed in his death and rising how different the Father's righteousness and power was from even the devout Jew's idea of righteousness and power, but also because, by being both the obedient Son who is raised from death *and* the Lord now 'seated at the right hand of the Father', the Lord who will 'come again and be our judge', Jesus had given the word 'resurrection' a new range and profundity of meaning.

We cannot imagine what that death and resurrection was like for him. But there are hints that he himself, looking ahead towards that end, did not make our neat distinctions between his giving up of himself, his rescue from death by the Father, and 'the end of the world'.[38] For him these were one mighty act, affirming the triumph of God. If he died as the servant of God depicted in Isaiah 53, as the first Christians bear witness, then, from all that is known of Israel's understanding of sacrifice and atonement we can be sure that he would have seen his martyrdom as having *unlimited* atoning power (cf. Mk 10:45; 14:24) . . . *in other words, as ushering in the End* (marked initially by 'times of distress' when all who followed him would suffer too).[39] The New Testament writers do not see Jesus's resurrection to glory as an isolated event, one link in the chain of history. For them such an interpretation simply would not make sense. For them Jesus's resurrection can only mean the dawn of a new creation (2 Cor. 5:14-17).[40]

This does not imply however, that the first Christians 'experienced the *parousia*' (in other words, Christ's return in glory at the end of all the ages),[41] for it is impossible to 'experience' something outside one's categories of thought and this 'end' was as much outside their categories of thought as it is outside ours. They believed that 'the form of this world is passing away' (1 Cor. 7:31); they were as well aware as we are that it had not yet 'passed away' (cf. e.g. 1 Cor. 13:12). But more mistaken still is the idea that for those first Christians it was Jesus's resurrection that mattered, not the expected parousia.[42] His resurrection is a reality that began to transform people's lives in an open as distinct from a hidden way from a particular moment in time, but it is not a historical event in the sense that, say, the Battle of Waterloo or the Wall Street Crash are – both of them events which are quite properly to be seen as just two links in the interminable chain that ties time together. The resurrection (and, behind it, the cross, Jesus's proclamation, and – at the culmination of the process of reflection – the divine Incarnation) is, as St Paul in particular stresses, *to be understood in the light of the parousia ... and perhaps only to be so understood.* 'If there is no resurrection of the dead, then Christ has not been raised' says Paul (1 Cor. 15:13). Christ is 'the first fruits of those who have fallen asleep' (1 Cor. 15:20). In other words, his resurrection is the beginning of 'the great resurrection'. His appearances to his disciples are not, then, *substitutes* for the parousia but, on the contrary, announce it.[43] It is not a case of there now being no more to come, no more to hope for, but that now what is hoped for is not immeasurably distant and uncertain, as it had been for the Jewish apocalyptists, for he whose resurrection is the pledge of our hope is not a vision but one 'we have heard ... looked upon and touched with our hands' (1 John 1:1). 'In that one man the future of the new world of life has already gained power over this unredeemed world of death'.[44] Whereas the Jewish apocalyptists yearned that the future might break into the present, the Christian claim is that it already had.

Yet although this means we are living in the 'last days' (Heb.

90

1–2), which effectively is in Christian terms the same as saying we need no longer be subject to the 'powers of this world', creation has still to be 'set free from its bondage to decay' (Rom. 8:12). If you doubt this, look around you! Christian expectation, then, should not be 'less lively' than that of the Jewish apocalyptists but, if anything, 'more lively'. Shouldn't it?

V THESE LAST DAYS

THERE WAS NO shortage of 'lively expectation' in the church of Pentecost.

It would be wrong to say Christian expectation and the presence of the Holy Spirit are one and the same thing. But they are very closely associated. 'The Holy Spirit leads to the resurrection of the dead.' – an ancient Jewish rabbi wrote that.[45] Is it, then, surprising that the former Pharisee Saul, now Paul, told the Christians in Rome 'If the Spirit of him who raised Jesus from the dead dwells in you, he who raised Christ Jesus from the dead will give life to your mortal bodies also through his Spirit which dwells in you' (8–11)? The Spirit, by leading us into the 'fellowship of the sufferings of Christ' (cf. 2 Cor. 1:5), leads us into a sure hope.

But can such a claim, however firmly founded, be obvious to anybody today?

There are, in fact, a number of people alive today, people who (for one reason or another) were effectively walled off from Christianity throughout childhood but stumbled on it later and as adults got baptised, for whom clearly Paul poses fewer problems than he does for a lot of us. They have understood straight away the import of those things he says about 'dying' and 'rising' in baptism and the work of the Spirit there – things which to most present-day Christians seem so mysterious and remote. Why? Not because they are extraordinary people or have read all the right books but because (often to their own amazement) after their own baptism they actually *have* 'seen the world with new eyes', even if the freshness of the new insight has quickly gone. So, to them, the assertion that the Spirit is simultaneously both *pledge* and *power* is not a dry theological statement which does not touch 'real' life, but is an assertion their own experience vividly confirms. They know what it means to say the Spirit is the pledge of God's triumph, the ever-present assurance of that final fulfilment, universal and individual, which has even now been realised in Christ Jesus but is destined to encompass all mankind . . . the ever-present assurance given to us for our guidance (cf. John 14:26). They know what it means to say the Spirit is also the power we need if we are to undergo the suffering which all of us must endure who respond to the summons the Lord has given to us to participate in his mission and in his love (cf. Acts 20:22 ff).[46]

In the first decades of the Church's history baptism, that momentous entry into Christ's death 'so that as Christ was raised from the dead by the glory of the Father, we too might walk in newness of life' (Rom. 6:3 f), was always (except in exceptional circumstances) seen as being accompanied by the giving of the Spirit [47]. We are sure to misunderstand the sort of demands Paul is making on his raw converts and the essence of his fiery criticism of the erring Corinthian church[48] if our understanding of baptism has lost its eschatological dimension; if we have forgotten that it is drawing us under the guidance of the Spirit to a destiny beyond ourselves, beyond our cramping imaginings and desires, beyond our own concept of what 'heaven' should be like.

'Already you have reached satiety! Already you have become rich! Apart from us you have come to your kingdom!' So Paul was scathingly writing to the Corinthians less than a quarter of a century after the first Easter (1 Cor. 4:8). They had mistaken their spiritual elation for the fulfilment of the parousia, and this was a danger that constantly beset the church. It was only too easy to fall into believing that because of Easter all was already fulfilled, or else to go to the opposite extreme – like the 'Judaizers' in the Jerusalem church – and try to force the message of Easter to fit one's previous life-pattern. (How little the really basic things dividing and confusing Christians change!)

The circle of disciples had its roots in Israel's past, but had been changed by Easter; the church of the apostles was apocalyptic, but 'apocalyptic with a difference', We find the same salient features there, but see how they have altered. The cosmic element is present, but the idea of the 'times of distress' which usher in the End has been reinterpreted and developed: part of the church's vocation has been seen to be a call to suffer with its Lord (an idea perhaps most starkly conveyed in Rev. 11:7 ff.). The element of intense expectation is present, but transfigured by the Easter event, in which the End has already begun: it is expectation suffused with joy.

Above all, the most important feature of apocalyptic – the element of break – is present, but manifested not merely in signs traditionally associated in apocalyptic with the coming of the End-time, but also in signs that burst the traditional categories of apocalyptic by stressing that something wholly new is happening which is breaking the old barriers – the barriers between peoples, the barriers between man and man. The miracle of Pentecost initiates the reversal of the scattering of the nations after the building of the tower of Babel and prophesies fulfilment of the summons to obedience which, according to tradition, had been given by God on Mount Sinai to the whole wide world but had hitherto been ignored by all the nations except Israel.[49] And the pictures which Luke gives us of the early Jerusalem community, in which 'all who believed were together and had all things in common' and 'there was not a needy person among them' (Acts 2:42-47; 4:32-37), anticipate the life of the Kingdom, in which the sons of the Resurrection will be equal to the angels, freed from the bonds of mortality, neither marrying nor being given in marriage (Luke 20:35 f).[50]

Even more startling, though, is the way apocalyptic's antithetical motif recurs. Paul announces Jesus Christ as he who 'gave himself for our sins to deliver us from the present evil age' (Gal. 1:4). Moving from a contrast between death and resurrection, he contrasts the old life with the new, weakness with power, foolishness with wisdom, 'this age' with 'the age to come'. Arguably among those first Christians 'radical reversal' was a commonly shared experience.[51] By its very nature this could not be just a private conversion experience, for the 'radical reversal' is in fact an overturning in the history of the cosmos, something bigger than we can possibly conceive.

The first Christians had this experience of 'radical reversal' because they were privileged to confront a *wholly novel situation* so a fairly common thesis goes. The disappearance of 'primitive Christianity' and the hope which manifested itself in the sort of workings of the Spirit which crowd the New Testament's pages – mighty signs radically challenging the world and its oppressive values and assumptions – is linked, then, with the next generation's lack of that great privilege. The so-called 'problem of the delay of the parousia': it was this more than anything that undermined the credibility of the apocalyptic element in Christianity . . . [52]

Now, remembering all that was said in section II, is this really the case?

Just talking of the 'delay of the parousia' immediately calls up a mental picture of the church as a queue of people at a bus stop, waiting for a bus that never comes. Hours pass, hopes fade. Some turn homewards disconsolate, some find taxis, some angrily telephone the bus company, some argue with each other over the timetables and a few sit down on the pavement and pretend the bus has arrived and already taken them to their magical destination.

This may depict fairly accurately the waxing and waning of some of the millennial movements of later time, but the primitive church never in fact resembles anything like a tidy static bus queue. Firstly, it is always a church in the making, a church groping towards an understanding of itself. We cannot in fact point to any one moment or place and say 'That is it! *There* is the primitive church!' Secondly, it is always a church on the move, and the One whose manifestation is so ardently awaited is the One who leads it. Mankind is not, as it were, a passive audience waiting for the curtain to rise on a celestial gala performance. The parousia is much more than that. It is 'the hour of the harvest' (cf. Rev. 14:5 Mat. 13:30) when all creation is brought to its fulfilment, its ultimate destiny. *All* creation. Therefore the time of that 'harvest' cannot be fixed from within this world, from inside 'our' time.

The 'apocalyptic with a difference' which colours the thought of the New Testament writers pushes them to what is essentially the same conclusion. Notice how we find them simultaneously emphasising the imminence of that 'harvest' and the fact that we cannot fix the time of its coming. Paul, in one of his most dramatic antitheses, warns his flock that 'When people say "There is peace and security", then sudden destruction will come upon them' (1 Thess. 5:3). And the seer John says in Revelation that he 'saw a great white throne and him who sat upon it; from his presence earth and sky fled away, and no place was found for them', (20:11). God's majesty and judgment is not something *set alongside* this creation, but is at the end seen to be the one and only reality, and this end, 'whether it be temporally "near " or "far", is essentially very near to everybody. For it is one with Christ, the Crucified and Risen Lord. It is there, where Christ is.'[53] So all Christians, of every age, live 'in the one last hour, in a world and time which is destined to pass away',[54] and because every man who is called is called under the guidance of the Spirit to share in Christ's death and resurrection – a summons which is a central part of the Easter faith – it is equally true to say that the 'novelty' of Easter is not an exclusive possession of the first generation of Christians but should be known by us all.

Should be. . . .

Turning back to hard reality from the reassurance given by one or two texts and a little theologizing, why, then, *was* there a loss of that vital sense of expectation and urgency, that sense that something new was happening? If the parousia's delay is an inadequate explanation, is Christianity's spread through other cultures a better one? The faith wove westwards, through societies which did not share the Jewish sense of history nor the profound awareness that the first Christians had of the unattainability of heaven in this kind of world – societies in which the apocalyptic notion of a break in history was wholly alien[55] and in which much more emphasis was placed on the individual, so that it was easier to see salvation in private rather than cosmic terms.

Very well, but is that an explanation at all – a basic one? Are we not nearer a basic explanation if we look more carefully at what we are trying to explain . . . in other words, take a harder look at what I have called the 'hard reality', the seemingly evident loss of the young church's liveliness? Is it not nearer the truth that even from as far back as the days of that young church – from the time the church first began to be conscious of its own identity and Paul waged war against the spiritual grip of places such as Corinth – the Christian has had to live with the tension between apocalyptic and the way of looking at the world presented by conflicting factors in his own culture? Surely apocalyptic, *just because of its instrinsically divisive nature,* cannot flourish perfectly peacefully in *any* culture, and has only come close to being wholly identified with a culture when a people has been in the throes of a cultural crisis (as, for example, Israel was in Jesus's time). The apocalyptic in the pages of the New Testament came out of the mouths of martyrs or would-be martyrs, men who saw themselves as aliens in their world (cf. e.g. 1 Peter 2:11) and were consequently often stamped out by that world. It is surely this that is one of the basic things which gives the message of the young church its terrifying power; that perhaps more than anything accounts for the feeling of vitality and newness that come over in its writings. It is not basically because of their euphoria (real though

96

that was), nor because they were privileged to be 'there, at the beginning' or had grown up in the world in which Jesus lived out his mission, that these men convey a feeling of being part of a church exploding with lasting life, but because for them *Easter hope and participation in Christ's death indeed actually were one and the same thing,* and time and again this meant that theirs was a message they found themselves eventually being driven to scrawl out in their own blood, so disruptive and yet so compelling it was.

It is thus the Spirit works, and though few of us are summoned to follow those early Christians that far, the tension between whatever happens to be the prevailing culture and apocalyptic, which puts a question mark over the whole order of this world, questioning every culture, is a tension every Christian has to cope with. It has shown itself to be a creative tension, and western man has been the poorer when it has broken down. (Here I am taking up again the themes of section II). When Christianity's apocalyptic element has been virtually absent the result has been a diminished and anaemic form of Christianity. And when the very opposite situation has arisen and this apocalyptic element has been so dominant that it has been seen by some men as alone supplying sense and meaning to their entire world, justifying a wholesale rejection of external reality, these men have normally experienced disorientation (sometimes of violent and destructive proportions) and eventual disillusion, resolved in rare cases by flights into utopianism. Such, it would seem, is the human cost of the outbreaks of millennialism that have recurred from time to time in Christian history, important although the social transformations brought about through the agency of these millennial movements sometimes may be.

Yet the very fact that these outbreaks do go on occurring – yes, even in our own age – makes it clear that apocalyptic's salient features give expression in a powerful way to certain abiding truths and drives. These are, however, ones which academic theological language can do no more than locate or circumscribe, for reasons we shall shortly see. Just how much, then, can be put into cold print?

In apocalyptic, so averse to pure abstractions, elusive notions 'come alive'; they become concrete. First, the apocalyptic notion of 'break' in concrete forms radically challenges an assumption even more prevalent in our secular technological society than in the past – the assumption that we can, if only given sufficient back data and adequate expertise, calculate (and so ultimately dominate) the future shapes of the lives of individuals, the economic destinies of whole peoples, maybe even what will lie at the end of man's jump to the stars. The assumption that individuals, peoples, humanity itself, are no more than clusters of events in an inexorable internally-conditioned evolutionary process – this is what it challenges. It says 'No!' to an assumption which, in the long run, far from liberating man for the future shackles him to the past. In Christian terms, it affirms concretely *the primacy of grace*, the 'transcendent novelty poured into our lives as the gift of Jesus Christ',[56] in whose death-and-resurrection man is freed from his own hopeless striving against the limiting conditioning forces of what has been.

Second, apocalyptic expectation concretely affirms *the hope which, for the Christian, makes sense of the 'truths of faith'*. When the 'Christ event' is not seen in the light of the parousia either it is divorced by us from history and turned into myth or else it is seen just as one more event in the middle of a series of events, and when that happens it is comprehended as something remote, static.[57] Faith then ceases to be Easter faith. Hope sustains a dynamic element in our understanding of the truths of faith and by doing that protects faith, which is under the constant attack of 'the powers of this world'. Today the most immediate threat to faith is rarely naked evil or radical doubt; what should trouble us more is the astonishing ease with which the things of faith may now be diminished, trivialized, appropriated. A faith that is not whole, a faith that is not Easter faith, can be quickly measured up, captured and turned into an instrument with which man can dominate fellow-man and lessen him. The 'man of faith' whose faith is Easter faith, the man who is also a 'man of hope', is always free, whatever the 'powers' try to do to him; yes, however subtle and aggressive is the evil that assaults him.

Third, apocalyptic's depiction of the working out of our destinies as part of a great cosmic drama affirms concretely *the mutual involvement of all creatures* in interrelationships which may be creative or destructive: although apocalyptic only emerges when men become aware of themselves as possessing personal destinies as well as sharing a tribal destiny, 'salvation' is never seen in apocalyptic as something wholly private; transfigured, the ancient Jewish idea that salvation for the righteous means sharing in the Kingdom lives on. We can only go to heaven in a crowd . . .

But, however important and urgent the points written down in the last three paragraphs may be, it is most unlikely that any of us, reading these strings of sentences, have made those insights in any sense *our own*. In that case what chance is there of mediating them to a wider world, even a wider Christian world, let alone the genuine wide world? Theology, which claims to address man concerning the things that move him most deeply, has dwindled into a game clever clergymen play with each other, complete with a set of rules and terminology only meaningful to the players. At least, that is how virtually all non-theologians see it. It tries to trap and freeze the ineffable within neatly rounded-off propositions written for cool reading: that at any rate is what non-theologians think theologians are trying to do, and by and large the non-theologians are right. Is it surprising, then, that so few of them want to join the clever clergymen's game? Above all, is it surprising that this century's debate over the place of apocalyptic should have touched the lives of non-theologians so little?

For apocalyptic, in spite of its literary roots, basically conflicts with the methods and presuppositions of what is accepted in academic circles as being 'modern thought'. If we forget that in apocalyptic 'the language is part of the happening',[58] if we forget that even when it is speaking of the particular it is revealing the 'total, cosmic and ultimate'[59] (and consequently the unanalysable), and if we forget that in apocalyptic the voice we hear is the voice of man cornered, man against a confused and hostile world,[60] then we may take possession of the apocalyptist's words but in our hands they become mere lifeless pawns for our game.

Discovering that modern academic theology has short-comings – that should not disconcert us excessively. What should disconcert us is that this theology can be seen as a positive threat not merely by the millennialist who, tapping her bible, said to me 'Forget all the theories and just keep on reading this', or merely by the fundamentalist groups who, following the exhortation in Mark 13:14 to 'flee to the mountains', now reside at high altitudes in the north west United States, well away from theologians, but that it should also be distrusted by, for example, some Latin American freedom fighters fired with apocalyptic expectations. With good reason, too. For, like the European brands of 'theology of liberation' I spoke about in section I, our attempts to fit the insights of apocalyptic into our theological framework can be seen only too easily as yet another appropriation of the hopes and expectations of the oppressed by the 'intellectuals' . . . those master-assimilators who have so often proved themselves to be the most subtle enemies of a genuine counter culture. It would seem that these insights are not in fact susceptible of a theological formulation, if we mean by 'theology,' something that can be put into a book. They do not belong to the world of the book. They constantly burst out of the bindings.

Then are these insights incommunicable? It is here that Pentecostalism perhaps has something to say to us.

VI 'WHERE TWO OR THREE ARE GATHERED ... '

'WE KNOW, LORD, that thou shalt surely come and that again thy holy city Jerusalem shall be the centre of all the earth. Yea, Lord! And that there thou shalt surely reign and all the nations of the earth shall bow down before thee. Yea, and longingly, we look longingly, Lord, to that Day of thy great and terrible Coming. Longingly, Lord! Bless Jerusalem, thy holy city! Bless Israel, thy people, Lord!'. Now other voices swiftly mingle: staccato utterances echoing and re-echoing each other across the shadows. 'Amen!' 'Come, Jesus!' 'The Lord comes!' 'Praise the Lord!' The words slip over bowed heads tight pressed together and once more the first voice rings, 'Bless Israel, thy people! Come quickly, Lord, come quickly! Praise God! Praise the Lord! ...'

So a young woman was praying in a recent meeting of 'classical' Pentecostals. It is a prayer of a kind still quite common among members of Pentecostal churches, if not so common among neo-Pentecostals in the main denominations, but the sort of thinking it reflects was even more prominent in the early days of the modern Pentecostal movement. One of the leading pioneers of Pentecostalism near the beginning of the century, A. J. Tomlinson, was sure that, just as in the early church 'the full blaze of light beamed forth from the Pentecostal chamber and shined forth with radiant glory in the early morning of the Gospel day', so (the true church having at last been rediscovered) 'the evening light, the true light, is now shining, and the sheep are hearing His voice and are coming from every place where they have been scattered during the cloudy and dark day'.[61]

'The evening light', 'the latter rain' – phrases like these express the great hopes of many a Pentecostal of Tomlinson's time. And apocalyptic expectation is still very much alive today among, say, young Pentecostals in the United States who are Jesus people; since 1967 no group of Christians has done more to make the eschatological prophecy of Joel 'I will pour out my spirit upon all flesh' yet again one of the most often-heard bible texts. Among many of the Pentecostals in the Third World apocalyptic expectation is more lively still. In the slums of Santiago 'a kingdom beyond this world is preached which will break through in the imminent future' and its existence is 'guaranteed as from this moment by the conviction that one's sins are pardoned and is often confirmed or made visible by a physical sign, healing'.[62] But here, already, in this mention of conviction of forgiveness and an awareness of the living power of God prompted by some visible sign reminiscent of the New Testament, is a hint of one of the most important things that distinguishes Pentecostalism from the adventist sects (from the Jehovah's Witnesses, for example): namely that it was not apocalyptic expectation which brought about the birth of twentieth-century Pentecostalism and which has sustained it; rather, the expectation grew out of the Pentecostals' identification of themselves with what they understood to be the 'apostolic church'.

'First-century Christianity was more a state of being than a doctrinal system', the Pentecostal, David du Plessis, recently said, and Pentecostals 'consider that the doctrines and religious experience of the apostles are constant standards that should not change ... If the patterns of the early Church are the only true expression of real Christianity, then the Church should make every effort to return to these patterns ... It was exactly this truth that brought about the Pentecostal movement.' So says du Plessis.[63] What, though, is the ground for these beliefs? It is deep certainty that (in the words of a Pentecostal hymn)

> The pow'r that fell at Pentecost, when in the upper room
> Upon the watching, waiting ones, the Holy Ghost had come,
> Remaineth evermore the same;
> Unchanging still ...'.[64]

Clearly a stirring vision of the church, drawing millions, it raises basic questions in the minds of many other Christians, particularly in the Catholic tradition. But all we need take note of for the moment is the fact that through 'Spirit-baptism' (that widely-discussed distinctive Pentecostal doctrine, provoker of even more basic questioning[65]) a growing group of people have come to an understanding of what it means to be 'in Pentecost'[66] and these people believe their own experience confirms that the risen Lord's promise to his disciples, 'You shall receive power when the Holy Spirit has come upon you and you shall be my witnesses' (Acts 1:8), extends to them also.

Modern Pentecostalism was initially a development within a major religious movement of 19th century America, the Methodist Holiness movement. Spread by the roaming bible salesmen who so often became its leaders, the Holiness movement was grounded in the profound optimism which was one of the great strengths of that frontier society: the optimism which helped to give birth to the big reform and protest movements of the time, both secular and religious [67] Unlike nearly all of these, it insisted that the perfection of the world would only be realized with the second coming of Christ and the institution of the millennium, but this never obscures the fact that its central distinctive doctrine is *perfectionism* – in other words, a certainty that *even now* by grace men can share fully the life of the upper room of Pentecost. [68] And (because of a thorough-going biblicism) *sharing fully in the life of the church of Pentecost* inevitably meant for the more radical members of the Holiness churches and, even more, for the early Pentecostals, *sharing the expectation of the church of Pentecost* . . . which, as we have seen, was rooted in apocalyptic.

This was not, of course, something academically reasoned out. Like the first Christians, these men could not but help 'bear witness' to their expectation. They did it, however, in their own way – in what surely all that has been said here so far suggests is the one and only way the message could be conveyed really effectively to modern man. *They did it, namely in and through their worship.* As Abdalazis de Moura, research assistant to Archbishop Helder Camara, has said about today's Brazilian Pentecostals, 'Their theology is not in their books. We must see their theology in what they do, in their prayer and in their programme of self-help.'[69] The expectation grew in the newcomer not simply as an outcome of 'announcement' by a preacher speaking at the newcomer in his seemingly godless isolation from 'over there', but as an outcome of the newcomer's active participation: in other words, as an outcome of group worship fired (it was stressed) by the presence of God even here and now in the workings of his Spirit, group worship in which the newcomer was *drawn to share.*

Today this may no longer be an accurate description of a lot of white pentecostal churches in the United States and Britain. But the future crucible of Christianity is likely to be not the northern world but Latin America, and there, where the spread of Pentecostalism has been most dramatic, what I am saying about the first modern Pentecostals still largely holds true. Two points have struck onlookers. Firstly, as has been said with particular reference to Chile's Pentecostals, 'There are no isolated person in Pentecostalist society ... Either the individual is completely integrated ... or else he is not a member of the congregation.'[70] Secondly, the Pentecostal emphasis on the oral – its 'oral theology' – 'allows for a process of democratization of language by dismantling the privileges of abstract, rational and propositional systems' as Professor Hollenweger has put it.[71] This (he thinks) has consequences spreading far beyond the church walls for the millions of the poor, who make up the vast majority of Latin American Pentecostals and do not belong to a primarily literary culture.[72] What, however, solely concerns us here is the awakening of consciousness and of awareness of oneself and of others that clearly does come about as a result of this stress on fellowship and oral communication.

Pentecostal worship's most arresting feature is the 'astonishing degree of communication'[73] that can take place in it. The sound of the subtly regulated to-and-fro between preacher and people. The discovery that you have been been led unknowingly to pray the prayer of somebody else in the group – somebody too frightened and confused to put his needs into prayers. Only when you have experienced things like this for yourself do you begin to realise how astonishing the degree of communication can be, it seems. And that the message heard (and the expectation it enkindled) should be mediated through *this* particular way of worship was no accident, at least to the minds of the pioneers. 'Belief' and 'worship style' were not, for them, two separate things, either of which could be thought of wholly apart from the other.

Apocalyptic made elusive notions concrete, and Pentecostalism scandalises western intellectuals because it responds so directly to the concrete: it only too easiiy sees in material bodily objects the imprint of the eternal. 'The Pentecostalist needs a concrete faith attested by material signs in the form of some vital change'.[74] The man who said this was thinking particularly of Chile, where a healing is often that 'vital change', but he could equally well have been generalising. In absorbing apocalyptic, Pentecostals have not been absorbing something alien.

Remember what I have pointed to as the three salient features of apocalyptic, and see the place they have in the Pentecostal world-view.

First, the notion of break. The experience of 'radical reversal' – experience of some Other breaking into one's life and, so it seems, turning everything upside down – has, throughout Pentecostalism's history, commonly accompanied the original powerful conversion experience (the 'Spirit-baptism') and been continually recalled liturgically. And entering life 'in Pentecost' can in some third-world countries be experienced as a dramatic break not merely spiritually but socially. For example, it has been shown how, for the members of the Pentecostal church at Ixmiquilpan in Mexico, religious conversion was the only way of escaping the confines of traditional social structures.[75] It has been shown how the outlook of peasant migrants in Chile has been transformed by going 'into Pentecost', with its egalitarian character . . . egalitarian in spite of the power of the pastor, for (to the humble newcomer) is it not evident that power 'in Pentecost' is distributed according to the charisms God gives a man, and these God bestows irrespective of wealth, class and learning?[76] And even for a number of present-day Pentecostals in the United States and Europe the *whole* of life has similarly radically changed.

It certainly so changed for many of the very first twentieth-century Pentecostals. And, interpreting from 'within Pentecost' the apparently mainly hostile world surrounding them, after a conversion experience which in some cases had most dramatically sharpened in their eyes the contrasts between things black and white, those men and women, many of them very poor and with no hope of ever achieving what this world counts as 'success', had as little difficulty as the apocalyptists of old in discerning in current events signs of cosmic import heralding the coming of the Lord.

A prophecy of 'awful destruction' was given at the Azusa Street meeting house, centre of the momentous Los Angeles revival, immediately preceding the great San Francisco earthquake of 1906. The tremors of that earthquake, which shook the entire Californian coast, were felt by the gathered worshippers, and 'the natural earthquake in San Francisco was followed by a "spiritual earthquake" on Azusa Street'.[77] As a Pentecostal was later to say, 'In all

God's great moves, nature sympathizes with Him'.[78] And this way of thinking spontaneously about the local and particular in cosmic terms, a way of thinking stimulated by worshipping in closely interrelated groups, continues today. The Common Market. The World Council of Churches. The now defunct magazine *New Christian*. All in recent years have been discerned as signs of the approaching End![79] Preposterous? No doubt. But the Pentecostal's tendency to see surrounding us witnesses to the final fulfilment of all things reminds us, surely, of an alternative world-view which few late 20th-century westerners are in a safe position to scoff lightly.

Tongues and prophesy. The freshly-found zeal to praise God (how striking are the parallels between the 'doxological utterances' of modern Pentecostals and ancient apocalyptists!). Exorcism, that practice so potentially dangerous if dabbled in, if extracted out of its eschatological context. Spiritual healings. The deep fellowship found in worship (which was – against the norms of the America of the time – interracial during the Azusa Street revival and for a brief period afterwards[80]). The hardness of heart of the world. . . . By the early Pentecostals all these were seen as 'signs'.

If they understood their world in cosmic terms much more spontaneously than do most of today's neo-Pentecostals, and very many of today's classical Pentecostals, here is a glimpse of a reason for the shift. In a Pentecostal chapel in England's industrial Midlands a preacher is saying: ' "The prize of the high calling of God in Christ Jesus." Do you know what that is? One of the tragedies of the Pentecostal churches is that the idea has got around in some of them that you have Baptism in the Holy Spirit and then you have tongues and all that . . . and then the door is closed. You've arrived! You've got it all! Have you? Listen to the apostle Paul. What every one of us needs is a vision! It's the vision Paul kept in front of him all the time. "I press toward the mark for the prize of the high calling of God in Christ Jesus. Let us therefore, as many as be perfect, be thus minded." That's what he tells us. It's a vision, this one, so small that with it you can meet anything tomorrow brings. Anything. But – and this is important – it is also a vision so big you will only see the whole of it in all its glory when you stand before the Lord, on that Last Day. So big, so small, it's yet one and the same vision.'[91]

The early men in particular sensed that 'So big, so small, it's yet one and the same vision', and so it was no more difficult for them than for the ancient apocalyptists to accommodate the supernatural, including the 'truths of faith' recorded in the bible, in a very down-to-earth world view. And this shaped their experience of the other salient feature of apocalyptic: hope, and more particularly Christian hope. The Spirit of God was already demonstrably bringing in the consummation of the world in their very midst; the evidence was there, they were certain, for everyone to hear and see. It was not necessary for these men to banish God into the future in order to 'live in hope'. Today neo-Pentecostalism has become so extraordinarily popular in Britain because (thinks Professor Hollenweger) the people of Britain 'feel let down'.[82] Are we, in fact, seeing them at present groping intuitively through neo-Pentecostalism for the hope-made-concrete which, to peoples 'let down', has already been mediated so many times in the past by apocalyptic? If so, the 'charismatic movement' might be the beginnings of something with repercussions spreading well beyond Britain's Christian ghetto.

However, the presence of a strong apocalyptic element in Pentecostalism also meant that from the start there were in Pentecostalism several half-hidden intractable tensions. First, between protestantism's traditional emphasis on the private and individual and the emphasis inevitably given to the group and to the cosmic by all whose prime object it is to live 'the life of the church of the apostles' Second, between the emphasis on God's immanence inherited from Methodism (with the important place it gives to 'inner feeling') and that emphasis on God's transcendence which even in Paul's time was being forgotten by the Corinthians – that looking-forward to the parousia in the light of which Jesus's life, death and resurrection can alone be properly understood. Third, between Pentecostalism's emphasis on the past, on what was 'at the beginning' (in fact, the archaism of Pentecostalism rooted in Acts 11:15), and its emphasis on the future when 'we shall always be with the Lord' (1 Thess. 4:17).

These tensions are not peculiar to Pentecostalism, of course. Every Christian has to live with them. It just happens that within Pentecostalism, because of its very nature, they are particularly severe. But if they are not sustained or if (and this is commonly the case in sects having no developed ecclesiology) they can only be sustained within a sealed-off universe of meaning, within a windowless fortress, the result can be a stultifying other-worldliness and passivity. Today from many a Pentecostal assembly prayers soar that curdle the blood of anyone who thinks labouring to bring about

107

a more just society is a vital way of witnessing to the coming of the Kingdom of God. Pentecostalism should not, admittedly, be judged simply on its own evidence, but on what it is likely to contribute in the long run to the building up of God's people. Nevertheless, it has been criticised for its narrowness, its apparent lack of social concern and its customary preference for the status quo even by people who recognize that it has been able to convey to multitudes of the earth's hungry and bewildered a message of dynamic power which the members of the main denominations have in recent times rarely been able to put into words that live outside the confines of text-books.

Does this mean that in modern society this message is only likely to be *really* effectively conveyed spasmodically? For example, during Pentecostalism's first years in the United States, when the prophet Joel was leaping with life in black back-street mission halls, and the heavens were about to open, and the process of taming and de-eschatologizing had still to begin? Or, today, among the youth who have turned their backs on what they see as a doomed culture and taken refuge in communes? Or among frontier folk of the third world – groups on the fringes of society undergoing radical change?

I do not think so.

I have just spoken of the difficulty sects with no developed ecclesiology have in sustaining certain tensions. The Pentecostal doctrine of baptism in Holy Spirit is a partial substitute for an ecclesiology, but only partial. I believe one reason why I am a Roman Catholic, not a member of a Pentecostal church, is that Catholicism has a developed ecclesiology and classical Pentecostalism does not. But where does that take us? Anywhere?

There is in fact *nothing* in those positive aspects of Pentecostalism I have concentrated on here that does not recall *some* aspect of the authentic tradition of the 'Great Church', even if tradition often hidden today or underdeveloped.[83]

To sum up, one of the things Pentecostalism has done for a number of us in the 'Great Church' has been to bring us to a new awareness of disturbing but clearly central elements of the primitive gospel message which most of us have half-forgotten or neutralised, and to show us how these can again become alive for us and transform our way of looking at the world. They are elements that call sharply into question the values of the highly-privatized consumer society which we have been taught to assume is 'our world' –

the only 'really real' world, but a world we now see beginning to fall apart – and they show that we need not be in bondage to those values. They incidentally also call into question a method of doing theology which is heavily dependent on certain presuppositions found in that society, and suggest that there is again a large area of theology which cannot be done 'in a vacuum' but only in the context of worship and human meeting, of prayer and praise, of preparing a way for the Lord by sharing with men their pain and want and their thirstings after justice.

Even more important still, these elements of the gospel message give us a promise that prevails. While staying true to our own tradition, we nevertheless now hear as if with new ears the mighty prophecies in the liturgy of Advent and the risen Lord saying at the close of Revelation 'I am coming soon'. As one great Catholic theologian, St Thomas Aquinas, said, 'We should hope for nothing less from God than his very self'.[84] As another, Karl Rahner, has lately said, hope alone is the locus of God as the One 'who cannot be controlled or manipulated', and so of God as such.[85] This hope, we see, is not something to be found in flight, something divorced from our humdrum commonplace lives, but can only grow in the sheer earthiness and ordinariness of the place 'where two or three are gathered together'. It is as members of one people that we can truly claim to be standing at the end of time in more than a metaphorical sense, and the One who binds us together is the One whose promise of his certain and imminent coming we have been given. Providing we do not break the bonds of love that hold us together expectation fired by that great promise will not lead us into fantasy. Surely the very opposite is the truth? Only when we are living in certain hope of the fulfilment of that promise have we the power to face realistically the uncertain days ahead.

For inspiration or criticism or both thanks are due to Professor John Bowker, Professor Walter Hollenweger, Mrs Joan Steele, Dr Bryan R. Wilson, and my fellow-Dominicans Antony Archer, Cornelius Ernst, Rob van der Hart, Timothy Radcliffe, Mary Esther Selo, Lewis Jerome Smith and Richard Woods of Chicago.

The notes below basically consist of citations and matter not integral to the main argument of the essay. By the incurious they can be ignored altogether.

[1] Cf. G. R. Beasley-Murray, *The Book of Revelation*, London 1974, p. 50.

[2] Cf. N. Cohn, *The Pursuit of the Millennium*, 3rd edn, London 1970, p. 33.

[3] For ET of text and introduction by H. Duensing cf. Hennecke – Schneemelcher-McL. Wilson. *New Testament Apocrypha* vol. 2, London 1965, p. 755-798.

[4] Cf. C. Evans, *Cults of Unreason*, London 1973, Part 2.

[5] Cf. F. E. Manuel, *The Religion of Isaac Newton*, Oxford 1974.

[6] Cf. N. Annan, 'The Strands of Unbelief', in *Ideas and Beliefs of the Victorians* (BBC talks), London 1949, p. 150; O. Chadwick, *The Secularization of the European Mind in the Nineteenth Century*, Cambridge 1975, p. 150f. But cf. on the term 'secularization' B. R. Wilson, *Religion in Secular Society*, London, 1966, p. 114; M. Hill, *A Sociology of Religion*, London 1973, pp. 228-251; R. Gill, *The Social Context of Theology*, London 1975, p. 67 ff.

[7] Cf. M. Argyle & B. Beit-Hallahmi, *The Social Psychology of Religion*, London 1975, p. 12 f. Quantifying belief and its shifts is a dangerous business. Between 1947 and 1965 surveys found that while about 80 % of the British population believed in God, only about 45% believed in an after-life (37% in 1973), Of the sample of believers in an after-life surveyed by G. Gorer (*Exploring English Character*, London 1955) only '13% referred to a scriptural heaven and hell, with judgment, plus another 9% without judgment; 15% had very material ideas of heaven as being like this life with the unpleasant features omitted and with endless leisure (e.g. no washing-up); 25% believed in some kind of reincarnation; and 12% looked forward to re-joining loved-ones; some used more than one category' (Argyle & Beit-Hallahmi, p. 13). Yet according to a 1973 survey (Argyle & Beit-Hallahmi, p. 26) about one-fifth of the British population believes in hell. Figures for USA are very much higher than for Britain (cf. Argyle & Beit-Hallahmi, pp. 26-29), but it can be argued that British and American figures are not comparable owing to the differences in the character of religion in the two countries and in its roles in society.

[8] Cf. D. Hay, 'More Rumour of Angels', *The Month*, Dec, 1974, pp. 796-803, where it is suggested – probably rightly – that one reason for the phenomenon of an apparent decline in religion in the West may be that 'religious' or 'transcendental' experience, although not absent, is largely hidden (and so undiscerned) in our society because so many people, with the exception of those on the fringe of society, lack sufficiently credible available 'system of significance' to which they can attribute their deeply felt inner perceptions.

[9] E. Käsemann, *New Testament Questions of Today*, London, 1969, p. 102. For the discussion of the truth of this famous statement and its implications between Käsemann, G. Ebeling and E. Fuchs see *Journal for Theology and the Church* 6, 1969 pp. 17-133. See also n. 31 below.

[10] On the cosmology in the language of which some of the central Christians doctrines were first expounded, cf. J. Daniélou, *A History of Early Christian Doctrine* Vol. 1, London 1964, pp. 173-181.

[11] Cf. G. von Rad, *Old Testament Theology* Vol. 2, Edinburgh 1965,p. 101.

[12] *Jesus' Proclamation of the Kingdom of God*, ET 1st edn, London 1971, pp. 131 133.

[13] Cf. D. S. Russell, *The Method and Message of Jewish Apocalyptic*, London 1964, pp. 221-3.

[14] Cf. O. Plöger, *Theocracy and Eschatology*, 2nd edn, Oxford 1968, p. 43.

[15] Cf. M. Hengel, *Judaism and Hellenism* Vol. 1, London 1974, pp. 47-57.

[16] Cf. in this context, on 'the problem of God's immanence', J. Bowker, *Problems of Suffering in Religions of the World*, Cambridge 1970, p. 7 ff.

[17] E. Bloch, *Das Prinzip Hoffnung*, Frankfurt am Main 1959, p. 1324.

[18] Some of the symbolism in this writing may be Iranian. Some of the structure of the thinking shows Greek influence. But *all* late Jewish religious thought, even that consciously most opposed to foreign influences, was to some extent 'hellenistic', for 'hellenism' was the spirit of the age (M. Hengel's main thesis: cf. op cit., p.311). H. D. Betz's argument that 'Jewish and, subsequently, Christian apocalypticism as well cannot be understood from themselves or from the Old Testament alone, but must be seen and presented as peculiar expressions within the entire development of Hellenistic syncretism' ('Religio-Historical Understanding of Apocalypticism', *Journal for the Theology and the Church*, 6, p. 155) must be read with this in mind.

[19] Cf. E. Käsemann, *New Testament Questions of Today*, London, 1969, p. 96ff., where it is suggested that here are the beginnings of a new literary form which was to find its ultimate expression in the gospels.

[20] Apocalyptic ideas were current among all classes in Jesus's time, although the vast majority of the people who held these ideas (often in a popularised debased form) did not hear, let alone read, the 'apocalypses' in which these ideas were assembled. Far from being opposed to each other, Torah – the Law of Moses – and apocalyptic were complementary influences forming the religious world in which Jesus was born. Only after the destruction of Jerusalem by the Romans did apocalyptic cease to be part of 'normative Judaism' (cf. D. S. Russell, op. cit., pp. 84-8; J. Jeremias, *Jerusalem in the Time of Jesus*, London 1969, pp. 237-242).

[21] Cf. L. Hartman, *Prophecy Interpreted*, Lund 1966 p. 51f. On the prevalence of esotericism in Judaism in the period before and including Jesus's time (and its influence on primitive Christian practice), for a brief account see J. Jeremias, *The Eucharistic Words of Jesus*, London 1966, p. 125 ff.

[22] D. S. Russell, op. cit., p. 17

[23] Contra ibid. p. 18

[24] Cf. F. M. Cross, 'New Directions in the Study of Apocalyptic', *Journal for Theology and the Church*, 6, p. 165 n. 23; L. Hartman, op. cit., pp. 105-9; D. S. Russell, op. cit., pp. 161-6; M. Hengel, op. cit., Vol 1, p. 207, Vol. 2, p. 137.

[25] E. Stauffer, *New Testament Theology*, London 1955, p. 258 n. 3.

[26] On the relation between anomie and apocalyptic expectation cf. A. N. Wilder, 'The Rhetoric of Ancient and Modern Apocalyptic', *Interpretation* Vol. 25 no. 4, p. 440f; B. R. Wilson, *Magic and the Millennium*, London 1973, p. 494f; C. G. Jung, 'Answer to Job', *Collected Works* Vol. 11, London 1958, p. 465.

[27] Few of these writers (the exceptions are Book of Jubilees 23:31, perhaps The Assumption of Moses 10:9 and perhaps 1 Enoch 91-104) believe that

men in Paradise are shorn of bodies. For sight is hardly ever lost of the ancient idea that salvation for the righteous means sharing in the Kingdom, and in Jewish thinking a disembodied soul would not be able to participate fully in this sharing. And, because it is as fully men, with bodies as well as souls, that the wicked must be judged and punished, many of the apocalyptic writings say the wicked as well as the just will be raised (exceptions are Psalms of Solomon 3:13f; 1 Enoch 83-90).

[28] E. Käsemann, op. cit., p. 105.

[29] Cf. also 1 Enoch 41:7f; 43:1-4; 75:1f; 80:2.

[30] Luke 7:22 par.; cf. Isaiah 35:5ff; 29:18f; perhaps 26:19; 61:1f. On these texts cf. J. Jeremias, *New Testament Theology* Vol. 1, London 1971, pp. 103-5; also cf. J. Moltmann, *The Crucified God*, London 1974, p. 98 f.

[31] E. Käsemann, *New Testament Questions of Today*, London 1969, p. 102. On this see n. 9 above. Kasemann qualifies what he is saying by emphasising that it is the primitive church he is speaking of, not Jesus himself, for Jesus's preaching cannot, in his opinion, be classed as 'theology' and in any case does not, he believes, bear 'a fundamentally apocalyptic stamp' (op. cit., p. 101). But the reason he gives why Jesus's preaching is not apocalyptical – that although Jesus made 'the apocalyptically determined message of John his point of departure' the whole emphasis of his message was 'the immediacy of the God who was at hand' and that the giver of such a message would not be prepared to wait for the acting-out of an apocalyptical scenario – is hardly satisfactory. Leaving aside the question of how 'remote' the apocalyptists thought God to be, we find that even if we deny that the 'eschatological discourse' which appears in a number of forms in various places in the NT (Mt 24, Mk, 13, Lk 17, 1 Cor. 15, 1 Th. 4, 2 Th. 2) had its origin in genuine dominical sayings, against e.g. L. Hartman, who suggests that the discourse had its origins in a 'midrashic' interpretation of Daniel by Jesus himself, we are nevertheless confronted with e.g. Mk 10:38 (the authenticity of which has been argued by V. Taylor against R. Bultmann &c.), a text that seems to indicate that associated with the triumph of God will be a 'time of distress' for those who have been 'baptized' with Jesus's 'baptism', and also with Mt. 10:34. We are, of course, entering here an area of fierce controversy among scholars, particularly in Germany. For what the author himself calls 'a polemical work' summarising the attitudes of 20th-century theologians and scripture scholars to apocalyptic, see K. Koch, *The Rediscovery of Apocalyptic,* London 1972, and particularly Ch. 6: 'The Agonised Attempts to Save Jesus from Apocalyptic'. N. Perrin, in *The Kingdom of God in the Teaching of Jesus*, London 1963, provides a useful fuller review of the history of the interpretation of Jesus's conception of the Kingdom during the 70 years after Weiss's *Die Predigt Jesu vom Reiche Gottes* appeared, and gives more mention to British and American work.

[32] Cf J. Bowker, *Jesus and the Pharisees*, Cambridge 1973, p. 15f; p. 30f; pp. 43-5.

[33] 'Paul, far from distorting the teaching of Jesus, expressed and continued it with great accuracy.' (J. Bowker, ibid. p. 45). In the parable of the prodigal son it is the 'righteous' elder brother who rejects his father's invitation to the banquet (Lk. 15:28f); Jesus insists that God's love extends to

sinners and aliens (cf. Mk. 2:16f; Mt 8:11f); in cleansing lepers he restores to the human community men regarded by his contemporaries as total outcasts and so virtually dead (cf. Josephus, Antiquities of the Jews, 3:264). Similarly, his miracle of the feeding of the five thousand (like his table-fellowship with tax-collectors) would be seen as an eschatological sign: it emphasises that *all* may share at the banquet in the coming Kingdom.

[34] Because (arguably only because) they are inheritors of the Kingdom, his disciples may address God as *'Abba,* 'Father'; the nucleus of the special prayer he gives them – 'Thy kingdom come' – petitions for the reign already being actualized (cf. J. Jeremias, op. cit., pp.193-203); he assures his followers that, without strenuous efforts of their own, they will have the strength they need to fulfil the command they have been given that they should devote every part of their lives to witnessing that the reign of God has dawned, for 'a city set on a hill cannot be hid' (Mt. 5:14) (cf. G. von Rad, The Problem of the Hexateuch and other Essays, Edinburgh 1966, pp. 232-242).

[35] Reconciliation is coming, then, through a human being, not, as some Jews (including some apocalyptic writers) were expecting, through an angel (cf. Qumran War Rule col. XVII; Testament of Levi 5:7; Phil, *de confus. linguarum* 28).

[36] Cf. W. Pannenberg, 'Did Jesus Really Rise from the Dead?' *Dialog* IV (1965), p. 135: 'Please understand me correctly. Only the name we give to this event is symbolic, metaphorical, but not the reality of the event itself. The latter is so absolutely unique that we have no other name for this than the metaphorical expression of the apocalyptic expectation'. Also cf. W. Pannenberg, *Jesus – God and Man,* London 1968, pp. 88-106. For reviews of modern approaches (both Catholic and Protestant) to the hermeneutical questions raised by the Easter narratives, see the review of X. Leon-Dufour's *Resurrection and the Message of Easter* by G. Turner ('Varieties of Resurrection *New Blackfriars* No. 661, June 1975, pp. 272-276) and R. E. Brown, *The Virginal Conception & Bodily Resurrection of Jesus,* London 1973, 69ff (especially pp. 125-127).

[37] Cf. J. Jeremias, op. cit., pp. 102, 205.

[38] Cf. e.g. C. H. Dodd, *The Parables of the Kingdom,* London (Fontana Edn) 1961, pp. 74-82.

[39] Cf. J. Jeremias, op. cit., pp. 286-299 and citations there; C. H. Dodd, op. cit., pp. 45-58.

[40] Cf. J. Jeremias, op. cit., pp. 308-311.

[41] Contra ibid. p. 310.

[42] Contra R. N. Longenecker, *The Christology of Early Jewish Christianity,* London 1970, p. 148f.

[43] In *that* sense it is right to say that the appearances must have been experienced 'as an eschatological event, as a dawning of the turning point of the world' (J. Jeremias, op. cit., p. 309). E. Käsemann, op. cit., p. 114: 'The Easter happening came only at a relatively late date to be restricted to Jesus himself; originally it had been understood as the dawn of the general resurrection and therefore interpreted apocalyptically and not as an isolated

113

wonder. We bar our own access to the primitve Easter kerygma if we ignore its apocalyptic content.'

[44] J. Moltmann, op. cit., p. 171.

[45] R. Phineas ben Jair (*Tos. Sotah* 9:15).

[46] Bearing in mind how Jesus's death and resurrection were comprehended by the first Christians, it would not be surprising if some of the NT texts seemed to witness to a link between the appearances of the crucified and risen Lord and the coming of the Spirit. For a cautious but sympathetic discussion of the evidence see J. D. G. Dunn, *Jesus and the Spirit*, London 1975, pp. 95-134.

[47] J. H. Schütz, *Paul and the Anatomy of Apostolic Authority*, Cambridge 1975, p. 278, argues that what Paul ultimately based his authority as an apostle on was this *commonly shared* experience – the experience of being 'called', of receiving the Spirit in baptism. It was, says Schütz, for this reason that he was able to urge the entire church to 'imitate' him . . . namely, to be a vessel receptive to the fullness of God's power, that power which never is to be separated from weakness and suffering (cf. ibid. p. 231).

[48] Cf. ibid. 188f. On the relationship between apocalyptic and enthusiasm (of both the Jerusalem and Corinthian varieties) see *Journal for Theology and the Church* 6: G. Ebeling, 'The Ground of Christian Theology', 54f.; E. Kasemann, 'On the Topic of Primitive Christian Apocalyptic', 100 n. 1; 108 n. 7; 119; 125 n. 17; 126; 127-133.

[49] Cf. J. M. Ford, 'Towards a Theology of Speaking in Tongues', *Theological Studies*, March 1971, 25ff.

[50] On the relationship between the Lucan account of life in the early Jerusalem community and eschatological expectation, see J. D. G. Dunn, op. cit., especially p. 158 ff.

[51] Cf. J. H. Schutz, op. cit., p. 279ff.

[52] The thesis notably of M. Werner, *The Formation of Christian Dogma*, London 1957

[53] P. Althaus, *Der Brief an die Römer*, Göttingen 1949, p. 117, quoted by G. R. Beasley-Murray, *The Book of Revelation*, London 1974, p. 48

[54] ibid.

[55] Virgil's celebrated proclamation of the dawn of future salvation in Eclogues 4, 39ff, written in 40BC, while it 'gave expression to the unvoiced thought of millions' (*Cambridge Ancient History* Vol. 10, 1934, p. 150), was composed under the influence of the oriental-Jewish Sibyls – i.e. apocalyptic – and, although the influence of the sybilline literature was rapidly expanding through all classes in the Roman empire at that time, Jewish theism and the Jewish understanding of the process of history was not taken over with it.

[56] J. P. Jossua, review of C. Ernst's *The Theology of Grace (New Blackfriars* No. 664, Sept, 1975, p. 428).

[57] In this context cf. n. 43 above; J. Moltmann, *Theology of Hope*, London 1967: *The Crucified God*, London 1974, 162f. p. 166; W. Pannenber *Jesus – God and Man*, London 1968, p. 82f.

[58] A. N. Wilder, 'The Rhetoric of Ancient and Modern Apocalyptic', *Interpretation* Vol. 25 no. 4, p. 446.

114

[59] Ibid. p. 450.

[60] Cf. ibid. p. 440.

[61] *The Evening Light and Church of God Evangel*, 1.3.1910, 1; quoted by H. V. Synan, *The Holiness-Pentecostal Movement in the United States*, Grand Rapids, Mich. 1971, p. 85.

[62] C. Lalive d'Epinay, *Haven of the Masses*, London 1969, p. 47. This book was based on a thorough survey of Chilean Pentecostalism carried out for the World Council of Churches. But it is unwise to generalize too hastily from observations of this kind. It can be difficult to classify the religion of some ethnic or cultural groups laying great stress on healing. And it cannot be assumed that what may be a reliable description of (say) Santiago's Pentecostals is able to be safely used to describe all or any Latin American Pentecostalism, because to different persons, all identifying themselves as Pentecostals but living in different societies, something like healing may well signify different things. See B. R. Wilson's description of the interrelationship and conflict between Pentecostalism and shamanism among Toba Indians, in *Magic and the Millennium*, London 1973, pp. 121-3.

[63] 'The Historic Background of Pentecostalism', paper given at the 2nd meeting of official Roman Catholic – Pentecostal Dialogue, Rome 1973, published in *One in Christ*, Vol. 10 no. 2, 1974, 176f. Cf. also E. P. Paulk (a Pentecostal), *Your Pentecostal Neighbour*, Cleveland, Tenn. 1958, p. 20, where Pentecostals are defined as people who 'receive the same experience as those "on the day of Pentecost" (Acts 2:1-4)'; also W. T. H. Richards, quoted in Peter Hocken's essay in this book (p. 36). Cf. also M. Harper (the Anglican who has done much to pioneer the spread of neo-Pentecostalism in Britain's main denominations), *As at the Beginning*, London 1965, p. 18: 'When Billy Graham was once criticised for taking the Church back fifty years, he complained afterwards 'Why, I'm trying to take the Church back 1900 years.' Again and again there has been this desire to return to the shining certainties and primitive simplicity of the age of the apostles.'

[64] C. H. Morris, *Redemption Hymnal* 1958, no. 219, quoted by W. J. Hollenweger, *The Pentecostals*, London 1972, p. 330.

[65] See Peter Hocken's essay, n. 11, and Simon Tugwell's essay, n. 12

[66] 'He has been to California and got Pentecost and speaks in an unknown tongue.' – extract from Thurman Carey's memoirs, quoted by H. V. Synan, op. cit., p. 117.

[67] Cf. H. V. Synan op. cit., 55ff, p. 219; R. M. Kanter, *Commitment and Community: communes and utopias in sociological perspective*, Cambridge, Mass. 1972, p. 32ff.

[68] Something different from 'attempting to *re-live* the experience of Pentecost', which George Every, in his essay in this book, rightly sees as not an authentic feature of Pentecostalism, p. 163ff.

[69] Quoted by W. J. Hollenweger, 'The Morning is Full', in P. Kami ed., *Pentecost and Politics* (pamphlet published by the Student Christian Movement's periodical *Movement*) Bristol, 1975, p. 5.

[70] C. Lalive d'Epinay, op. cit., 56f.

[71] *Pentecost and Politics*, 2. Cf. also W. J. Hollenweger, *Pentecost between Black and White*, Belfast 1974, p. 32: 'The ecumenical problem of the immediate

115

future is not the relationship between catholic and protestant but between "oral" and "literary" theology,'

[72] *Pentecostalism, eschatology and liberation in the third world: a Note:* In *Pentecost and Politics,* p. 6, Professor Hollenweger says that the consequences for social and political alphabetisation 'go far beyond the influence of some so-called pressure groups which are so often just a new form of foreign ideology, based on some middle-class revolutionary romanticism. The latter's revolution is by and large a paper revolution and will be reactionary in the long run, because it can never win against the overwhelming technical resources of any internal or external colonial power'. In *The Pentecostals,* p. 165, he says (speaking of the African independent churches) 'Emotional worship seems everywhere in the world to be able to bring about a desire to change the outward conditions of life.' In certain circumstances it does seem that there can be not merely a development of mutual help within the church community but a growth of political awareness. 'The gospel must be concerned with bread', the Brazilian Pentecostal Manoel de Mello is quoted as saying, in *Pentecost and Politics,* p. 18. Writing before the time of the Allende government, C. Lalive d'Epinay, op. cit., p. 143f. described the Pentecostal Iglesia Wesleyana Nacional of Chile, a condition of membership of which was to belong to a trade union and be an active member of a party of the left. Cf. also what, much more recently, P.Kami has had to say about the Cuban Christian Pentecostal Church, in *Pentecost and Politics,* 14f, On the black Pentecostal churches of the USA (some of which regard political involvement and picketing as a gift of the Holy Spirit), in addition to what Hollenweger says in *The Pentecostals,* p. 469f., in 'Pentecostalism and Black Power' (*Theology Today,* 30-3, October, 1973, p. 234), and in *Pentecost between Black and White,* p. 13ff, see also L. Gerlach & V. Hine, *People, Power, Change: Movements of Social Transformation,* Indianapolis & New York, 1970, and R. Gerloff, 'Black Power and Pentecostalism ' in *Pentecost and Politics,* p. 11ff.

But writers like Hollenweger, who believe that on a long-term basis Pentecostalism may well show itself to be a socially and politically liberating force, are still very much in a minority. (Hollenweger himself, in *The Pentecostals,* p. 467, quotes early 20th-century members of the Holiness movement as saying 'For the converted, are not most so-called social problems resolved?' . . . 'No one can save a man by filling his belly. Bring him into contact with Jesus and he will soon be able to buy his own dinner.') Writers on the third world of the opposite and prevailing opinion include E. Willems (*Followers of the New Faith: Culture Changes and the Rise of Protestantism in Brazil and Chile,* Nashville, Tenn. 1967), G. Lewy (*Religion and Revolution,* New York 1974) and C. Lalive d'Epinay, who says 'Underlying the expansion of Pentecostalism is a social protest which never, in this religious movement, assumes the form of revolutionary action; the Kingdom of God is still regarded as a transcendent, other-worldly kingdom, of which the congregations are the visible symbol, but they have no relation of continuity with the thing they symbolize. The Reign of God will come from the Heavens; it is radically other and cannot be regarded as a continuation of any human activity. This eschatological conception symbolizes (rather than determines) Pentecostalist socio-political passivity.' (op. cit. p. 124). The viewpoint of E. Willems (op. cit. p. 134) is rather different. He considers that one of the distinguishing marks of Pentecostalism in Latin America is that its message is *not* the Second Coming but 'the far more appealing prospect of an immediate coming of the deity' (i.e. the descent of the Spirit) – which is why G. Lewy (op. cit. p. 271f.) sees revolutionary millenarism as 'not a viable option' in Latin America. But it can be argued that, at least in the long run, not even in popular religion containing substantial non-Christian elements can either of these doctrines (namely, 'the Second Coming' and 'the descent of the Spirit') be jettisoned without weakening the other. It is fashionable to contrast Latin America's Christian freedom fighters and its 'charismatics' and overlook how much they have in common.

Here leaving aside the question (which I have touched on elsewhere in this essay) whether the notion of a radical eschatological break is stultifying or liberating, it would seem that many of the differences among scholars about the social and political role of Pentecostalism in the third world have their origins primarily in differences of method and emphasis. The majority draw their conclusions simply on what they hear these Pentecostals saying today, and what they see them doing, and are reluctant to allow in their projections for a significant shift. On the other hand Hollenweger, drawing on his deep first-hand knowledge of how Pentecostals think, does not conclude, in spite of the persistence of 'other-worldly' influences, that Pentecostalism is *in practice* automatically world-negating: the ideology of self-help which it inculcates is in certain societies potentially a liberating force. In the quotation opening this note he excessively underplays the importance of current 'theology of liberation', but his basic criticism is right. Maybe it will be in the area of apocalyptic that the forces inspiring 'liberation theology' and Pentecostalism in the third world will discover their common ground ... ground not necessarily there only for them to fight each other on.

In reply to the question whether Pentecostalism in Latin America was a potentially revolutionary force, A Sapsezian, a Brazilian attached to the World Council of Churches, said that for Pentecostals 'eschatology is a living hope ... Of course, we can always say that they transfer, they extrapolate this hope to the beyond. This I'm not sure ... There are signs of a gradual development, that this eschatological hope has something to do with the present suffering of these people. And to my view the consciousness of suffering and this eschatological hope are moving to each other, and my understanding is that when these two things touch each other we will have a very explosive situation among Pentecostals ... ' (Interview originally published by the United Society for the Propagation of the Gospel and the Methodist Missionary Society, London; reprinted in *Pentecost and Politics*, p. 24).

[73] W. J. Hollenweger, *The Pentecostals*, p. 466.

[74] C. Lalive d'Epinay, op. cit., p. 207

[75] Cf. M. J. Amerlinck y Assereto, *Ixmiquilpan: un estudio comparativo de evangelistas y católicos* (Anthropological thesis, Universidad Iberoamericano, Mexico 1970), quoted by W. J. Hollenweger, *Pentecost between Black and White*, p. 48.

[76] Cf. E. Willems, op. cit., p. 108; C Lalive d'Epinay, op. cit., pp. 35-39, 128ff.

[77] H. V. Synan, op. cit., p. 108.

[78] Quoted by H. V. Synan, ibid. p. 108.

[79] Cf.W. J. Hollenweger, *The Pentecostals*, p. 416.

[80] 'Not only did blacks initiate the Azusa Street meeting which is now recognized as a 'watershed' in Pentecostal history, but for many years maintained inter-racial ties during a crucial period in the history of American race relations.' (Leonard Lovett, President of the Theological Seminary of the black Pentecostal Church of God in Christ, quoted by R. Gerloff in *Pentecost and Politics*, p. 14.)

[81] Guest preacher at Hockley Pentecostal Church, Birmingham, December 1972.

[82] Interview on BBC programme, The Powers of Darkness, 27.10.75.

[83] See Peter Hocken's essay in this book, pp. 46-8, and cf. Simon Tugwell's essay, pp. 121-4, and H. V. Synan, op. cit., p. 217. (*Note:* These are citations to references to the 'similarity' and the 'otherness' of pentecostalism compared with Catholicism and to Synan's observation that the lineage of pentecostalism goes back through Arminianism to Catholicism placing it outside the Calvinistic reformed tradition.)

[84] *Summa Theologiae*, 2a2ae. p.17, 2. Also cf. Augustine, *De Civitate Dei*, XXII, p. 30.

[85] *Theological Investigations* ET Vol. 10, London and New York, p. 225

The Speech-Giving Spirit
A dialogue with 'tongues'

SIMON TUGWELL OP

CONTENTS

INTRODUCTORY: WHOLESOME DIALOGUE

He who believes will not be in a hurry.
(Isaiah 28:16)

ARISTOTLE DENIED THE possibility of love at first sight; the most he would allow was that one might conceive an immediate desire to make friends with someone.[1] But actually becoming someone's friend takes time. And it takes time because coming to love someone involves coming to know them, really know them; and that entails piercing through first impressions, through surface appearances, even through real insights, for

> those who know her, know her less
> The nearer her they get,

as Emily Dickinson wrote both of nature and of her sister-in-law.[2] Only so does person really meet person, the mystery of each touching the mystery of the other; only so can true love displace the mere convenience of mutual benefit and exploitation.

And something similar is surely involved in oecumenical dialogue. Theologians are not infrequently accused of unnecessarily complicating the project of christian unity; but, at least at their best, what they are trying to do is to ensure that the dialogue is real, that it gets beyond superficial and partial mating, so that churches and confessions meet one another whole, as they really are.

If oecumenism is to bring us all together in the love of Christ, then interchurch sightseeing is not enough. It is not enough to go round each others' churches simply collecting similarities and curiosities.

We must ask what each element is doing, what part it plays in the whole system of the other man's belief and practice. Only so will our encounter be true and respectful.

And in the particular meeting which is oecumenism, there is a further factor of inestimable importance: the truth of any church is not its own, but God's. No church has any truth but His. However comfortable it might be for us simply to assemble a church of our own devising, taking bits and pieces from all our various denominations, the Word of God forbids it utterly. It is God who defines and identifies his church. If our dialogue is to be truly christian, then it must involve not only respect for our own and each others' integrity, but also attentiveness and fidelity to God's truth.

And it is not enough to hear: we must listen, long and deeply. This is why the Second Vatican Council was so adamant that there can be no true oecumenism without conversion. [3] Whatever else it may be, the oecumenical movement is a call to conversion, conversion to Christ, the Lord of us all.

If the challenge of oecumenism is indeed one of the ways in which God addresses his word to us, then listening will be a major part of it. And the Vatican Council says precisely that. In oecumenical dialogue, instead of hurling abuse and accusations at one another, we must now be prepared to learn from one another: 'nor must we overlook the fact that whatever is achieved among our separated brethren by the grace of the Holy Spirit can contribute to our up-building too. Anything that is genuinely christian will never be hostile to the true treasure of the faith; rather it can help to bring about a more perfect realisation of the mystery of Christ and the church ... Because of the divisions between christians it is harder for the church herself to express the fullness of her own catholicity in every respect in actual life'. [4]

We are to listen, then, to be attentive to what the Holy Spirit may have for our own edification in what he is doing among Christians of other denominations. But such edification will, nevertheless, always have the result of making us better, more adequate, precisely as catholics. In one sense, we shall recognise whatever we find of good in other churches as already ours, already part of our own catholicism though maybe we had overlooked it or even tried to hide it and do away with it. So, paradoxically, the voice of God that appears to come to us from outside, will always be found also to speak to us from within our own heritage as catholics. This is why it is so important not just to pick up bits and pieces from each others' religion, but to find them in relationship to what we already have, to see them proceeding from our own faith, not as alien bodies, but as a newly discovered channel of grace flowing from the one source. It is from deep within ourselves that the Lord promised that rivers of living waters would flow (Jn. 7:38), and this is always characteristic of his authentic works.

But this need to situate what we learn from others always in the context of our own faith as catholics in no way lets us off trying to see also how it fits into the whole faith of the other churches. The Vatican Council was most insistent that other christian bodies cannot any longer be regarded simply as accidental collections of catholic fragments. They are recognised as having a real importance for salvation precisely as structures, as systems.[5] It is in meeting other churches as a living whole that we will be challenged by the Holy Spirit to rediscover aspects of our own living wholeness.

It is perhaps particularly important, and peculiarly difficult, to remember this in connexion with our dialogue with Pentecostalism, where the whole is so elusive and unfamiliar, not to say startling, while some aspects are, at least to some people, so appealing and exciting. The temptation is strong to a kind of 'smash and grab' oecumenism, seizing upon one or two bits, without examining too closely what they actually signify, and then making our get away as quickly as possible. I suspect that some of the problems that have arisen so painfully in the churches in connexion with what they now like to call the 'charismatic movement' are due in part to this excessively impatient shelving of the oecumenical dimension, whether by pretending that the problem is already solved ('We are one in the Spirit'), or by banishing it altogether – this has been done so successfully in some parts that I met recently a lady who expressed some interest in a Catholic Pentecostal group some seventy or eighty miles away; but when I mentioned to her the Elim Pentecostal Church just next door to her, she said, 'Oh, they're not real Pentecostals; they're just one of those sects'.

Apart from the incivility involved in smash and grab oecumenism, it results also in a seriously impoverished understanding of the bits brought home as booty. Pentecostalism is notoriously open to misunderstanding among those who are unsympathetic – witness the worldwide and quite unjustified confusion with spiritism. But maybe even its friends are sometimes prone to jump to conclusions. As

Professor Hollenweger, an acknowledged authority on world Pentecostalism, has pointed out, the same religious practice can have very different meaning in different situations[6] Just because Catholics have started speaking in tongues now, it does not mean that they are necessarily doing the same thing as the Pentecostals. How easily, in our meeting with Pentecostalism, we assume that what they are interested in is charisms and charismatic renewal. How easily, and how unfairly! A well-known Pentecostal pastor, George Canty, has written: 'we are interested in many things beside speaking by the Spirit in unlearned languages. We are not just "tongues people". However that fact of "tongues" is significant for every part of the Christian creed. Pentecost is far more than a "charismatic renewal" ' " ('Pentecost', in Pentecostal parlance, refers often to the experience of Pentecostalism, rather than to the historical event of the first Whitsunday). 'That is only its percussion cap. If truth is one whole, then Pentecostal truth should help us to see truth – it should provide new strands of unity for all Christian belief.'[7]

If we treat tongues, then, simply as the kingpin of a charismatic structure, we may be missing precisely what the Holy Spirit is saying to us through the meeting with Pentecostalism because for the Pentecostals glossolalia is *not* the kingpin of a network of charisms, but a way into the whole of christian doctrine. They value it so supremely, not because they regard it as peculiarly important in itself, but because for them it is the sign that takes the lid off the whole of christian truth.

From our meeting with Pentecostalism then, it may or may not result that we shall ourselves start speaking in tongues, and – surely a point well worth achieving – it will not matter too much either way. What we shall find is that we are confronted with the challenge of christian integrity, the wholeness and cohesiveness of christian truth. And that matters a great deal.

In this essay I propose to explore, from a catholic point of view, tongues, not as a phenomenon in itself, but as part of a whole system of christian practice and belief. This can, I hope, get us beyond the initial feeling of fascination or revulsion usually evoked by the topic of tongues-speaking, and may help to clear the way for us to discern part of what the Spirit is saying to the churches at this time.

* * *

But first, by way of a cautionary tale, let me illustrate my remarks about method with an instance from antiquity, which brings out clearly both how easy and how misleading it is for us to jump too quickly to conclusions.

A fourth century Syriac writer, Aphrahat, preserves for us in one of his Demonstrations what is now usually taken to be a liturgical fragment from a local baptismal rite, or at least an echo of traditional baptismal homiletic material, which indicates that, for a time, in some church in Persia at any rate, only celibates were admitted to baptism.[8]

That is, of course, by now a safely dead letter; but suppose we were to find ourselves engaged in oecumenical dialogue with such a church, how would we proceed?

The first and easiest blind alley would be simply to take the isolated phenomenon by itself, and perhaps get very excited about it. Well yes, we might say, of course we do tend to baptise far too many people far too readily, and it might be a very good idea only to baptise, not celibates exactly, but people really zealous and dedicated to being full-time christians. After all, we have now progressed beyond the narrowly individualistic concept of salvation which made it so vital for everyone individually to belong explicitly to the church . . . In some such vein one might go on, taking a hint, certainly, from antiquity, but not really listening to it.

More probably we should simply say, 'Bosh! How could you have a church which restricted baptism to an élite like that?'. And that would be the end of our discussion; we should then probably launch out into an easy diatribe on how all the early christians were so afraid of sex – after all, they were all really Manichees, weren't they?

It is so easy for us to jump to conclusions, and celibacy, after all, is rather a raw nerve for us. And in fact the great Estonian scholar who first identified the nature of our passage in Aphrahat, Arthur Vööbus, at once interpreted it in the light of such denunciations of marriage as one finds in the Acts of Judas Thomas, where marriage is simply denounced as filthy, so that there could be no question of combining the filthy intercourse of marriage with the spiritual intercourse of union with Christ.[9]

However, as usual, jumping to conclusions leads to wrong conclusions. Our passage quite explicitly does not regard marriage as filthy. It invites anyone who wants to get married to go and do so, and specifically says that there is no blame attached to so doing.

Only if they want to get married, they cannot also be baptised.

The whole passage is in close imitation of the Deuteronomic instructions for the Holy War (Deut. 20:5ff), in which only those warriors are allowed to take part who have no pressing concerns to distract them; those who have just acquired property or wives, for instance, would be likely to waver in the time of crisis. It is not necessary for the Lord to have many men to fight in his war, but those he has must be wholehearted and free from fear because of their trust in him.

It is well known that the early Syrian church very readily saw the christian life in terms of the Lord's war against spiritual evil; here we see a rather curious, but not illogical, application of this concept to baptism. There is no suggestion that getting married is evil; only it is a distraction, as St Paul says too (1 Cor. 7:32ff). What our passage is saying is not that nobody may get married, but that not everybody needs to be baptised. The christian life is essentially interpreted in the light of the Holy War: it is not necessary for everyone to be a fighter, but whoever does sign on must be able to pledge himself to it body and soul, with no other commitments to hold him back. Hence the obligation of poverty and celibacy upon candidates for baptism.

Especially if von Rad is right that 'in all probability the biblical demand for faith has its proper origin here in the Holy War of ancient Israel',[10] it is hard to deny that there is a certain cogency in all this.

In terms of one of our best known modern mythologies, it is necessary for somebody to go off and fight the hosts of Mordor; but one of the desired consequences of their valour is that most of the hobbits can stay at home, facing their own relatively unimpressive problems, and largely unaware of what is happening in the bigger world.

Christians are to be the 'salt of the earth' (Mt. 5:13), the preservative in the midst of the world which prevents the whole world from going off, like the putative handful of righteous men whose presence would have saved even Sodom and Gomorrah from destruction, had they been found. In a famous passage, the letter to Diognetus takes up the same thought, and H. I. Marrou in his commentary demonstrates how utterly traditional this understanding is: the christians, simply by being christians, keep the world together.[11] It is their fidelity which is their primary service to the world. Even if they are only few in number, the whole world will benefit from them. The loyal discipleship of the church is more important than its size.

But the christians had to face realistically, just as the Jews did, that even within their number not all could be relied upon to be utterly faithful. The Jews reckoned that in every age there is at least one good man, one *zaddiq*, for whose sake the world is preserved. Similarly the christians came to think that everyone, christian and pagan alike, benefits from the holiness of certain chosen ones in the church, such as the martyrs and ascetics. Marrou refers to Clement of Alexandria, for instance, who posits a select few, whose hidden lives do not impress the world, but yet they are the source of all its well-being.

Dialogue with our curious relic of christian Persian antiquity, then, leads us not, as we might expect, into much discussion of baptism - though the link between baptism and spiritual warfare is traditional and important – nor of celibacy, except indirectly, but into the area of indulgences and the communion of saints, the role of contemplatives in the church and in the world and how all of us benefit in hidden ways from the fidelity of the few. It leads us also to consider that maybe our most important service to the world is in being ourselves converted and faithful to our discipleship, rather than in more evident apostolic or social works.

This, admittedly rather way-out, illustration helps to make clear, I think, how deep dialogue can work. Seeing beyond the superficial issue can help to take a lot of the initial acrimony and suspicion out of the meeting, and can then lead us into a vision of the whole christian life which may be of value, whatever our eventual attitude to the specific point from which we started.

I suggest that the whole business of tongues, in the case of Pentecostalism is not unlike the question of celibate baptism in the instance we have been considering. Tongues in itself is not really the most important issue, and we need not expend too much emotional energy on it; but the importance of tongues for the Pentecostals is a very important issue. If we would enter into serious dialogue with the Pentecostals, we must learn how to see through tongues to a whole vision of christianity; if tongues, in the Pentecostal system, can lead us, as George Canty suggests, into 'new strands of unity for all Christian belief', from that, surely, all of us can hope to benefit.

'AS THE SPIRIT GAVE THEM UTTERANCE'

1. The Speech-giving Spirit

Sermone ditans guttura
(from the hymn Veni Creator Spiritus)

AS IS WELL known, Pentecostals regard speaking in tongues, as, at least, the normal sign that one has been, as they say, 'baptised in the Spirit'. An outburst of tongues, they point out, was the immediate result of the descent of the Holy Spirit at Pentecost, and they expect something similar to happen today when people receive the Holy Spirit.

The case against the whole doctrine of 'baptism in the Spirit' has been argued often enough, and, in particular, there is a cogent scriptural case against generalising the story of Pentecost into a doctrine of tongues as the initial evidence of reception of the Spirit. [12]

But that does not mean that our dialogue is over before it even begins. Far from it. There is good reason to think, both from scriptural evidence and from the witness of patristic tradition, that the Pentecostals are on to something in picking out inspired utterance as being in some way symptomatic of the whole working of the Holy Sprit in our lives, a typical fruit of the Incarnation.

That the actual vocal confession of faith is an integral part of our salvation is suggested by Romans 10:9f: 'if you confess with your mouth the Lord Jesus, and believe in your heart that God raised him from the dead, you will be saved; for in the heart one believes, and this brings righteousness, and with one's mouth one makes confession and this brings salvation' (this is one of those very compact phrases that St. Paul loves so much and which are the bane of translators: καρδίᾳ πιστεύεται εἰς δικαιοσύνην στόματι δὲ ὁμολογεῖται εἰς σωτηρίαν).

We find a similar, though more general, exhortation in one of the Odes of Solomon, that remarkable collection of ancient Syriac hymns, dated by its most recent editor as early as the late first century:[13]

> Open, open your hearts to the exultation of the Lord,
> And let your love abound from the heart to the lips,
> In order to bring forth fruits to the Lord, a holy life;
> And to talk with watchfulness in his light.
> Rise up and stand erect,
> You who sometimes were brought low.
> You who were in silence, speak,
> For your mouth has been opened. (8:1-4)

Song is the appropriate response to the coming of God's Truth into our world in the Incarnation:

> Let the singers sing the grace of the Lord Most High,
> And let them bring their songs.
>
> And let their heart be like the day,
> And their gentle voices like the majestic beauty of the Lord.
>
> And let there not be anyone who breathes
> That is without knowledge or voice.
>
> For he gave a mouth to his creation:
> To open the voice of the mouth towards him,
> And to praise him. (7:22-25)

The living, intoxicating waters of God's Spirit that we receive at baptism are characterised as 'speaking waters' (11:6), and they unlock speech in us:

> He has filled me with words of truth,
> That I may proclaim him.

(The word here rendered 'proclaim' is in fact the same in Syriac as 'speak' and 'talk' in the previous quotations)

129

And like the flowing of waters, truth flows from my mouth,
And my lips declare his fruits.
And he has caused his knowledge to abound in me,
Because the mouth of the Lord is the true Word,
And the entrance of his light . . .
By him the generations spoke to one another,
And those that were silent acquired speech.
(12:1-3,8)

The silence from which men are liberated by the Word of God is not a neutral silence, but, in a phrase of St Ephrem, A 'hateful, icy silence'. The Holy Spirit comes with his heat to thaw men who have been frozen into silence: 'Heat loosens the hateful bridle, the icy silence of frost upon the lips, and penetrates the mouth and the tongue, as did the tongues of fire which settled on the disciples. The Holy Spirit by his heat applied by the tongues, chased silence away from the disciples, that hateful, icy silence which, cowed by winter, dared not speak. For that people (i.e. the hostile Jews) being a sign of winter, a type of the frost, was altogether dark against the disciples. But the Holy Spirit by the tongues of fire which came loosened the might of the cold, and chased away fear from the disciples: and silence fled from their tongues by means of the tongues. Satan was condemned like winter, and the dark, raging people like a winter month. There the small birds on high burst into song (Literally 'speech' – the same word as the Odes of Solomon) with new voices, despising hawk and winter'.[14]

In one of his Hymns on the Nativity, in a midrashic passage on the various applications of the image of the Rock, Ephrem refers to our Lord's words about the very stones crying out, applying it to the conversion of stony-hearted men: 'the rocks became soft through him who is the Rock, and acquired tongues that could speak'.[15]

Unyielding rocks, frost-bound earth, these are potent images of the deathly life that is without God. And the end of such a life is to go down into eternal silence, from which we can only be delivered by the gracious purpose of God that men should live, not die, and live to praise him.

If the Lord were not to help me,
I would soon go down into the silence.
(Psalm 94:17, Grail)

The dead shall not praise the Lord,
Nor those who go down into the silence;
But we who live bless the Lord
Now and for ever.
(Psalm 115:17f, Grail)

In later Jewish tradition, in fact, Silence (Duma) came to be the proper name for 'the angel presiding over Gehinnom' (Hell).[16]

This is why it is possible for the author of the Odes of Solomon to claim:

Death has been destroyed before my face,
And Sheol has been vanquished by my word. (15:9)

The ability to praise God is regarded, especially in monastic circles, as one's essential sign of life in face of demonic onslaught. Alexander Akoimetes calls psalmody the monk's 'whole armour'[17] (and psalmody means praise. The Hebrew word for 'praise' in Ps 115 is related to the word for 'psalm'). And a Syriac poem ascribed to St. Ephrem, on the pilgrim life, says of one who falls away:

Then his tongue is silent,
Satan has robbed him of his weapons.[18]

In an admittedly obscure passage in the Letter of Barnabas there actually seems to be an identification made between the Lord opening our mouth, and his opening the door of the heavenly temple to let us in (16:9):

Opening the door of the temple for us, that is our mouth,
and giving us repentance, he brings those who had been death's
slaves into the everlasting temple.

The context makes it clear that some kind of utterance is to be understood:

How does God dwell in us? His word of faith, the call of his promise, the wisdom of his precepts, the commandments of doctrine – he himself prophesying in us, he himself dwelling in us . . .

131

God, it seems, opens our mouth so that we may speak his own word, and this utterance of his word is the means by which we are brought into the everlasting temple. (Compare the passage already quoted from the Odes of Solomon 12:3: 'the mouth of the Lord is the true Word, and the entrance of his light'.[19])

In another rather unclear passage, this time from the Valentinian Gospel of Truth, we seem to find a similar idea: 'Truth came into the midst. All its emanations knew it. They saluted the Father in truth and perfect strength which joined them with the Father; for everyone loves truth, because truth is the mouth of the Father. His tongue is the Holy Spirit which joins him to the truth, joining him to the mouth of the Father by means of his tongue when he receives the Holy Spirit.[20]

J. E. Ménard is surely right, in his commentary, to see here a reference to the tongues of Pentecost. The Holy Spirit unites us with the Father's Mouth (which is his Truth, his Word, which came into our midst in Christ), so that we speak his own Word in union with him.

Thou art my God, falsehood and death are not in my mouth;
Only perfection is thy will.
And vanity thou knowest not,
Because neither does it know thee.

And thou knowest not error;
Because neither does it know thee.

And ignorance appeared like dust,
And like the foam of the sea.

And vain people thought that it was great,
And they became like its type and were impoverished.

But the wise understood and contemplated,
And were not polluted by their thoughts;

Because they were in the mind of the Most High,
And mocked those who were walking in error.

And they spoke the truth,
From the breath which the Most High breathed into them.

Praise and great honour to his name.
Hallelujah.
(Odes of Solomon 18:8-16)

It seems clear, then, that there was a tradition, even if not a central or well articulated one, in the early church, which viewed salvation as involving the opening of our mouths by the Holy Spirit released into the world by the incarnation and sacrifice of the Son of God, so that we may utter God's Word in union with him, in praise and proclamation of him, and so escape from the hateful silence of death and damnation.[21]

And since there is, prima facie, a marked resemblance between this tradition and that of Pentecostalism, it is at least worth looking to see whether it can, as Pastor Canty suggests in connexion with tongues, provide a 'strand of unity' for an entire vision of christian truth and practice. To this end we must, in the next chapter, examine both theologically and psychologically the role of speech in man's creation and nature.

2. Man the Word-bearer.

Eala seo wlitige heofoncund þrynes,
þa mid ryhte sculon reordberende,
earme eordware ealle moegene
heregan healice . . .
(Advent Lyrics, 378ff)

Man is a talking animal, that is plain enough, and we might see little reason to get excited about it. But it is a curious fact how endlessly our ancient poets return to it. In Homer men are regularly characterised as μέροπες or αὐδήεντες , both of which simply mean 'endowed with speech'. Similarly, and presumably independently, our own Anglo-Saxon poets often refer to man as reordberend, 'bearer of speech'. In a poem addressed to Bishop Abraham of Nisibis, Ephrem refers to his flock as the 'speech-endowed sheep'.[22]

133

In Jewish thought, man's ability to talk takes on considerable theological significance. A Rabbinic tradition going back at least to the second century teaches that God created man 'with four attributes of the higher beings (i.e. angels) and four attributes of the lower beings (i.e. beasts). The four attributes of the higher beings are: he stands upright, like the ministering angels; he speaks, like the ministering angels; he understands, like the ministering angels; and he sees, like the ministering angels' (this last is developed to mean that man, like the angels but unlike the animals, can look sideways!).[23] Speech is an angelic, a supernatural, endowment. This is brought out even more emphatically in a largely parallel text from the Talmud, which says that human beings 'converse in the Holy Tongue like the ministering angels'.[24]

That man's capacity for speech is something marvellous, something one would not have anticipated, something therefore that unmistakeably indicates the effect of divine intervention, is stated in a fragment of Valentinus: 'fear fell on the angels in the presence of this creature when it uttered things greater than its own creation, because of the one who had invisibly deposited in him seed of the substance above and was expressing himself freely ($\pi\alpha\rho\rho\eta$-$\sigma\iota\alpha\zeta\acute{o}\mu\epsilon\nu o\nu$)'.[25] Stripped of its Gnostic doctrine of creation, this derives from a Jewish tradition that man's capacity to name the animals demonstrates his superiority to the angels, who, in one version, retreat in dismay, and begin to plot his downfall.[26]

According to an ancient Jewish version of Genesis 2:19,[27] it is 'in the language of the sanctuary' that man performs this feat of naming the animals. And this is surely the same as the 'holy tongue' which man is privileged to speak, and this in turn is identical with the very 'tongue of creation', the 'holy language by which the world was created at the beginning'.[28]

It was by his Word that God created the universe, and man, made in his image and likeness, is called to share with God in the utterance of that Word, to speak the very language in which 'he spoke and it came to be'. This is why the naming of the creatures is considered to be so important – and it is worth noticing that one account specifically adds the detail that Adam also names himself:[29] it reveals that man is uniquely privileged to share in God's own creative act, in a way surpassing the role even of the ministering angels.

But man sinned, he abandoned that communion with God for

134

which he was made. And so eventually he lost the ability to share God's language. According to Jewish legend, in the confusion of men's language at Babel, the knowledge of the holy tongue was lost.[30]

And so the language of creation fell silent in the world till Abraham was found worthy to be retaught it. As the book of Jubilees tells the story, Abraham suddenly realises one night the futility of astrology, and prays: 'my God, God Most High, Thou alone art my God, and Thee and Thy dominion have I chosen and Thou hast created all things, and all things that are are the work of Thy hands. Deliver me from the hands of evil spirits who have dominion over the thoughts of men's hearts, and let them not lead me astray from Thee, my God'. In return, God bids an angel: 'open his mouth and his ears, that he may hear and speak with his mouth the language which has been revealed'. The angel does so, and 'began to speak with him in Hebrew, in the tongue of creation'. This opened the way for Abraham to begin studying 'the books of the fathers', under the supervision of the angel.[31] Man can once again study God's truth and his commandments.

If the Word of God is already given to man in some way in the Old Testament – that Word which involves creation, revelation, precept and promise – how much more fully is it given in the New Covenant, when the Word actually becomes flesh and dwells among us. Now, by the grace of the Holy Spirit making us one with him, we are flesh of his flesh and bone of his bone (Eph. 5:19, Vulg and some Greek MSS).

The church has traditionally seen Pentecost as the definitive divine remedy for Babel; for instance, at the beginning of his Pentecost kontakion, Romanos the Melodist writes: 'when he came down and confused their tongues, the Most High divided the nations; when he distributed the tongues of fire, he called all men into unity', Against the background of Jewish legend, this takes on an even richer significance. Men need no longer be separate from one another by barriers of language, and that is wonderful enough; but, even more wonderfully, we need now no longer be separated by our language from God. God gives back to us the privilege of actually speaking with him in the language in which the world, ourselves included, was created. Man is no longer condemned to be out of harmony with the deepest truth of creation, the deepest truth of his own creatureliness. He can once more declare his own name and that of all his fellow-creatures, and know that they are not divided from that Name in which God has made himself known.

It is God's Word that is always effective, never frustrated (cf. Isaiah 55:11). 'His every word is actuality' (Enoch 14:22 Gk. Πᾶς λόγος αὐτοῦ ἔργον).

But man, when he loses the ability to speak God's word, is condemned to speak 'mere words', words which carry no weight in reality, words which therefore express nothing and leave man empty and frustrated.[32]

Man was created precisely for this sharing with God, this 'conversation' with God, as St Athanasius says.[33] Deprived of it, he is deprived of his own meaning. And not only man: it was man's role in the universe to be its poet, its orator, to speak God's word for it. Because of man's sin, 'creation was subjected to futility'; therefore 'the whole creation groans in travail to this present day (Rom. 8:20,22).

Man, created by the Word of God, created to speak that Word in which he was created back to God, is as it were pregnant with an utterance that he cannot achieve, once he is separated from God by sin. 'Like a woman with child, who writhes and cries out in her pangs, when she is near her time, so were we because of thee, O Lord; we were with child, we writhed, we have as it were brought forth wind, we have wrought no deliverance in the earth' (Isaiah 26:17f RSV).

The Odes of Solomon combine precisely this image of travail with inability to utter the word of truth:

The chasms were opened and closed;
And they were seeking the Lord as those who are about to give birth ...

And all of them who were lacking perished,
Because they were not able to express the word so that they might remain.

And the Lord destroyed the devices
Of all those who had not the truth with them
(24:5, 9f).

But now the time of birth has come. 'The earth has yielded its

136

fruit',[34] the Word of God, by the faithfulness of a virgin, has been born of our race. And in us too, who have received the first instalment of the Spirit, in us too the Word has begun to be formed, begun to be uttered. The awful dumbness of Hell has been overcome.

* * *

The Word with which we were pregnant is, of course, the Word of God. But it is also our own word, that word which God spoke to call us into being, that word which is the secret of our identity. Each one of us is a unique echo of the one Word in which God utters the fullness of himself and the fullness of his creation; it is our role in life to find and to speak that word, that word which is both ours and God's. That word which is ourself, spoken from the eternal silence of God, yet always prone to collapse into the silence of death and damnation.

'Expression is the need of my soul,' declares Don Marquis' famous and delightful cockroach poet,[35] and it is increasingly recognised that a certain freedom to express oneself is an essential factor in human maturity and sanity. Many of our deepest emotional and psychological problems seem to arise because we have something we have never dared utter, something we needed, maybe a very long time ago, to 'get off our chest', and could not. It may often be something that upset us as very small children, and its utterance will then be pretty basic and inarticulate – what Arthur Janov calls a 'primal scream'.[36] a concept curiously reminiscent of St.Paul's reference to the 'groaning' of the whole creation, subjected o futility and emptiness and unreality by sin.

Again, there is good evidence that what is usually called schizophrenia is not, or not simply, a malfunctioning of an individual's psychosomatic system, so much as a drastic response to a social situation, in which a person is ruthlessly denied the right to be himself, until eventually he does not himself know who or what he is, and does not know what his own thoughts, his own feelings, his own experience, are. It is interesting for our purposes to notice how important in one of the cases investigated by Laing and Esterson always having to 'take somebody else's word' for things is.[37]

And quite apart from major personality disorders, have not most of us sometimes experienced the acute frustration of wanting to say something and, for one reason or another, not being able to?

When we are hurt, it so often helps just to be able to say so to someone sympathetic, whom we can trust not to despise or molest us. And at moments of great joy too our pleasure is enhanced immensely if we can share it with a friend. Even if we are by ourselves, we can hardly help murmuring 'Isn't this nice?'. Man was not made to be alone, and words are as basic to us as thoughts. It is as true to say that thoughts are internalised words as it is to see words as externalised thoughts.

But so often we dare not speak, To speak, truly to speak, to speak from the heart, is to give ourselves, and if that gift is spurned or slighted, we soon loose the courage to try it again. Then our words, instead of expressing ourselves, will be distorted to express only our desire to please, to be accepted; we shall say only what we think we are expected to say. And the gift of ourselves will remain ungiven. And that is an almost inconceivable tragedy, because man is only himself when he can give himself.

That is why it is so wonderful when we are blessed with a companion, a friend, a brother, to whom we can speak freely, without always wondering anxiously whether we shall be accepted. As the Rabbinic proverb says, 'either companionship or death'.[38] Life without a companion is not worth living.

The Holy Spirit, who comes to free us from dumbness, restores our confidence to speak. As St Ephrem, in the poem already quoted, realised, the chasing away of silence must go hand in hand with the chasing away of fear.

This is expressed very precisely in one of the words used in the New Testament of our confident access to God: παρρησία, which means literally 'being able to say anything and everything'. In Christ we have such a trusting relationship with the Father that we can speak freely with him, getting things off our chest without fear of inhibition. Whatever we may find ourselves saying, God's love will not be defeated by it, however outrageous it may be.

The Holy Spirit frees us from the necessity always to put on a good show, the need always to keep a few masks handy lest we be found without our face on. Christian prayer should not be a smooth public performance, our Lord tells us (Mt. 6:5ff); it goes on in the intimacy and secrecy of a closed room, where we can speak, however shyly and crudely, to him who has called us his children and invites us to call him 'Abba, Father'.

Professor Hollenweger has suggested that the major contribution of Pentecostalism is, in fact, precisely here, in its ability to use means of communication that come easily and naturally to people. 'An astonishing degree of communication, never achieved in other churches, takes place' in their services. 'In Pentecostal worship – which only a casual observer could describe as unstructured and un-liturgical – everyone can express himself with the means of speech at his own disposal. The criterion is not conceptual clarity, but com-municability . . . It is here, in a sphere of liturgy and preaching, that the Pentecostal movement seems to me to have made its most impor-tant contribution, and not in the sphere of pneumatology, as is con-stantly and quite wrongly supposed'.[39]

If Professor Hollenweger is right, then we find here confirmation that we are on the right track: for our dialogue, it is not the pneumatological interpretation of glossolalia that is fundamental, so much as its role in freeing people to communicate with whatever means they have at their own disposal.

And perhaps it is relevant that St Paul says that someone speaking in tongues 'builds himself up' (1 Cor. 14:4). After all, having lost the confidence to say whatever we want to say, we rapidly pass on to a stage where we do not even know any longer what it is that we wanted to say. This is why, sometimes, the breakthrough into com-munication comes in the form of violent weeping or 'primal screaming'. Why should it not also sometimes come in the form of glossolalia?

But the important thing is that, however it comes, we learn to speak ourselves truly, at least to God. This does not mean that we need to know all about ourselves, so that we could present God with a thorough diagnosis of our situation! As Dom Georges Lefebvre has written recently: 'we do not need to see clearly what is in our hearts in order to offer it simply and with confidence'.[40] But it does mean that we stop hiding, and present ourselves to God's knowing. (Notice that in Galatians 4:8f St Paul implies that the crucial ele-ment in being a believer is not that now we know the God whom previously we did not know, but that now *he knows us*).

139

3. The Two shall be One

Mea doctrina non est mea
(Jn 7:16)

We are pregnant with a word from God, which we were created to speak, and it is easy to state, in principle, that this must be the deepest thrust behind our evident need for self-expression; yet there still remains a certain tension between these two things, a tension between originality and obedience, independence and creaturely receptivity.

This tension has sometimes been resolved heavily in favour of obedience. It is not so very long ago that we used to hear and talk a lot about the centrality of mortification in the christian life, the importance of denying ourselves.

But then, perhaps, we began to suspect that all we were doing was to produce people who were, no doubt, very meek and unassuming and generally harmless, but who were not, really, all that alive, let alone happy; which made us wonder what had happened to the life more abundant that our Lord had promised, and why christians seemed so oblivious of the commandment to rejoice in the Lord always.

The pendulum accordingly began to swing in the other direction, so that now the great commandment is that we must be, above all, authentic, even if we can only be authentically beastly. And one may, perhaps, venture to suggest that all we are doing now is to produce a lot of people who think a lot of themselves and shout very loud, and who find it necessary to remind us (or themselves?) as often as possible how very free and enlightened they are.

This is a caricature, of course, but if there is any truth in it at all, it shows up just how very difficult it is for us to grasp the significance of our Lord's high paradox that if we would find ourselves, we must lose ourselves (Mt. 10:39).

There is certainly a wrong way of losing ourselves; a tidy, orderly, prim array of stuffed dummies is not the intended result of the resurrection of Christ. We must not sacrifice our identity simply in the interests of conformity to some abstract model.

But, curiously enough, if we would be genuinely free to be ourselves, we must be prepared also to be free from ourselves.

This was the great mystery that St. Paul learned from his own ex-

140

perience. He had been a Pharisee, and a very successful one, but he realised, in retrospect, that the perfection he had as a Pharisee – a real enough perfection in its own way – was too small; so he threw off that righteousness that was simply his own, in favour of a totally different kind of righteousness that did not belong to Paul but to God (Phil 3). And so he learned to say, 'I live now not I, but Christ lives in me' (Gal. 2:20), a statement whose 'I live' balances exactly its 'not I' just as our Lord forces the finding and losing of ourselves into a strange and potent synthesis.

Beyond both self-assertion and self-denial lies a wonderful synergy, a working together, a *being* together, of God and man.

George Canty testifies that, for the Pentecostals, speaking with tongues 'is a tremendously suggestive idea involving the whole doctrine of the nature of man, of creation, and the style of God's fellowship with man'.[41] For them it discloses the truth expressed by St Augustine in his famous phrase: 'tu eras interior intimo meo':[42] God *belongs* in us. For God to dwell in our hearts, taking up his residence there as in his temple, ruling there by his Spirit, 'is not an invasion from outside so much as a glorious possession of the Temple from within', as George Canty says; 'utterance comes as a sign of the sweet agreement of God's Spirit and ours, and is a relaxing thing, devoid of the stress which would come if we were being invaded by a strange power'. 'To speak with tongues means the Bridge has been taken into the embrace of the Divine Bridegroom'.[43]

Any attempt at self-expression that is not rooted in God's self-expression is really doomed at the outset. But it is also true that any attempt to speak God's Word which does not proceed from the depth of our own freedom is foolishness, and may even be blasphemy.

The word which we must utter is a word which comes from deep within us; but it is a word which we do not choose for ourselves: it is a word that is given to us. We are a word that God speaks.

St Augustine makes the point well in his discussion of our Lord's apparently contradictory statement: 'my teaching is not mine, but his who sent me' (Jn. 7:16): 'what is the Father's teaching? Surely, the Father's Word. So Christ himself, being the Father's Word, *is* the Father's teaching. But a word must be somebody's word; so he said that his doctrine is himself, but not his own because the word is the Father's. For what is so much yours as yourself? Yet what is so little yours as yourself, when your very being is another's? ... In a nutshell, I think our Lord said "My teaching is not mine" as if to say "I am not the source of myself" ".[44]

In Christ there is no disunity or disharmony between the Word that he is and the word that he speaks; but in us it may require much patience and labour before the two come together as one. We must expect to grow through immaturity to maturity, and there may be a great deal of immature and agressive self-expression that we shall have to work through before we find how to utter ourselves entirely and freely in the utterance of God's Word.

That is why our progress towards true freedom and fulfillment involves both that we should be encouraged to say whatever we want to say· (παρρησία), and that we should be silenced, unable to go on simply uttering our own words. The Syriac poet Cyrillona in his free interpretation of our Lord's farewell discourse says:

The Spirit will come
with his tongues. . .
A new utterance
will dwell in you . . .
Your tongue will be silent
and will conceive.[45]

The way for us to enter into newness of life is by dying with Christ; we must go down with him into Sheol, the place of silence, to be reborn of water and the Holy Spirit.

We may recall that at the very beginning of creation, 'God created the heavens and the earth; and the earth was without form and void (tôhû wābôhû) . . . and the Spirit of God hovered over the waters' (Gen. 1:1f). In union with Christ's descent into Sheol, we too are brought back into the primeval waters, the chaos before the Word was spoken that formed the world into order and multiform beauty. And the Spirit of God hovers over the waters, waiting to bring us forth again into a new world, a world that is, once again, subject to the Word of God, within which we can learn again how to speak the language of God's creation, naming even ourselves with the new name that God has given us.

Before the new birth comes the dying, before the recovery comes the breakdown, before the new wisdom comes the lapsing into folly (cf. 1 Cor. 3:18).

Understanding the ways of God takes time, and will be perfected only at the very end, when we shall know him even as we are known by him (1 Cor. 13:12). First we must be prepared to speak the words that he gives us without always insisting too much on understanding them.

It has been plausibly suggested that our Lord very probably used the normal teaching method of his time, making the disciples learn his doctrine off by heart;[46] but he also promised that in due course the Holy Spirit, reminding them of all that he had said, would introduce them into the understanding of all truth.

Doctrine, objective doctrine, entrusted by the Father to Christ, and by him to the apostles, from whom in turn we have received it in the church,[47] is essential precisely as a means by which we are brought out of the blindness of a worldview or a theology determined simply by our own preconceptions.[48]

But, as Père Congar points out, the genuine tradition of the church is not just doctrine, administered dispassionately and extrinsically. It is a whole language, learned, as language always is, from a whole experience of life. The church's tradition is never adequately mediated in the form of fragmentary words, items of doctrine, because it is a living whole, a language of worship and celebration and mystery as well as doctrine and theology.

'Nothing,' says Congar, 'is more educative for man in his totality than the liturgy ... The liturgy is 'the authentic method instituted by the church to unite souls to Jesus'. The sort of christian produced by an enlightened and docile participation in the liturgy is a man at peace and unified in every fibre of his human nature, by the secret penetration of faith and love in his life, throughout a lifetime of prayer and worship, during which he learned, as if at his mother's knee and without effort, *the church's language:* her language of faith, love, hope and fidelity ... This is something quite different from mechanical obedience. It concerns the inner sensitivity (il s'agit de ce tact intime) that unites us to the thought and feeling of Christ's Bride.'[49]

As our hearts and minds are penetrated more and more by the words of teaching and worship that the church gives us, faith should grow gently into knowledge, just as tongues should lead into interpretation (1 Cor. 14:13). But true faith will not assume that it has an immediate right to knowledge, it will not be in a hurry (cf. Isaiah 28:16). That, after all, was the sin of our first parents, to arrogate knowledge to themselves, instead of waiting for the right time. –

143

such, at least, is how St Theophilus of Antioch understood the story of the fall, and the idea was taken up and developed by St Irenaeus.[50]

The Holy Spirit, who enables us to call Jesus 'Lord' and to make profession of true faith, also gives us peace and patience. Faith already senses obscurely that God's truth and man's truth are ultimately one; there is a kind of homeliness about revealed truth even before full understanding dawns. As Karl Rahner says: 'the holy Mystery is the one thing that is self-explanatory, the one thing that is its own self-sufficient reason, even in our eyes'.[51] It is a little bit like the way in which poetry can sometimes speak powerfully to us even when we cannot quite identify what it is saying; indeed, we are perhaps more likely to be gripped, haunted, fascinated by a poem that is not immediately clear, but retains some mystery to itself.

With his usual flair for revelatory paradox, G. K. Chesterton called one of his best books 'Orthodoxy – a personal philosophy'. And it must be so, because it is only God's truth that is large enough to evoke a genuinely personal response that is adequate to what we are. The Holy Spirit, leading us into God's truth overcomes the separation between God's truth and ours, so that we come spontaneously and even creatively to see things God's way. The Holy Spirit places God's word in our mouth and in our heart, giving us the mind of Christ to be the core of our own minds, renewed by faith.

Just as we discover our full freedom in being docile to God's will, so we discover our own creative originality in being docile to his truth. An orthodoxy which is frightened of thought and originality is not yet fully orthodox; a faith that must be protected by obscurantism is the very antithesis of faith. But equally thought that can acknowledge no master outside itself is not yet really thought.

As we grow in Christ, entering more fully and maturely into the language of the church, the divine language given to us by the Holy Spirit, we shall discover that it is a language in which we can express ourselves fully, but also that it is a language in which we are not separated from God or from one another.

Unity of language – the very opposite of Babel – is a characteristic of the Messianic Age,[52] and so must rightly be characteristic of the church of Christ. When St Paul exhorts the Corinthians to overcome their party rivalry, he tells them, literally, 'all to say the same thing' ('Ἵνα τὸ αὐτὸ λέγητε πάντες) (1 Cor. 1:10). The Holy Spirit should free us from that compulsive 'originality' which prohibits us ever to use the language of others. He will make us free even to use age-old even to use age-old formulae, though the church's unity of language probably does not actually consist of this. He will give us an instinctive sympathy for the different ways in which christians have spoken down the ages, uniting us intimately with the church as a worldwide and millenial fellowship.

The Pentecostals, on the whole, are uneasy with what they understand to be the Catholic view of Tradition, and they tend to regard fixed liturgies as an unreal way to worship, But all the same, I think that their experience of speaking in tongues, and the way in which it leads them into discovering both the synergy of God and man, and the cohesiveness of the christian community, can suggest to us important reflections about tradition and liturgy, and especially I think it can help us to overcome the facile and misleading antithesis between spontaneity and liturgy, free thought and traditional orthodoxy.

4. Man the Poet

who were so dark of heart they might not speak,
a little innocence will make them sing
(e.e. cummings)

Reference has already been made to a certain similarity between words of faith and words of poetry, and even though this is only a partial similarity, it is by no means a merely accidental one, as Karl Rahner brings out in his beautiful and deservedly famous essay, *Priest and Poet*,[53] in which he shows the natural convergence of the vocation of the poet, to whom words are specially entrusted, and that of the priest, to whom the Word of God is specially entrusted.

Words, he reminds us, are not just inessential garments in which thoughts have to be clothed. 'The word is the embodied thought, not the embodiment of the thought' (p. 295). Much less are they simply conventional tools which can be manipulated at will. 'There are words which divide and words which unite; words which can be artificially manufactured and arbitrarily determined and words which have always existed or are newly born as by a miracle; ... words which by a kind of enchantment produce in the person who listens to them what they are expressing ... words which render a single thing translucent to the infinity of all reality. They are like sea-shells, in

145

which can be heard the sound of the ocean of infinity, no matter how small they are in themselves. They bring light to *us*, not we to them. They have power over us, because they are gifts of God, not creations of men. Some words are clear because they are shallow and without mystery; they suffice for the mind; by means of them one acquires mastery over things. Other words are perhaps obscure because they evoke the blinding mystery of things. They pour out of the heart and sound forth in hymns. They open the doors to great works and they decide over eternities. Such words, which spring up out of the heart, which hold us in their power, which enchant us, the glorifying, heaven-sent words, I should like to call primordial words (Urworte) ... No matter what it is they speak of, they always whisper something about everything' (pp. 295-7).

This is why there are words which 'have every right to be, indeed must be, obscure' (p. 299). 'There is a knowledge which stands before the mystery of unity in multiplicity, of essense in appearance, of the whole in the part and the part in the whole. This knowledge makes use of primordial words, which evoke the mystery. It is always indistinct and obscure, like the reality itself which by means of such words of knowledge obtains possession of us and draws us into its unsounded depths. In the primordial words spirit and flesh, the signified and its symbol, concept and word, things and image, are still freshly and originally one – which does not mean, simply the same. "O Stern und Blume, Geist und Kleid, Lieb', Leid und Zeit und Ewigkeit!" ("O star and flower, spirit and garment, love, sorrow and time and eternity!") exclaims Brentano, the Catholic poet. What does this mean? Can one say what it means? Or is it precisely an uttering of primordial words, which one must understand without having to explain them by means of "clearer" and cheaper words?' (pp. 297f).

If it is in any sense true that man was created to speak God's language, then man must be the poet-priest of creation, uttering aloud the word by which God created each thing and all things in the silence of his heart. 'Everything is redeemed by the word. It is the perfection of things. The word is their spiritual body in which they themselves first reach their own fulfilment' (p. 300).

But the poet is silenced when words are strait-jacketed into false clarity; Adam the royal priest becomes man the tyrant, whose words bring no fulfilment, only falsehood and exploitation.

The Holy Spirit leads us away again from false clarity, he brings

146

us safely through the allurements of false mystical obscurity, and teaches us real words, words which heal us and restore a truer relationship with God's creation.

If it is true, as the work of Professor Hollenweger suggests, that Pentecostalism is more a rediscovery of natural religion than of supernatural, then this again reassures us that our dialogue is on the right track. And we may recall that George Canty bears witness that for the Pentecostals speaking in tongues does actually lead into the whole doctrine of creation.

Our words have been corrupted by sin, and so tend to prevent us from seeing the world or ourselves in truth. They slide too glibly into apparent but false wisdom, as in slogans and clichés and propaganda generally; or they simply serve to keep us unaware of mystery, of transcendence, of gospel newness, as when we use words merely as killers of silence.

Fr J. P. Manigne suggests that it is only when words become opaque again for us, so that we notice words as things in their own right, that we shall learn how to talk again, how to let things be without having to twist and oppress them. [54]

There are words which have power simply because they express man's domination, man's tyrannical power over things; but such words have no depth, no peace, in them, because man's domination must collapse like the tower of Babel.

It is in the poverty and weakness of words which play no part in our system of falsehood which we proudly term 'realism', that true words of power, words of God's power, are waiting, wooing us to rediscover them.

This is why the healing of our minds brings us through folly to wisdom, and involves a complete reappraisal of our use of words. In St Ephrem's hymn, quoted earlier, the disciples at Pentecost are compared to small birds bursting into song; the words released in us by the Holy Spirit are primordial words, words which spring from our creatureliness as deeply and simply and inexplicably as birdsong. They have a strange power over the minds of those who speak them and those who have ears to hear them.

There is no doubt that people have sometimes experienced speaking in tongues in the same way, as a speaking of words that have a strangely deep power, and that are at one with the 'words' of birds and beasts.

But this must not be rationalised again into 'magic', into a new way of manipulating and mastering things. It is always, unfortunately, possible for us to abuse God's most precious gifts, including the gift of new speech. New speech is not given to us, surely, as a new power in 'this world': it is in the new world, the new heaven and new earth of God's kingdom of whose powers we already have a foretaste, it is in the 'other world' that our 'other tongues', our new speech, is at home, giving us who speak it citizenship in heaven.

This is why the new speech given to us by God is so typically a song of praise, not of utility. Praise of God, contentment with God, is the link which paradoxically unites radical detachment from all creatures, with a deep, instinctive awareness of oneness with them, a combination found strikingly in St Francis and St John of the Cross. It is only in detachment that we can really hear what creation is saying to us, and we shall find that it is inciting us to join in, and indeed to lead, the universal hymn of praise.

There is a rather fine statement of this in the *Ignea Sagitta* of Nicholas of France, who succeeded St Simon Stock as Prior General of the Carmelites in the latter part of the thirteenth century. His latin, like that of St Bernard, is untranslateable, and we must be content here with the merest paraphrase, relegating the latin text to the notes: 'In our life of solitude all God's creatures come to help us. The beauty of the sky, with its dazzling array of planets and stars, draws us heavenwards. Birds, like angels, sing for our consolation. The mountains 'drip sweetness' and our friends, the hills, flow with milk and honey, which the vain lovers of this world can never taste. When we sing psalms in praise of the Creator, the mountains are our choir, praising the Lord with us in elegant counter-point. Roots germinate, and grass grows green, leaves rejoice on the trees in their own way, glad at our praise. Flowers, wonderful flowers, rich in a wonderful fragrance, strive to smile on us joy to comfort our solitude.'[55]

Poetry discloses this world to us precisely by not being taken in by worldly 'realism'. As J. R. R. Tolkien suggested so provocatively, fantasy is 'the most nearly pure form of art'.[56] 'Fantasy remains a human right: we make in our measure and in our derivative mode, because we are made: and not only made, but made in the image and likeness of a Maker'.

The 'other worlds' of human imagining, far from being an illegitimate escape, are, as Tolkien claims, one of the surest ways of being confronted with the divine truth in things that are.

And within these other worlds, new languages, new possibilities of speech, can play a very significant part. If we had to select one single feature from Tolkien's marvellous trilogy, one element which haunts and stirs us, might we not well choose the elvish poems as constituting at least one of the points where the whole power of Tolkien's creative vision is concentrated?

A! Elbereth Gilthoniel!
silivren penna míriel
o menel aglar elenath,
Gilthoniel, A! Elbereth! [57]

Maybe our own world and the language in it are too far gone in the service of the 'prince of this world' to be easily rescued. Perhaps it is only in 'other worlds' and 'other tongues' that the Holy Spirit can open our eyes to see the world of God's creating, and our mouths to speak the words of God's own language.

'Suddenly he was aware of a man clothed in white who watched him through the falling water of the fountain. As their eyes met, a bird sang aloud in the branches of the tree. In that moment Ged understood the singing of the bird, and the language of the water falling in the basin of the fountain, and the shape of the clouds, and the beginning and end of the wind that stirred the leaves: it seemed to him that he himself was a word spoken by the sunlight ... The Archmage looked at Ged and looked away, and began to speak in a tongue that Ged did not understand, mumbling as will an old old man whose wits go wandering among the years and islands. Yet in among his mumbling there were words of what the bird had sung and what the water had said falling. He was not laying a spell, and yet there was a power in his voice that moved Ged's mind so that the boy was bewildered, and for an instant seemed to behold himself standing in a strange vast desert place alone among shadows. Yet all along he was in the sunlit court, hearing the fountain fall'. [58]

II THE SACRIFICE OF PRAISE

Sacrificium laudis honorificabit me
(Ps 49:23)

OUR ENQUIRY SO far has shown that, even where at first sight there appeared to be little or no common ground between Catholics and Pentecostals– for, until recently, glossolalia played no part at all in Catholic self-awareness – deeper investigation discloses significant areas of encounter, where we may have much to learn and maybe also much to give.

Let us now see whether our method can also help us in a rather different situation, where Catholics and Pentecostals do appear to have common ground, but have diametrically opposed understanding of it. Catholics and Pentecostals appear to have at least two sacraments in common, in that both practise baptism and the Lord's Supper; but in fact there are crucial points of practice and doctrine in connexion with both of them about which there would seem to be not even sufficient agreement to serve as a basis for dialogue. Pentecostals, even with goodwill towards Catholics, find it difficult to see that our practice of baptism does not imply a magical view of sacramental efficacy. We, on the other hand, cannot help but be profoundly shocked by the apparent reduction of baptism among the Pentecostals to 'water baptism' like that of John. Similarly the Pentecostals have difficulties over transubstantiation and all that goes with it, while we must be deeply perplexed by what appears to be the total subjectivising of the eucharist among Pentecostals.

But if we look more deeply, not just at isolated phenomena, but at the structural whole of the Pentecostal and Catholic religions, the problem becomes more tractable. Our difficulty comes at least in part from the assumption that the proper correlative of Catholic

150

baptismal practice must be Pentecostal baptismal practice, and so on. But this may not in fact be the case.

Although the chapter on sacraments in Professor Hollenweger's magisterial book is devoted largely to the Lord's Supper and baptism, with a brief note on the practice in some Pentecostal churches of foot-washing, this is really rather misleading, because for the Pentecostals neither baptism nor the eucharist are sacraments, at least not in any sense of the word 'sacrament' current in Catholic theology. They are not regarded as divine acts, dependent upon divine ordinance, but as human acts, signs of human faith and obedience. This is not to say that they are unimportant, nor that they are not regarded as real occasions of grace; but simply that they are not, in the Catholic sense, sacraments. If we are to understand Pentecostal baptism, we shall probably do better to consider the immersion of pilgrims at Lourdes, stressing more the repentance side of it than the healing of the sick; in some ways, at least, this is much closer to what Pentecostals understand by baptism, and this may help us also to see a way through the urgent pastoral problem of Catholics seeking rebaptism at the hands of Pentecostal ministers.

On the other hand, the Pentecostals have a strong sense of the sacramentality of the Word of God. For them the baptism of infants does not, in general, make sense, because they do not reckon an infant capable of repentance or obedience. For us it makes sense, because we regard baptism not simply as a human act, but as a divine act, an act of God, which creates the condition for the infant to grow into a converted, obedient believer. Infant baptism, for us, reflects our belief in the prevenience of God's grace. And the Pentecostals also believe in the prevenience of God's grace, but they see it evidenced, not in sacramental baptism, but in the efficacy of the word of preaching, which may touch a man's heart far below the level of consciousness, and only long afterwards bear manifest fruit.

And in a very special way the Pentecostals believe in the sacramentality of speaking in tongues. I think it would not be too far wrong to suggest that for them speaking in tongues is a sacrament in the fullest catholic sense of that word, in that it is a human act given to men to do, in which however, according to their belief, we may unequivocally and without reserve identify an act of God himself.

According to St Thomas Aquinas[59] the Incarnate Word is the basis of all the sacraments, so that in different ways all the sacraments express the union of man and God which is founded on the hypostatic union in the person of Jesus Christ.

According to George Canty, 'at Pentecost God and man rejoice together as one in the charismatic language. To 'speak with tongues' means the Bride has been taken into the embrace of the Divine Bridegroom, and is completed in Him. The Baptism with the Holy Spirit reveals the dual nature of Nature' (pp. 14f. I am not quite sure what Pastor Canty means by this, but, in the context, it appears to refer to the capacity of created nature to be united with the divine nature, which, as he says, is 'the secret now brought to light' in the mystery of the dual nature of Christ).

Pentecostal 'eucharistic' devotions are somewhat reminiscent of Catholic meditations on the Passion – for Pentecostals in general the eucharist is simply a commemoration of Calvary. It is not a real making present of the act of God in the sacrifice of Christ, and so even Holy Communion is not a real embodied communion with Christ, but only a sign of spiritual communion. It is speaking in tongues that, for a Pentecostal, really embodies the act of God made present here and now.

And it is quite erroneous to suppose that it is all sheer emotionalism. Emotion may be involved, but need not be. The essential attitude is one of trust. Here, in their view, there is an act of God, validated by God himself, and therefore safe. It provides the occasion for the believer simply to rest in God, without being anxious about his own response, his own participation. If emotion results, it will come from this resting in God, and therefore will, normally, be genuine and unforced.

Now it is easy for us to say that the Pentecostals are wrong to trust tongues in this way. As at least some Pentecostals themselves have had to realise, speaking in tongues does not necessarily come from God, and is found in spiritist religion, for instance, where it may well be actually demonic. And sociology and psychology can suggest other hazards too: tongues may be simply expressive of a more or less unfree need to identify with a particular group, or it may be used in the interests of spiritual one-upmanship, for example, hazards which however arise particularly in connexion with neo-Pentecostalism.

But then it is equally easy for the Pentecostals to remind us of the dangers of trusting in our sacraments. We can rest in the objective sufficiency of the sacraments in a way which is just lazy and complacent.

In neither case is it a sufficient answer just to subjectivise everything, and put all the stress on active participation and full involvement. After all, we cannot, of ourselves, offer ourselves to God. As the third eucharistic prayer reminds us, we are a gift that Christ offers to the Father.

Dom Jean Leclercq, in a rather attractive little essay on 'Le mystère de l'autel'[60] reminds us that, once the easy communication between God and man in Paradise was broken by sin, it could only be restored by God's initiative, and God took this initiative by giving to man a symbolic altar. In Paradise man needed no altar, no symbol of his self-offering to God in response to God's self-giving to man. But now he does need an altar, a symbol; he needs something he can do that, by God's ordinance, will count as sacrifice, as self-offering. Otherwise he cannot offer himself, he cannot even find how to attempt to offer himself.

All other altars are fulfilled in Christ, in whom the meeting between God and man has definitively taken place. But we still do not see God face to face, and so we still need symbolic means to express our part in the union restored in Christ, in the self-offering of humanity accomplished perfectly in him who is both God and man.

Christ has made himself our self-offering, and so it is only in him and by him that we are offered to God. And so the symbolic acts which, by God's ordinance, will count as our self-offering must be acts not simply chosen and appointed by ourselves. They must be acts that we can, indeed, undertake, else there would be no point in them, but which nevertheless do not in any way depend upon ourselves for their validity and efficacy.

This is why the concept of validity is so important in all discussion of sacraments. It is inseparable from objectivity. It must be possible to know beyond all reasonable doubt whether or not the sacramental act is being performed, so that we can truly rest it in faith, without being anxious about our own feelings, or worthiness, or whatever.

It is in this spirit that the Pentecostals value speaking in tongues, as a human act which God accepts as a sacrifice of praise, independently of our own effort. Unless we are actually contradicting it by some actual sin or sinful purpose of our own, speaking in tongues is 'valid', that is to say it can be trusted to look after itself. Even if we are cold and tired and distracted, it is still worth doing.

I think this can high-light for us how important it is for us not to play down too much the objectivity of our sacraments. Of course

153

they are not magical, and they will not save us if we persistently contradict them in our other behaviour and attitudes. And rubrical correctness should not be made an end in itself (leading to all kinds of anxiety, which is quite unnecessary, since the church has always insisted that, in routine matters, *ecclesia supplet,* provided we are genuinely trying to accomplish the church's purpose); it should, in fact, be a restful thing, freeing us from anxiety, so that we can be tranquil, trusting in God's act and letting it be in us a wellspring of life, hope, strength and joy.

The Pentecostal 'sacrament' of tongues brings out clearly that there are wrong ways of resting in ritual. There can, for instance, be a wrong orientation, as when tongues is used to bolster one's sense of indentification with a desired group. This is perhaps not unlike the Anglo-Catholic temptation to 'go to Mass' at least partly to spite the evangelicals; or the latinophile temptation to go to a latin Mass more as a protest against vernacular than to enter into the *admirabile commercium* of God and man sharing in each other's lives. No doubt there would be a great sense of satisfaction, and even a kind of peace, there; but it would not be exactly a resting in God!

But the hazards should never make us lose sight of the fact that, in the sacraments, what is essential is not what we put into it (or what we get out of it, even), but what God is doing. Our basic response, then, must be one of trust, of contentment with God.

Once again, then, it seems that a look beneath the surface discloses an area of dialogue which we might not have expected to find, an area which does indeed point out to us something of importance for our own catholicity, as well as for our oecumenical relations with the Pentecostals. From it we may or may not learn to speak in tongues – and even if we do learn to speak in tongues, we must realise that our tongues-speaking will inevitably function differently in the total context of catholicism, for our good or ill, so that it may be of little oecumenical significance, and we may actually have little to learn from Pentecostal glossolalia about Catholic glossolalia.[61] What we can gain, surely, from our dialogue is encouragement not to give in to the tendency to subjectivise the sacraments and seek meaning in them by importing into them all kinds of secondary meaning of our own choosing; instead, we should be able to trust the meaning that is there by God's appointment and let them therefore look after themselves. Sacraments are meant to be human acts, in which human words are spoken; but they should also be a means by which we are brought to realise that human acts are only fully human in so far as they get beyond mere self-assertiveness, and find their roots in the act of God himself; and that human words only carry weight, for our good and blessing and for the good of the whole of creation, in so far as they proceed from the Word of God which itself proceeds eternally from the Silence of the Father.

This essay is based on a talk given on January 25, 1975, at Mount St Benedict, Trinidad. I am grateful to Fr Bernard Vlaar (now the Abbot) for inviting me to speak there and for arranging to have my talk taped and transcribed; and to Mr and Mrs Cuthbert Mejias and Miss Jean Gomez for actually doing the transcribing.

[1] Eth. Nic VIII, 1156b29ff.
[2] Poems 1400.
[3] Decree on Oecumenism, § 7.
[4] Ibid., § 4.
[5] Ibid., § 3.
[6] Walter J. Hollenweger, The Pentecostals (London, 1972), p. 507.
[7] George Canty, In my Father's House (London, 1969), p. 9.
[8] Dem VII, 18-20 (PS 1. 341-6, ed. J. Parisot). See Arthur Vööbus, Celibacy, a Requirement for Admission to Baptism in the Early Syrian Church (Stockholm, 1951); Robert Murray, The Exhortation to Candidates for Ascetical Vows at Baptism in the ancient Syriac Church (New Testament Studies 21 (1974), pp. 59-80). It is only fair to add that a great deal of uncertainty remains in the interpretation of these texts; see now T. Jansma, Aphraates' Demonstration VII 18 and 20 (Parole de l'Orient 5 (1974), pp. 21-48).
[9] Vööbus, op. cit., p. 27. The reference is to Acts of Judas Thomas, 88.
[10] Studies in Deuteronomy (London, 1953), p. 48.
[11] Letter to Diognetus, 6. See the edition by H. I. Marrou (Sources Chrétiennes 33, 2nd ed., Paris, 1965), pp. 137-176. For further evidence from the Syriac tradition, see Robert Murray, Symbols of Church and Kingdom (Cambridge, 1975), pp. 87[n.4], 114ff, 251. For Jewish belief, see R. Mach, Der Zaddik in Talmud und Midrasch (Leiden, 1957): the preservation of the world is due to the presence, merits and prayers of the righteous in each generation (pp. 134-7); it is occasionally claimed that even one zaddiq may suffice (p. 109). The zaddiq, like the Syrian ascetic christian, must engage in spiritual warfare against the evil *yêtzer* (pp. 26-31, 94, 150); his life is ascetic and penitential, and he looks for treasure in the world to come, not in this world (pp. 32-40, 87f, 94-6). He is a pilgrim and a stranger in this world (p. 150). Although the rabbinic picture of the zaddiq has parallels in Hellenistic sources and may be influenced by them, Mach is surely right

that this is essentially an autonomous Jewish tradition (p. 57). It is surely this tradition that underlies the view of Clement and others that it is the special christians, the martyrs and saints, rather than the whole church, whose merits sustain the world; it is not, as Marrou suggests, due to 'l'aristocratisme spirituel des Gnostiques', though both probably derive from the same Jewish belief. The democratisation of it in Diognetus comes from an awareness that Christ is the true and ultimate zaddiq, and that the church, by his grace and appointment, continues his office in the world.

[12] See for instance F. D. Bruner, A Theology of the Holy Spirit (London, 1971); Simon Tugwell, Did you Receive the Spirit? (London, 1972); Simon Tugwell, Reflections on the Pentecostal Doctrine of Baptism in the Holy Spirit (Heythrop Journal 13 (1972), pp. 268-81, 402-14); and now F. A. Sullivan, 'Baptism in the Holy Spirit' (Gregorianum 55 (1974), pp. 49-68).

[13] The Odes of Solomon, edited with translation and notes by J. H. Charlesworth (Oxford, 1973). I quote from his translation.

[14] Hymns de Fide 74:18-26, translated by J. B. Morris, Select Works of S. Ephrem the Syrian (Oxford, 1847); the translation has been revised in view of Dom E. Beck's authoritative edition and translation in C.S.C.O. 154-5 (Louvain, 1955). The use of winter as a symbol of this world, and summer as a symbol of the world to come, is probably traditional: cf., Hermas 52f; Gospel of Philip 7; Philip 109 (in connexion with baptism): 'when the Holy Spirit breathes, then the summer comes'. Cyril of Jerusalem regards it as significant that baptism and its immediate preparation occur during the spring (Cat. 14:10). Cf. J. Daniélou, Bible et Liturgie (Paris, 1958), pp. 389ff. Notice too that the English word 'lent' is simply the medieval word for 'spring'. In the background of all this is Cant 2:11f, and it is interesting that the Midrash Rabbah (II 12,1) applies it to the Exodus and to circumcision.

[15] Hymns de Nativitate 24:19. On the whole passage, see Murray, Symbols, pp. 211f.

[16] Zohar I 8a.

[17] Life of Alexander, 7 (PO VI, p. 662).

[18] Homilie über das Pilgerleben 24. Ed., A. Haffner, Sitzungsberichte der k. Akad. der Wiss., Wien, phil.-hist. Classe, 135 (1896) IX

[19] There is presumably also a reference to the same symbolism in the first hymn in the Acts of Judas Thomas, 6: 'her mouth is open fittingly . . . her tongue is like a veil over the doorway which is flung aside for those who enter'. The Syriac, here generally taken to be secondary, expands and interprets: 'her mouth is open and it becometh her, wherewith she uttereth all songs of praise . . . her tongue is the curtain, which the priest raiseth and entereth in'.

[20] Gospel of Truth, 26:28-27:4. Translated by K. H. Kuhn in Foertser/Wilson, Gnosis II (Oxford, 1974), slightly revised. See also the French version with commentary by Jacques-E. Ménard (Leiden, 1972).

[21] This is naturally not to say that the early church was unaware of the positive value of silence. St Ephrem in particular has a profound understanding of the interplay of speech and silence. It is characteristic of infidelity to be silent when it should be bursting into song (e.g. HNat 24:14); it is characteristic of heresy not to know when to be silent before the mystery of

God (e.g. HFid 38). A proper balance between the two is in accordance with nature, and makes us like God (HFid 38:8f; cf., below, n.32).

[22] CNis 19:3 (see Murray, Symbols p. 191); the same phrase occurs in HEpiph 7:5 HEpiph 13:13 refers to 'speech-endowed fruit' (which picks up a comparison in HParad 6;6), and HNat 2:10 to 'speech-endowed springs'. It is fascinating to consider to what extent the tradition we have been studying affected and was affected by the theological exploitation of the Greek word λογικος ; Clement of Alexandria, as Beck and Murray point out, also talks of λογικα προβατα in Paed. III Hymn 29, in connexion with their shepherd/bishop. But C. Mondésert (Rech ScRel 42 (1954), pp. 258-65) denies that, for Clement at any rate, retains any connexion with λογικος meaning 'word'. However, Cyril of Jerusalem does seem to retain a sense of this connection in Cat 4:8: Λόγος υἱός, λογικῶν ποιητής, Λόγος ἀκούων τοῦ Πατρὸς καὶ λαλῶν αὐτός. This might encourage us to see a similar point in Cat 10:3, where Christ is called πρόβατον . . . . οὐκ, ἄλογον, ἀλλὰ . . . τό ἀλόμενον ἐνώπιον τοῦ κείροντος καὶ γινῶσκον πότε δεῖ σιωπᾶν. There is reference in the same paragraph to λογικὰ πρόβατα, but it appears to be exactly equivalent to νοητὰ πρόβατα, which is also found (e.g. Cat 14:23). In the Acts of Judas Thomas 39 ἄλογα ζῶα corresponds to Syriac 'animals that have no speech'; 'the miraculous endowment of the ass (a proud descendant of the family of Balaam's ass!) with speech is, at least if we follow the Greek version (the Syriac is ambiguous) drawn into connection with the familiar Syrian theme of the divine silence made vocal in and through Christ (cf. below n.32): Christ is addressed as ἡ ἡσυχία καὶ ἡ ἠρεμία(Syr: O thou quiet and silent One), καὶ ἐν τοῖς ἀλόγοις ζώοις (Syr: animals that have no speech, meltâ) νῦν λαλούμενε (Syr: methmalal). This whole enigmatic episode is very probably intended as a dramatic parable, and the same can be said with even more confidence of the penitent leopard in the Acts of Philip 96ff (an evident descendant of the famous lion baptised by St Paul in the Acta Pauli); it is a dramatised statement of the conventional idea that faith in the Lord turns 'wild beasts' of men into true humans (cf. Clem. Alex., Strom. VI 6,50,3-6; also Acts of Judas Thomas 87). At least in the Acts of Philip, the power of speech is an integral part of the transformation: the leopard and the resuscitated kid end up giving praise to God 'who remembered us in this desert place, and changed our wild, bestial nature into gentleness, and gave us the divine word, and put a tongue and a mind in us, so that we could speak and confess your name' (100).

[23] Genesis Rabbah 8:11.

[24] Hag. 16a;

[25] Clement of Alexandria, Str II 8, 36, 2-4. Valentinus fr. 1 in Foerster/Wilson, Gnosis I (Oxford, 1972), trans. by David Hill; I have slightly modified the translation.

[26] Genesis Rabbah 17:4; Pirqê dRabbi Eliezer 13.

[27] Targum Neofiti ad loc.

[28] Jubilees 12:26; Targum Neofiti and PsJonathan, Genesis 11:1.

[29] Genesis Rabbah 17:4.

[30] Jubilees 12:25.

157

[31] Jubilees 12:19ff.

[32] Even though the overworked game of pitting Greek and Hebrew thought against each other seems, mercifully, to have died the death, it is still amusing to notice that whereas Greek regularly contrasts 'word' (   ) with 'deed, reality' (   ), the Hebrew *dābhār* means both 'word' and 'deed, reality', St Ignatius of Antioch is also concerned that 'inner' and 'outer' should be reconciled, that word and reality should coalesce, and he connects this with Christ who is the effective Word of God; he articulates this chiefly by reference to the silence from which the Word is spoken, the silence of the deeds of God and of men (ad Eph. 15:1f, ad Rom. 3:2f etc). A very close parallel to Ignatius' thought here is provided by Ephrem who also treats of Christ, the Voice of the Father, proceeding from the silence (HNat 3:3). in whom the 'silent nature' of Godhead is hidden (HNat 4:147), and who, even while babbling away in his mother's lap, is still conversing with the Father in the intimate silence in which they communicate with each other (HNat 5:22, HFid 11:7f). In him silence itself becomes audible (HFid 11:9). One must therefore know how to respond to speech, to words: to take mere words by themselves leads to blasphemy (HParad 11:5-8). Silence and speech interpenetrate at every level, divine, human and natural (cf. HFid 11:6) (cf. above n.21). Cf., also Martyrium Petri 10, in which the unreliability of the external voice of the body is contrasted with the intellectual voice by which the spirit speaks in silence. For a modern exploration of this theme, see the beautiful book by Max Picard, Die Welt des Schweigens (Zurich, 1948). 'Man hört durch das Wort das Schweigen hindurch, das rechte Wort ist nicht anderes als die Resonanz des Schweigens' (p. 21).

[33] Contra Gentes 2.

[34] Psalm 66:7, as interpreted by St Bernard, for instance, in Super Missus Est, Hom. 1:1.

[35] Don Marquis, Archy and Mehitabel (London, 1958).

[36] Arthur Janov, The Primal Scream (London, 1970).

[37] R. D. Laing and A. Esterson, Sanity, Madness and the Family (London, 1964), especially their first case.

[38] Babylonian Talmud, Taan. 23a.

[39] Hollenweger, op cit., p. 466.

[40] Georges Lefebvre, Simplicity (London, 1975), p. 25.

[41] Canty, op. cit., p. 94-95.

[42] Confessions, III 6.

[43] Canty op. cit., pp. 103, 15.

[44] In Ev. John. tr. 29:3-5.

[45] Cyrillona III 159-178. Italian trans. by Costantino Vona (Rome, 1963).

[46] See the monumental, though very one-sided, study by B. Gerhardsson, Memory and Manuscript (Uppsala, 1961), and the very judicious critique of it by W. D. Davies, The Setting of the Sermon on the Mount (Cambridge, 1963), Appendix XV. For Rabbinic evidence, see J. Bowker, Targums and Rabbinic Literature (Cambridge, 1969), p. 49.

[47] Cf. Tertullian, de Praescr. Haer. 21:4.

[48] Cf. M-J. Le Guillou, Le Mystère du Père (Paris, 1973), especially, pp. 1-55.

[49] Y. Congar, Tradition and the life of the Church (Fact and Faith, no. 3), p. 128. I have slightly revised the translation.

[50] Theophilus, ad Autol. II 25; Irenaeus, adv. Haer. IV 38-9; see also Greg. Naz., Or. 45:8. Cf., Murray, Symbols, pp. 304-6.

[51] Theological Investigations IV, p. 57.

[52] Tanhuma Noah, 19: quoted in Everyman's Talmud, p. 354.

[53] Theological Investigations III, pp. 294-317.

[54] J. P. Manigne, Pour une Poètique de la Foi (Paris, 1969); briefly summarised in a review by the present writer, Clergy Review 56 (1971) pp. 220-3.

[55] *In solitudine omnia nobis prospere patrocinantur elementa. Firmamentum miro ordine planetarum ac siderum mirabiliter decoratum, nos ad superiora miranda sua pulchritudine allicit et invitat. Aves angelicam naturam quodammodo induentes, suavem cantus melodiam ad nostrum solatium dulciter modulatur. Montes autem iuxta Isaiae prophetiam nobis mirificam stillant dulcedinem; sed et colles, nostri consortes, fluunt lac et mel, quae mundi huius amatores fatui non gustabunt. Nobis autem ad laudem psallentibus Creatoris, montes circumstantes, fratres nostri conventuales, iuxta identitatem vocis nostrae, linguae polite plectra percutientes, ac versus organice in aere modulantes, una nobiscum tono concordi resonant collaudantes. Germinant radices, virent herbae, frondes et arbores nobis suo modo laetantur applaudentes; sed et flores mirabiles, qui quadam fragrantia redundant mirabili, nobis solitariis consolationis gratia satagunt arridere.* (Ignea Sagitta, chapter 11). Part of this text is quoted by Marrou, op. cit., from the French version by François de Saint-Marie (Les Plus vieux Textes du Carmel, Paris, 1945). There is now a critical edition by A. Staring, O. Carm., in Carmelus 9 (1962), pp. 237-307.

[56] J. R. R. Tolkien, Tree and Leaf (London, 1964), pp. 50, 44.

[57] J. R. R. Tolkien, The Return of the King (London, 1955), p. 308.

[58] Ursula Le Guin, A Wizard of Earthsea (Harmondsworth, 1971), p. 47-49.

[59] Summa Theologiae III, q. 60, Introd.

[60] In Dom Jean Leclercq, La Liturgie et les Paradoxes Chrétiens (Paris, 1963) pp. 133-145.

[61] For a catholic view of speaking in tongues, see Simon Tugwell, Prayer in Practice (Dublin, 1974), pp. 127-40.

Prophecy in the Christian Era

GEORGE EVERY

CONTENTS

IN THIS ESSAY I will try to show that Pentecostal and 'charismatic' movements are misunderstood if they are regarded, as they often are by their followers, simply as attempts to repeat the experiences recorded in the New Testament, especially in the *Acts of the Apostles* and in *1 Corinthians*. Rather they continue a kind of prophetic activity that is found in all periods. Among Christians the typical exercise of prophecy is the spiritual interpretation of Scripture, of the Old Testament in the New, and of the whole Bible thereafter, but this spiritual or allegorical interpretation has never been limited to the Scriptures in any religion. Other writings[1] are read in the same way, and signs of the times interpreted spiritually, especially in hunches and intimations, dreams and visions. Every Christian who meditates on the work of Christ, and reads the signs of his presence in the Bible, in the history of the world and of the Church, and in the course of his own life, has some share, through the power of the Spirit, in the prophetic office of all Christians.

The Scriptures have spoken to the particular condition of Christians in every age, primitive, medieval, and modern. But in groups where attention is paid to the exercise of prophecy by particular members and by the group collectively, in the selection and exposition of passages of Scripture, and in other comments on the whole situation that seem to come from the same sources of inspiration, the Scriptures themselves appear in a fresh light. In perennial controversies about the relation of the Bible to the Church it has often been pointed out that the Church had a Bible from the beginning. The Law, the Prophets and the Psalms all spoke to the early Christians of Christ. All the epistles and gospels of the New Testament contain a great deal of 'prophetic' interpretation of Scripture.

163

At the beginning of *St Matthew* 'All this took place to fulfil what the Lord had spoken by the prophet', is a phrase used in substance four times in the first two chapters.[2] St. Paul in his letters to the churches interprets Scripture in a variety of ways, some of them evidently coloured by his Rabbinical background, as in *Galatians* 4,vv21-31, on the wives of Abraham considered as 'an allegory' of the earthly and heavenly Jerusalem.

Methods of allegorical exposition change. Modern scholars in all schools have done their best to distinguish betweem them and in particular between the methods characteristic of the Rabbis, including St Paul, and those of Jewish and Gentile students of literature at the Greek schools at Alexandria and elsewhere. Some students of Biblical theology have pressed these distinctions to the point of saying that any spiritual interpretation of Scripture which is not Rabbinical is not Biblical, and therefore not legitimate for a Christian. But in Pentecostal prayer groups, Protestant and Catholic, a wide variety of prophetic or spiritual interpretation is used, not only in the choice and exposition of texts from all the Scriptures, but in the interpretation of signs of the times in events of the day, in the situation of the group, and in particular intimations or hunches that may be given to members of it. Interesting instances are the series of prophecies that led to the formation of the interdenominational Community of the Word of God at Ann Arbor out of a small Catholic charismatic group,[3] No doubt in discerning what is truly of the Spirit in such prophecies the Bible is one of our standards, but one that can be misused. There is nothing surprising in the frequent use of the language of King James' version in modern prophecies, and no reason to regard them as fabricated imitations for this reason, but the emphatic 'Thus says the Lord' may betray uncertainty on the defensive rather than genuine faith, and direct citations from Scripture may often belong to the penumbra of the message rather than to the essential core of the meaning. In the discernment of spirits a wider range of comparison is needed than can be provided by the text of the New Testament and modern Pentecostal and Neo-Pentecostal literature.

It is my contention that the whole history of allegorical interpretation of Scripture is relevant, and with it the history of the other forms of prophecy that were practised in the Church in the age of the Fathers and the 'Dark Ages'. Our inherited distinctions between these and the Biblical period on the one hand, the age of the Reformation and the Counter-Reformation on the other, have been imposed upon us by the conditions of controversy in the West, and need to be looked at again in the more relaxed atmosphere of our present ecumenical dialogue. I propose therefore to introduce this essay by a short survey of the history of church history, before reconsidering the role of prophecy in the formation of Christian doctrine, and distinctions made by the schoolmen in the Middle Ages between types of prophecy and revelation.

1. The History of Church History.

The popular presentation of history always involves some simplification. In an historical religion, where faith is involved with historical judgement, some distortion of history is inevitable. The most dangerous arise out of an honest passion to be objective. In the Middle Ages, as in the ancient world, history was a branch of rhetoric. Lives of the saints and of other worthies were written for edification rather than information. In Geoffrey of Monmouth's *History of the Kings of Britain,* Lear, Cymbeline, King Arthur and his knights were on the same level with Romulus and Remus, Julius Caesar, Noah and Abraham, Solomon and the Queen of Sheba. The 'letter' of Scripture then meant the original meaning of the author, [4] and 'the inspiration of the letter' related to doctrinal rather than to what we should call historical accuracy. But in the 17th century a new kind of traveller's tale from those who had been to Niagara or to China demanded empirical verification. It became important to establish the truth of the Bible on this level, as a true tale. Sir Isaac Newton found there ancient science, obscurely expressed, and clues to future history, while others looked therefore for clues to chronology.

The first comprehensive collections of historical materials were made not in but after the controversies of the Reformation. [5] In the 17th century these gave place to a general Church history, composed largely by Gallican Catholics, who wanted to discover common ground with Anglicans, Lutherans, and French Huguenots. [6] They were agreed that the Bible was inspired, and that the historical books of Scripture were superior to any other authority as sources of ancient history. They were also agreed in revering St Augustine and in paying attention to what he said and to all that was said about him in the century after his death. After that the Dark Ages began, when miracles did not happen or, if they did, Protestants, and many Catholics, did not believe in them.

In the debate on the miracles of the Bible, which began in the 18th century and by the beginning of the 19th century was becoming a matter of intense popular interest, the difficulties of Catholic apologists in using the ecclesiastical miracles as motives for credibility in considering any aspects of the gospel story was accentuated by differences of opinion between them, not only on questions of historical criticism, but on the history of authority in the Church and especially on the history of Papal authority and on its contemporary operation.[7] Some of the most learned Catholic historians were involved in the debate on the terms in which the infallibility of the Pope and the inspiration of Scripture were defined at the First Vatican Council, and one of the most eminent[8] was unable to accept them. As a result of this crisis the Catholic contribution to historical debate was muted for some years. In this period when Catholic scholars read more Protestant than Catholic books they were even more inclined to minimise prophecies and miracles after the New Testament, but they had gone a long way in this direction in the 18th century, for reasons that had more to do with 'the age of reason' than with the materials in front of them. They did not wish to assert what would not be believed.

I do not suppose that any Catholic, or any orthodox Protestant, ever supposed that Harnack's *History of Dogma*[9] was an objective account of the development of Christian doctrine, but many learnt from him how to revise their history of the age of the Fathers. Harnack's own theological interest was not in doubt and deserved attention from all who thought that the manhood of Christ had been unduly neglected.[10] He was aware of his Catholic readers and adapted himself to their needs in a way that no doubt helped to increase the circulation of his book among patristic scholars, not only in Germany, but in France and England. He won their sympathy by his hostility to Arianism in all its forms and his admiration for St Athanasius, but concealed the way in which the saint's difficulties were increased, especially in the East, by his association with Marcellus,[11] whose theological sympathies were nearer to Harnack's than to his own. On the place of prophecy in the early Church, Catholic and Anglican scholars did not accept Harnack's judgement, but his way of putting the question.

2. Prophets in the Church Orders.

A new debate on this began with the discovery of the *Didache*, 'the Teaching of the Apostles', in a library at Constantinople belonging to the Patriarchate of Jerusalem in 1875. Its original editor, Philotheus Bryennios, was a Greek scholar and an Orthodox metropolitan, who believed that it had been written towards the end of the 2nd century to recommend an orthodox view of the nature of prophecy and to encourage discernment of spirits, at a time when Montanists were troubling the churches of Asia and elsewhere with a new and exciting kind of ecstatic prophecy. But as soon as he published it in 1883 a debate began about its relation to the New Testament and to other early Christians books, especially *The Shepherd of Hermas* and the *Epistle of Barnabas*.[12] In the matter of date Harnack agreed with Bryennios that the *Didache* must be later than these, but in the matter of the intention of the book he agreed with other Protestant scholars who found there valuable evidence of the emergence of the Catholic institution out of a much much more flexible association of Christian groups whose ministries were charismatic, exercises of gifts of the Spirit, and not offices held for life. Harnack found more evidence of this in other early Church Orders, especially the *Apostolic Church Order,* sometimes called the *Constitutions of the Apostles,* which he put after the Didache in the same period, about 160 A.D.[13]

Catholics involved in the debate disagreed, at least at first, with both Bryennios and Harnack about the date, and with Harnack about the intention of the book. They saw that he and other Protestants had read into the text a conflict between the charismatic ministry of apostles and prophets and the settled ministry of bishops and deacons in the several particular churches. Harnack believed that the displacement of charismatic ministries by early Catholicism had taken a long time, and that Montanism could be a backlash against it. Catholics wanted to push the evidence for Catholic institutions back as far as they could. Since in the *Didachē* they are somewhat formless, at an early stage, either it must be as old as the New Testament, and older than parts of it, or it must be heretical, probably Montanist.

This choice was forced upon Catholics because the wandering prophets of the *Didache* were regarded by Protestants as itinerant evangelists. Their role in relation to the eucharist seemed to imply a

167

ministry of the Spirit, without any formal ordination.[14] Both Anglicans[15] and Catholics were shy about prophets outside the New Testament, because they shared with Protestants the common conviction that an important gap divided the age when revelations were given to apostles and prophets from the early Catholicism of the sub--apostolic Church. This could be shifted by Protestants like Harnack forward into the second century, or back into the apostolic age. Protestants are now more ready to recognise the presence of Catholic elements in the New Testament than they were in Harnack's time but Catholics were, and are, unwilling to move the gap forward, for fear that their claim to apostolic roots would be weakened. They would rather move it back and see in the *Didache* evidence of an apostolic tradition that did not become Scripture. J.-P. Audet, in his edition of 1958, made it contemporary with the New Testament. He believed that Hermas, the prophet who wrote the *Shepherd,* was on the fringe of the Church.[16] Like Fr Pierre Batiffol at the beginning of this century, he thought that 'prophets and prophesying virgins were soon found no more, except in dissenting conventicles, Marcionite or Montanist.[17] But Hermas reported his visions to the same Clement who wrote an important letter from the Roman Church to the Corinthian at the end of the first century, and according to the Muratorian fragment[18] Pius, who was Pope rather later, was Hermas's brother. Nothing in the *Didache* is directed against bishops on behalf of prophets, or against prophecy as such, although false prophets are a problem. The apostles indeed are unique as witnesses to Christ's resurrection, and the age of his revelation ends with their lifetime. But the apparent gap between this apostolic age and early Catholicism is an illusion of perspective.

Scripture in the beginning did not refer to a canon, but to a miscellaneous collection of inspired writing, old and new. The Law and the Prophets indeed were something apart, the Bible accepted by Jews in the time of Christ, and through the preaching of the apostles by the Gentiles in the Church. But the Church did not accept the division made by the Rabbis between some of the other holy books and all the rest. Her *Hagiographa,* on the edge of Scripture, was larger and more diverse than that of the synagogue,[19] and so came to include besides the four gospels and the *Epistles* of St Paul, another collection of letters by St Peter, St John, St James and St Jude, and in many places the *Apocalypse of St John The Shepherd of Hermas,* and the *Didache.* Eusebius, who provides sufficient evidence of this variety, refers in his summary of anti-Montanist polemic to a list made at the end of the 2nd century of those 'who had prophesied under the new covenant', and cites with approval the reproach of a Catholic writer against the Montanists that they have failed to produce new prophets of their own in the 14 years since the death of their prophetess Maximilla, whereas 'the prophetic gift must continue in the whole Church until the final coming.[20] The critical importance of Montanism is not that it provoked a reaction against prophecy, but that it provided a classic instance of false prophets who were not otherwise heretics. The bishops in the cities of Asia who set their faces against a general pilgrimage of Christians to the mountain village of Pepuza, there to await the second coming of Christ, were right in their conviction that this was a craze, parallel to cargo-cults in modern times.[21] But other churches suspected them of quenching the Spirit, and when Rome and the other Western churches finally decided to support the bishops of Asia, Tertullian was one of those who went into schism.[22]

Other evidence of the persistence of the prophetic office is in the various versions of *The Apostolic Church Order.*[23] This provides a blue-print for the organisation of a church in a place with twelve Christian families. They need a bishop, presbyters and deacons, a reader and three widows. Two of the widows are 'to persevere in prayer for all who are in trials and temptations, and to receive revelations where such are necessary'. One is 'to assist the women visited by sicknesses'. This is in the Greek, which is almost certainly the original.[24] At this point the Latin, Coptic and Syriac agree.[25] Only the Arabic and the Ethiopic, which are secondary and late, tone the revelations down, the Arabic[26] saying: 'They shall devote themselves to prayer for all who are in affliction, and who wish to tell them what it is', the Ethiopic:[27] 'Two shall devote themselves to prayer for all who are in affliction, and sufficient daily sustenance shall be given them'. This 'daily sustenance' is implied elsewhere in the other texts. It is clear from a number of places, including the *Acts of the Apostles* and the Pastoral Epistles in the New Testament,[28] that 'widows' were in most churches the chief charge on the church's own resources. They probably included some who had never been married, or had been deserted by their husbands, and some of the virgins who lived with them joined them. In the small churches envisaged by the *Apostolic Church Order* they were the paid staff, while the officers of the Church supported themselves by their own labours or out of their own resources.[29]

In one of the later Church Orders, *The Testament of the Lord*, the 'widows who sit in front'[30] are rather like elders. But they did not develop into presbyters, because as presbyters came to take the bishop's place in country churches, and in smaller churches in the cities, and to deputise for him in his own church if he were away, they came to be regarded primarily as potential presidents at the eucharist. Widows, who could not take the bishop's place, could be deaconesses, but not presbyters. Their institutional future lay in another direction.

The role of widows in the rise of monasticism has been obscured because on the whole nuns have been less important than monks in the history of the Church. But the *Life of St Macrina* by St Gregory of Nyssa, St Basil's brother, shows how important their sister had been in their lives and so in the whole development of monasticism in the Byzantine East from a seed-bed in his family, where their grand-mother, another Macrina, had been a remarkable visionary. As we have seen, the traditional role of widows had to do with exercise of prophetic and healing gifts, and with prayer for all Christians. In many places they kept vigils with others who prayed with them or at home. They prayed for everyone and from time to time, as need arose, received direction in the Spirit. We do not hear of them acting upon it, except in the matter of healing, which doubtless extended to exorcism, but they were consulted in situations which baffled other authorities.

3. Prayer and Prophecy in Vigils.

These communities of widows developed into monasteries. According to the Egyptian tradition of the 4th century, as reported by St Athanasius in his *Life of St Antony*, that father of hermits, before he went to live among the tombs in the desert, entrusted his sister to 'the care of some well-known, trustworthy virgins', living in a place called by the word for a convent in later Greek terminology.[32] In the Syrian tradition, which may be older, the 'Sons and Daughters of Covenant'[33] were an inner core of dedicated celibates, solitaries, who did not live in communities, but made themselves available for the service of the Church and of Christians generally.[34] In such monastic circles prophecy persisted. Not all prophets were celibates. Hermas, for instance, combined prophetic gifts with anxieties about his unruly family.[35] St Peter and other apostles were married, and inspired.[36] But it is reasonable to suppose that many of the wandering prophets whose activities we glimpse in the *Didache* were without commitments to a family, like St Paul and St Barnabas in the New Testament[37] and the Syrian 'Sons of the Covenant'. As the structures of the Church developed, and bishops as well as deacons and sub-deacons spent more time in her service, and less in their own occupations, more of them were chosen from the celibates, for obvious economic reasons, and they were more often involved in the organisation of vigils. On more and more occasions these developed under their direction into official gatherings on the model of the all-night vigils which in most Christian churches preceded the baptisms at Easter and Pentecost, and at other feasts as these were used for baptisms, but Christians continued to watch and pray night by night, as they had done since the earliest days.

The liturgical life of the Church, the canon of Scripture, and Christian doctrine grew up together. The role of spiritual gifts in this has been obscured by the general belief that the canon of Scripture preceded the creeds, and that doctrine developed through the kind of contentions concerning the meaning of texts that became familiar in the West in and after the Reformation. But this is a misunderstanding. The role of Scripture in the development of doctrine was indeed very important,[38] but the relation of Scriptures with one another came to be understood through prayerful reflection on their meaning, and especially on the relation between prophecies in the Old Testament and their fulfilment in the New.

It seems to be a mistake to think of the doctrine of the Incarnation as arising simply out of reflection on the historical evidence for the life of Christ in the gospels, without regard to the communion of Christians in his risen life, to their sense of the relationship between his humanity in the heavenly places and our own, between our resurrection and his, as this was perceived through participation in baptism and the eucharist,[39] and through the whole life of Christians at prayer in Christ and in the Spirit. In the same way the doctrine of the Trinity arises out of prayer in the Spirit to the Father through Jesus Christ his Son our Lord. This is not a consequence but a cause of the formulation of the doctrine. The *Gloria* for instance was modified from an earlier form: 'Glory be to the Father, through the

171

Son, in the Holy Spirit', because this had been used to support theories that the Son and the Spirit are creatures, and God only in a derivative sense. It was then changed to emphasise the equality of the three persons who received glory.[40] But the vision of the Trinity arises out of Trinitarian prayer, and not out of metaphysical speculation, although Christians took part in this with other philosophers of the time, and many of the terms of Christian doctrine were taken from Neo-Platonism. Their meaning, like the meaning of prophecies in the Old Testament, was transfigured by prophetic and mystical insight.

4. The Last Things.

In the doctrines of the Trinity and the Incarnation there is no contradiction between the emphasis that I have advanced on the role of experience in prayer, in and out of the liturgy, in the making of the canon of Scripture and of Christian doctrine, and the traditional view of the foundation of Christian faith in the Church's own understanding of apostolic tradition in Scripture. But there are places where prophecy has influenced the development of doctrine through visions subsequent to apostolic times. Prayer for the dead may indeed have support in the New Testament, more perhaps than Catholics have commonly used in argument,[41] but the general opinion seems to be that the doctrine of purgatory has not sufficient support in Scripture. Yet Catholics in East and West continue to believe it in rather different forms,[42] and in the last hundred years more and more Protestants have come to hold something like it.[43] If we look again at the experience on which prayer for the dead is based, we shall find it in visions received and seen by major and minor prophets, from St Perpetua at the end of the 2nd century, who saw in a vision her little brother, Dinocrates, comforted after death by her prayers,[44] to Dante, St Catherine of Genoa,[45] and Cardinal Newman, whose *Dream of Gerontius* has had an important influence on modern views of the after-life, Anglican as well as Catholic. We shall also see that in these visions more is involved than the condition of individual souls beyond the veil.

As the *Apocalypse of St John* is Scripture we have higher authority for reading it prophetically than we have in the case of the *Divine*

Comedy of Dante. But both are visions of judgement, where an ultimate meaning appears in the individual decisions taken, in the cities of Asia in the former, of Italy in the latter. The early Church saw all in terms of the coming of Christ to judge a breaking, falling world. The Roman empire fell, and he came to judge and reign, but not quite as they expected. In Dante's time Christians in the West were more aware of his judgement on souls departed. In the East too they were concerned with this from early times.

In the reign of the Emperor Heraclius (610-41), a well-to-do trader, Filentolus, who lived at Constantia in Cyprus, was generous to widows and orphans, and spent much money on hospitals. But he continued to live in sin with a woman who was not his wife, and died without repenting of this. The Archbishop and other bishops were in difficulties about his commemoration, and sent round to monasteries, stylites standing on pillars, and other anchorites, asking them to pray for a revelation. Kaioumos, a hermit with experience in the Egyptian desert and on Sinai, sent them a message that he had something to say. The bishops did not ask for his report. They went to his cell and heard that he had seen Filentolus suspended between heaven and hell, unable to enter either. He gave them no prescription for the terms of his commemoration. He simply reported what he himself had seen.[46]

Bede reports the vision of Fursey, an Irish ascetic who worked for the conversion of East Anglia,[47] how he was carried by angels towards heaven, and told to look down and see the fires that would consume the world, falsehood, cupidity, dissension, pitiless cruelty. These were gathered into a huge flame and came towards him, full of demons, but with the aid of the angels he passed through it, and saw the saints. On his way back to the body a soul was thrown at him, whose garment he had taken by way of payment at a deathbed, 'for the sake of saving the other's soul'. His cheek was scorched, and an angel told him: 'If you had not taken the goods of this man, his pains would not burn in you'. Another tale is told by Bede[48] of a Northumbrian householder, Drythelm, who after recovery from a long and dangerous illness, became an anchorite at Melrose. He remembered being taken into a broad and deep valley with fire on one side and hail and snow on the other, where souls were tossed across, but his guide told him: 'This is not the hell you imagine'. He came to a great pit and stood alone beside it, while great globes of black fire, full of souls, came out of it and fell back again into the

173

abyss. His fear increased as he heard behind him a gang of devils throwing in more souls, including a tonsured clerk and a woman. They thrust burning coals in tongs at his face, but his angel guide rescued him and took him away into the light. He saw a wall in front of him, of boundless height and without a gate, but suddenly found himself on top of it, in a beautiful field of fragrant flowers, full of rejoicing spirits in white. He saw a lovelier light in front of him, and heard distant voices singing. He smelt a surpassing fragrance, but he could not get into heaven, and with his angel guide went back the way he came.

These visions are prophetic in a double sense, of insight beyond our normal range of vision, and of reference to the future of those who are now alive. It is not unlikely that Drythelm's dream was responsible for the common opinion that there were two purgatories, one close to hell and the other on the way to heaven. [49] Such visions arising out of prayer and demanding prayer for others are scattered over the *Dialogues* of St Gregory the Great, where they form the basis of a number of good stories about souls in trouble, who want to get out of their present position as quickly as possible. [50] Other visions of a different kind shape the sayings of Caterina Adorno, St Catherine of Genoa, a widow in charge of a hospital there who died in 1510. She said that 'the souls in purgatory, so far as I understand the matter, cannot but choose to be there', and spoke of their joy as 'increasing day by day, as God more and more flows in upon the soul, which he does abundantly as every hindrance to his entrance is consumed away'. [51] In the long run her influence and Dante's on the theology of the last things has been at least as large as that of St Gregory the Great in his *Dialogues*. But in one respect this influence has been minimal, in the formal determination of doctrine. The definition of purgatory presented to the Greeks at the Council of Lyons (1274), revised at Florence in 1438-9 and for the Protestants at Trent in 1562, is in terms of supplementary satisfaction for repented sin, where penance cannot be completed in this life. Eastern Christians, lacking any developed doctrine of penitential works of satisfaction, were puzzled, but found it hard to frame their objections, [52] which were so far met that no description of purgatorial pains and penalties was given.

In the 16th century a further difficulty was created by the determination of one side of the controversy to treat Scripture as the necessary basis of all Christian belief. St Catherine's *Life and Doctrine* was published in 1551, by those who had been helped by her and hoped to help others torn between conflicting winds of doctrine. Someone in the 19th century maintained that there would have been no objections to purgatory if the idea had been presented in her terms.[53] But this was impossible. Not only was her book put on the index in Spain in 1583.[54] Visionary material of this kind was always open to objection if used in controversy, the more so after the Reformation, when Protestants insisted on the sole authority of Scripture.

5. Natural Prophecy.

The earlier history of the matter can be illustrated from controversies about prophecy in the 13th century. I propose here to examine the treatise De Prophetia of St Thomas Aquinas,[55] making use of related passages in the Summa, and of an article by Fr Victor White, O.P., on 'St Thomas's conception of revelation' in Dominican Studies I (1948). I shall also use The Influence of Prophecy in the Later Middle Ages by Dr Marjorie Reeves,[56] who does not refer to the De Prophetia, but does help to give it the right setting. She shows clearly that in the middle of the 13th century many people believed that Joachim of Fiore, a Calabrian Abbot who died in 1202, had prophesied a new age of the Spirit, and that his prophecy had been fulfilled, at least in part, in the rise of the orders of friars. He had expected an anti-Christ, in succession to other anti-Christs, the 'five heads of the dragon' in the Apocalypse of St John, to be born before the end of the 12th century, in Rome, which does not mean the city, but the imperialist party, for Joachim saw the empire as Babylon, the concentration of secular power. He would come near to victory, but his defeat would be followed by an age of the Spirit at the end of history.[57]

Like every vision of judgement, this had an immediate and a remote application. Joachim was well aware of the rising power of the empire in his own country, Naples and Sicily, where the Emperor Henry VI had married Constance, the heiress of the Norman kings of Sicily, and united her inheritance with his Swabian lands and the imperial dignity of the Holy Roman Empire. The anti-Christ to be born was in Joachim's mind their son, and in a real sense he was right. Frederick II was an able young man, who could never be manipulated by papal policy into becoming an instrument to divide the Sicilian kingdom from the empire. Rather he meant to use the popes for his own ends and to use them and his imperial claims to turn the Sicilian state into a strong monarchy over the whole of Italy, at the expense of the power and independence of the Papacy. He would in the end be defeated, by the resistance of parties in the Italian cities to his policies which, if successful, would have seriously limited their independence. The role of the friars in this was evident, and very important, but many feared the consequences of his failure for Italy and the empire, and even for the health of the Catholic Church.

In the middle of the 13th century the Roman empire and the Papacy seemed to be destroying one another. The future, if there was a future, lay with the friars, and not with the older monastic orders, or with the bishops and the secular clergy. Additions to Joachim's prophecies, some of them made by his own disciples before the rise of the friars and enlarged afterwards, circulated especially among some of the Franciscans, but in many other places as well. These made explicit reference to what had already happened in the rise of the Franciscan and Dominican orders.[58] It was not immediately obvious how much or how little of these prophecies were Joachim's own work. It is not easy now to distinguish this, or to determine the dates of the several additions.[59] If the prophecies were genuine, he had anticipated in considerable detail at or before the beginning of the century developments in the decade between 1216 and 1226. While some no doubt believed that some of the prophecies were spurious, and others that all were fantasies of his own, a number of people supposed that the rise of the friars was a direct result of his false prophecies, and stirred up by the same lying spirit. Friars were false prophets, luring away clerks from their lawful vocations, and making it more and more difficult for bishops to find administrators, or to conduct the affairs of their churches. William of St Amour, a distinguished Master of Arts in the University of Paris, contended in his *Liber de AntiChristo et eius ministris* (1254-5) against 'pseudo-preachers who make their way into houses, who dare to announce the imminence of ruin for the covenant of the Son of God, and the swallowing up of sacraments by gifts of the Spirit'.[60] This was part of his campaign against the threat that the friars might come to dominate the faculty of theology in the university if Thomas Aquinas was given his higher degree.[61]

At this critical moment the end of the Roman empire appeared to be near. Frederick II, to gain a free hand in Italy, had signed away imperial rights to bishops and princes in Germany. Now he and his son Conrad were both dead. The heir was a child and the imperialist party in some confusion, but the papal court was still in exile from Italy and would have difficulty in returning to Rome. The Tartars were a threat to the whole of Europe and their coming was commonly thought to portend the end of the world. In this atmosphere of doom estimates of prophecy demanded consideration. There were those who made the most of Joachim's prophecies, genuine and spurious, including men of exceptional intelligence, like Roger Bacon, who anticipated an anti-Christ from the East, able to make use of Chinese astrological learning.[62] Others regarded the friars as false prophets, who would never have swarmed if Joachim had not prophesied, and made the most of the condemnation of his criticism of Peter Lombard, the Master of the Sentences, at the Lateran Council of 1215, where the truth of the Lombard's doctrine of the procession of the persons in the Trinity had been confirmed against Joachim's criticism.[63]

The most important contribution to this discussion was made, as we might expect, by St Thomas Aquinas. As a Dominican he was in no way concerned, as were some of the Franciscans, to defend the whole corpus of Joachite prophecies. The Dominicans like to remember that he had underlined with a query, or crossed out, some passages in a book of Joachim's in a Dominican library.[64] But he could not avoid the question. It was essential for the friars to defend the role of prophecy in the Christian life, because the clamour against false prophecy was an attack on them, and in Paris in particular against St Thomas himself, not only against the 'spiritual Franciscans'. St Thomas brought to the subject his expertise as a student of the relations between human knowledge and revealed truth. He knew not only Aristotle in the Byzantine version as well as in the Arabian, but Muslim and Jewish philosophers, Avicenna, Averroes, Al-Ghazzali, Avicebron, Maimonides. Some of these had much to say about prophecies.

St. Thomas regarded prophecy as a universal phenomenon in all religions, and saw the Bible in this context. The original element in his *De Prophetia* is in the distinction between 'natural prophecy' and 'that type which the apostle numbers among the gifts of the Holy Spirit'.[65]

To follow the argument it is necessary to understand that all prophecy is insight, followed by judgement. A prophet is a seer, not only of future events, but into present situations. Prophets may have hunches about matters that can be discovered by other means, but 'the distinguishing mark of prophetic sight lies in the remoteness, the distance of what is seen from normal vision and cognition'[66] the capacity to see, as from far away, 'what is remote or opaque'. This is often associated with an aptitude or disposition, but it is not a habit.[67] No one is prophetic or 'psychically sensitive' the whole time, and prophecy involves more than this aptitude or sensitivity. In all prophecy, natural and in the Spirit, there is judgement. We may be inspired in judgements on knowledge that we receive in other ways, but the difference between natural prophecy and the gifts of the Holy Spirit is that knowledge 'derived from the pre-existence of events in the divine mind . . . is called a gift of the Holy Spirit, and it is not natural.[68] St Thomas nowhere implies that this is limited to the authors of holy writ, or those who hold office in the Church. He says in the *Summa Theologica*[69] (later than the *De Prophetia*): 'The gift of prophecy is granted to a man both for the use of others and for the enlightenment of his own mind,' and goes on 'These are they in whose souls divine wisdom by sanctifying grace comes to dwell, and makes them friends of God and prophets. On the other hand there are some who received the gift of prophecy solely for the benefit of others'. It is not clear that the first receive it only for themselves, but St Thomas did not use what Fr Karl Rahner calls 'the rather problematic distinction between the (purely) mystical vision and the prophetic (as well)'.[70] St Thomas knows that the gifts of the Spirit cannot be immediately or easily distinguished from natural prophecy. 'Certain movements can be impressed on the human imagination . . . by the power of the heavenly bodies, in which there pre-exist some signs of certain future events'. 'The illumination of the separated intellects' may also be at work.[71] Both kinds of prophecy 'elevate the human mind, so that it understands in a way similar to the separated substances, who understand the principles and the conclusion with the utmost certainty without deducing the one from the other',[72] by what we would call intuition.

St Thomas allows that 'the prophet must be transported out of his senses', 'whenever prophecy takes place according to the insight of imagination'.[73] This may happen 'through a proper physical cause, as through sleep', or 'in a vision, when the transport comes through some cause in the soul'. Here the word 'physical' is used much as we would use it, but in other places it means 'natural' and would include 'a cause in the soul when a man, from too much attention to the objects of the understanding or the imagination, is altogether abstracted from the external world', as we know from several stories that St Thomas often was.[74] The prophet knows that what he sees and hears on such occasions are not things, 'but in some way the likeness of things about which his judgement is certain because of the light of the mind'.

'The supernatural reception proper to prophecy is in the insight of imagination,'[75] and for this dreams are a good way of receiving prophetic sight. But what makes a prophet more than a dreamer is his capacity to interpret his vision. Some prophets are inspired in judgement, but not in reception.[76] They do not need to be transported in any kind of ecstasy, or even to see or to hear anything. They are simply inspired in judgement that this is the time to say what they know already. On the other hand what was wrong with the Montanists, as St Thomas understood the matter, was that they made it necessary that 'prophets, when announcing, should be carried out of their senses, as happens with those who are mad, or with those who talk in their sleep.[77] St Thomas allowed that some might prophesy without knowing it, as Caiaphas did about the death of Christ, and the soldiers did who divided Christ's garments,[78] but prophets normally announce a meaning, either of a situation symbolised, or in matters otherwise known.

The *De Prophetia* is in several respects a difficult book. The references to 'the power of the heavenly bodies' demand a knowledge of astrology as this was understood in the 13th century in the light of Arabian as well as of Greek sources. The 'separated substances' are 'the purely spiritual *daimones* . . . These could and would understand the heavenly bodies, and with them their determining activity in sublunary events'.[79] By 'sublunary' is meant in the earth's atmosphere, where the coincidence and opposition of the heavenly bodies had a large role in determining not only the weather, but the prevailing moods and therefore the thoughts of most men and women. The 'separated substances' might themselves act on the body, and through the body on the imagination. They might be benevolent, but they might not. It was dangerous to deal with them without knowing who they were, and impossible to be certain. St Thomas did his best to take the sting out of this debate, so that the

179

discernment of spirits might proceed with more calm.

Some friars may be dreamers, some in their dreams may be natural prophets, who pick up insights like those of the 'separated substances' into the influence of the heavenly bodies on the moods and movements of men and nations. Prophets do not always understand their own visions, and they may be deceived by their own moods, or fail to discern between an angel and some other sort of separated substance. Those inspired by the Spirit are not all saints, but they have a place in God's present plan.

We know that Dante agreed with this. In the *Paradiso* at xii, 140-1, he made St Bonaventura speak of Joachim as 'endowed with the prophetic spirit'. In his *Epistle to Can Grande* Dante recognised an affinity between his own inspiration and that of the Bible.[80] The whole of the *Divine Comedy* has a plurality of meaning. The literal sense is the state of souls after death, as in the visions of Fursey and Drythelm. The allegory is a vision of judgement. This goes beyond the intention of the author, and we can recognise it whatever we care or do not care about Italian politics in his time, or space and time in the afterlife.

Dante's fealty to Thomism on points of detail may have been exaggerated, but there is no doubt that he had a deep respect for the insight of St Thomas. I do not know if anyone has asked what St Thomas thought about Dante. In one sense the question is meaningless, since Dante was a boy of nine when he died. In another it is like asking what he thought of Siger of Brabant, who represents philosophy in the *Paradiso,* as Joachim represents prophecy, and is praised by St Thomas as Bonaventura praises Joachim.[81] When Dante saw within the eternal light 'ingathered, bound by love in one volume, the scattered leaves of all the universe, substance and accidents in their relations, as though together fused, in such fashion that what I tell of is one simple flame', he spoke of his mind as 'suspended', 'fixed, immoveable, intent, ever enkindled by its gazing',[82] describing prophetic vision as St Thomas believed that it could and did happen, and as it happened to him at the end of his life, when he could no longer write it down.[83] As he saw the problem in order to have this sort of insight it is not necessary to be good, or to be without bitterness, but only to see with the Spirit's aid into the divine intention. Much of Dante's prophecy was natural, in St. Thomas's sense, and not infallible, but in such places as this he was inspired by the Spirit to see into the mind of the Church triumphant and even into the relationship of the Three Persons in the Trinity. He was inspired to say as well as to see, but he saw more than he could say.[84] St Thomas's classification of prophecy probably helped him, and may help us, to understand how this could be, but it may be that it also contributed to link natural prophecy with other kinds of occult knowledge, and so in the long run to undermine its prestige.

Among these were the various forms of prognostication used in the Middle Ages. Astrology had the greatest intellectual prestige then and in the 16th and 17th centuries, but because it required instruments, professional knowledge of their use, and some skill in calculation, its use was not common outside learned circles before the invention of printing and the wide circulation of astrological almanacs. By a curious paradox, its widest popular vogue seems to have been in the second half of the 17th century,[85] after Ptolemaic astronomy had been outmoded, and in esoteric forms it remains popular today. In considering the attitude of the Church towards it, it is necessary to distinguish the theory from the varieties of practice. The theory that the heavenly bodies, themselves unchanging, have great influence on the changing elements beneath the moon, was an integral part of medieval science, and all forms of prediction, of the weather, of the condition of the crops, and of good and bad days, for instance for a journey or a wedding, were interpreted in the light of it. Many of these did not use scientific astrological instruments. Some who had reputations for cunning in these matters did not use any instruments at all. They observed the flight of birds or the fall of leaves, or they smelt the wind. But this was 'scientifically' explained as sensitivity to astral influence, and not altogether different from the kind of awareness of spirits that comes through prayer and meditation. No one had serious objections to the use of astrological instruments for general predictions, for instance for forecasts of the weather and of the crops, although it would be pointed out that these were not invariably reliable. In this insight might do better than instruments. Objections were made to the use of horoscopes to cast the nativities of particular persons, on grounds fundamentally analogous to modern objections to psycho-analysis. To find clues to the course of the lifetime in the position of the stars and planets at the hour of birth may easily produce undue depression or elation. The stars determine moods, but they do not compel us to act upon them. They are creatures of the good God, and the power of grace is greater than that of any natural spiritual influence. Moreover horoscopes may easily be wrong. The means used to determine them leave plenty of room for error, and more for interference by malevolent influences who want to delude us into depression or conceit. A bad horoscope might have the same effect on a medieval man or woman as may be produced in a modern by a suspicion, perhaps based only on inference, that his mother did not love him. But those who warn us not to be over-depressed by presumed traumatic experiences may yet allow that there is truth in the determination of character by social and psychological circumstances, by deprivation and care.

Many prophets used means of divination derived from a Christian understanding of the human condition at a variety of levels. In these it is never easy to distinguish between natural insight, aided by prayer in the Spirit, and the prophetic gift of the Spirit in the fullest sense, between Dame Julian of Norwich, whose *Revelations of Divine Love* had a small circulation among some of her friends, and Margery Kemp, the wife of a tradesman in King's Lynn, who reported her revelations to the Bishop of Lincoln and the Archbishop of Canterbury, as well as to Dame Julian, and to priests who gave her help in getting them recorded in a book that remained in manuscript for nearly five hundred years.[86] That Margery's revelations were a problem is obvious. It was not immediately obvious that Dame Julian's were of a different class, with those of St Catherine of Siena. The revelations of St Bridget of Sweden were the subject of controversies in which theologians of the 15th century took sides, or suspended judgement.[87] Now they seem more tied to the time than those of St Catherine and Dame Julian, but they led to her canonisation and brought great prestige to a new religious order, founded in effect by her daughter.

No doubt the methods used in discerning spirits had their limitations, but it is hard to see any strong bias against the possibility of revelations through the gifts of the Holy Spirit himself in the period when scholasticism was the dominant philosophy. To say of St Thomas: 'He did indeed discuss the influence of demons and particularly angels, but only in a most involved way as influences on the body, stirring up humors in the liver which present phantasms to the mind',[88] is to miss the point that these humours include much that we would now call unconscious influences, for in medieval medicine the soul is spread out all over the body, and is especially present in

182

the heart. Jung recognised this, [89] but Dr Morton Kelsey, who admires him, has missed the difference between reason in St Thomas and what Coleridge called 'the understanding', 'the faculty judging according to sense',[90] in Locke and the English philosophy of the 18th century. He imagines that experience through the senses (*nihil in intellectu nisi prius in sensu*) means the same in scholasticism as in English empiricism.[91]

St Thomas wrote poetry, but his prose does not remind us of Dante as Hooker reminds us of Shakespeare. Nevertheless he saw

'How the floor of heaven
Is thick inlaid with patines of bright gold;
There's not the smallest orb which thou behold'st
But in his motion like an angel sings,
Still quiring to the young-eyed cherubims.[92]

St Thomas's angels are natural, but not in our sense physical. He may never have succeeded in synthesising all his information about them, from the Bible and the Fathers, especially from the *Celestial Hierarchies* of Dionysius the (Pseudo-) Areopagite, as well as from Greek and Arabian science. His natural prophecy, like natural philosophy and theology, was a form of knowledge accessible to all men, including Muslims and 'the wild man of the woods', but his own experience of it was in Christians, including himself. No doubt he believed that the Holy Spirit was at work in him, but also in the possibility of confusion between the voices of holy angels and those of other 'separated substances', good, bad or indifferent, whose knowledge was derived from natural causes. Other communications with human persons, alive or dead, might come through the same channels of extra-sensory perception, as we would call it in our attempts to assimilate it to experience through the senses in the restricted sense of the 18th and 19th centuries.

6. Predestination, Science and the Scriptures.

Before the Copernican revolution displaced the angels from their spheres in the heavens, and compelled a revision of ideas about their nature and function, the crisis of the Reformation introduced some further complications. Luther's experience of justification by faith and preaching of belief in this as necessary to salvation was received sympathetically by many, especially in Italy and Spain, who could not follow him when in *The Bondage of the Will* he attacked Erasmus, and insisted on theological determinism. The conflict was not about the experience of justification, but about its explanation. Erasmus and others were anxious to balance the excessive influence of St Augustine on Western theology with new ideas from the East and from Christian antiquity, from St Irenaeus and Origen and the Greek Fathers generally. These were in harmony with distinctions made in the discernment of spirits between inspirations and fixed ideas. Objections to obsessions operated against a rigid interpretation of St Augustine on predestination, as they did against Luther's obsession with the one article of justification by faith, but the changes in astronomy replaced a jig-saw puzzle of malevolent, neutral and kindly influences, by a mechanical mill-wheel, the order of nature, which God occasionally stopped for a miracle, the question of freedom became more important.[93] Those whose reading of predestination followed the new mechanical model made much of the mighty acts of God recorded in Scripture, and denounced astrologers who pried into the divine decrees. In Calvinist communities they pursued witches with a fresh ferocity, but Protestants as well as Catholics were influenced by a moral theology and a spiritual literature that gave a larger place to human freedom.

As the debate on this crossed every ecclesiastical frontier, so did mystical writings.[94] The influence of these on the life and devotion of Christians generally increased with a wider diffusion of literacy. In the first great age of Protestant Bible reading mystical interpretation of Scripture continued, and developed. Protestant Pentecostals would probably say that the second half of the 17th century was the richest in spiritual gifts in Church history since the apostolic age, containing as it did *The Pilgrim's Progress,* George Fox and the other early Quakers, and the Protestant prophets of the Cevennes, many of whom took refuge in England after the Revocation of the Edict of Nantes in 1685.[95] But the influence of spirituality on controversy between Protestants and Catholics was minimal. In matters of doctrine Protestants rejected appeals to the experience of the Church and to mystical interpretation, and insisted on the letter of Scripture alone.[96] Calvinists rejected natural theology and natural prophecy as infiltrations from paganism into Christianity, and in many places subordinated the New to the Old Testament. While Catholics did not do this, and many Protestants had a place in their theology for freedom and for the natural knowledge of God, all were wary of coming into conflict with the letter of Scripture in debate, and of relying on traditions that could be proved to be late, and not apostolic.[97] This was one of the reasons why the literature of spiritual experience was neglected in the study of Church history, and came under a cloud in all the confessions at the end of the 17th century.

It seems to me that at the turn of the 17th and 18th centuries the fear of enthusiasm is a far more important reason for the eclipse of prophecy than any aridity in scholastic method, which is a symptom rather than a cause. One cause was fear of the decay of religious belief, especially among the poor. It is a mistake to suppose that establishments of religion always discourage zeal. When they are strong, they can provide a stimulus to spiritual movements as correctives to ambitions for preferment, as in the Christian Roman empire. But the fear of collapse and the failure of persecution brings anxiety, not only about heresy, but about any kind of ardour. One effect of the enactment of religious toleration in England in 1689 was to reveal the presence of a large minority, especially in and about London, without any religious allegiance.[98] It could no longer be assumed that those who did not go to church were dissenters or papists. The extent of disbelief among those of little education could not be explained by the small circulation of sceptical or anti-religious books. A better explanation was variety in religion, and this made for a deep distrust of enthusiasm.

In France there was no toleration after 1685, but those Protestants who had been dragooned into Catholicism were not converted. The wounds of the religious wars had left many in all classes, in Germany as in France, convinced that their conformity to a Church was the result of battle, not of conviction. The great Bishop Bossuet combined polemic against the variations of Protestantism and a genuine desire to explore the possibilities of reunion, with a deep distrust of spiritual movements seeking a deeper interior life and of the influence of Madame Guyon whom Fénelon, the Archbishop of Cambrai, defended. He also distrusted the *Maxims of the Saints*, collected by Fénelon from mystical writers, but condemned at Rome by Bossuet's influence in 1699. No doubt there were valid criticisms of the selection, as there were of Madame Guyon and her friends. What is characteristic of the developing situation, in England as in

185

France, is ecclesiastical distrust of anything that makes men and women in the pew ask searching questions about their own conformity to obligations which keep society together and fend off impending disorder.[99]

Other reasons for distrust of enthusiasts arise from the new philosophy and science, especially in England. English influence in Europe was never so strong as in the 18th century. In English science the master mind was Sir Isaac Newton, who spent a surprising amount of his time on the study of prophecy, especially of the *Book of Daniel* and the *Revelation of St John*, but published very little on this in his lifetime. His papers throw light, not only on his mentality, but on the mind of his age in relation to prophecy.[100]

His deepest convictions, which he shared with his friend, the philosopher Locke, arose out of his hostility to metaphysics. He believed that science and religion had been corrupted by Platonism. He was not in the modern sense a fundamentalist, since he saw in the Bible evidence of scientific secrets known to Egyptian and Chaldean priests, and preserved in the Hermetic writings and in works by some of the alchemists. But all this had been corrupted by pagan Platonists, Jewish Cabalists, and Roman Catholic theologians who had made a metaphysical system of theology. The reason why his papers remained unpublished was that in the controversies of his day his allies were not reliable. Those who agreed with him in antagonism to the Nicene and Athanasian creeds included friends who profited by his advice, but had theories of their own which did not agree with his reading of the Bible. He had more personal sympathy with the adherents of an older Puritan divinity, who took the Bible literally, if their interpretation was coloured by beliefs which the rise of science would in time remove. The science of the Bible was not metaphysics, but a record of history, past, present and to come, told in symbolic and figurative ways to edify and to please the unlearned. In his interpretation of prophecy Newton felt himself to be a prophet, translating these tropes, and foretelling the transformation of the world into the kingdom where Christ and his saints will reign over mortal men. 'The children of the resurrection'[101] will be in motion all over the universe as space travellers, but visible from time to time to regulate the affairs of this world.

Newton's interpretation was not altogether original. It owed a good deal to the divinity of the generation before him, especially to some who were learned in Rabbinical lore, and to the debate about the age of the world initiated by Joseph Scaliger in 1583, and continued by the Jesuit Petavius, Archbishop Ussher, and others. This belongs to the history of fundamentalism, as Newton's criticism of the creeds belongs to an early stage in the history of Liberal Protestantism. Both are hostile to the tradition of mystical interpretation, and to any understanding of the Bible that depends on the experience of the Church and of Christians at prayer. This was preserved in England by William Law, who studied the German Protestant mystic, Jacob Boehme, and earlier mystical literature, and had an influence on the beginnings of the Evangelical revival as well as of the Oxford Movement, but it became increasingly difficult to get a hearing for any argument not established by external evidence.

What was eclipsed in the 18th century was not reason or revelation, but natural prophecy.[102] It was still possible to believe that the Bible was the revealed word of God, attested as such by the Church and the sects alike, and in the Catholic Church and in some of the others that revelations might be made in the Spirit to good Christians, but 'to claim revelations of the Holy Ghost' was 'a horrid thing', not only to Bishop Butler, rebuking Wesley, but to Bishop Bossuet, rebuking Archbishop Fénelon for his favour to Madame Guyon. If such revelations were not of the Spirit, and miraculous, they must be of the devil, and delusive, or simply delusions.

The attempt to identify a common element in all inspiration, in Biblical and natural prophecy, the gifts of the Holy Spirit, the voices of angels, influences from the stars and the muses, foundered at the end of the 17th century, partly through changes in the scientific world picture, especially where the music of the spheres was concerned, and partly through fears that any comparison between the inspiration of the Bible and the work of the Spirit in the Church would be denounced by Protestants as undermining the authority of Scripture for sinister ends. The pioneers of Biblical criticism before Spinoza were all Catholics, and included Cardinal Bellarmine.[103] But Bossuet did his best to suppress the work of Father Richard Simon, whose impish attacks on Bibliolatry were bad for the Church's reputation among Protestants.[104]

The task laid down in the decline of scholastic science was resumed by Samuel Taylor Coleridge and his disciples, by F. D. Maurice and the great Anglican commentators, Hort and Westcott, who in the middle of the 19th century combined belief in the inspiration of

Scripture with honest attention to Biblical criticism but in the Church of England their work was confused and confounded by the very different approach of German Protestant scholarship, which did so much of the detailed work they used. This was based on the belief that the Bible must be evaluated first and last as historical evidence. This was not specifically a German notion. It is in Newton and in some Puritan divines before him, and no doubt it could be found in some of the Rabbis. But it is hostile to the whole tradition of multiple interpretation in the Christian Fathers and in the Middle Ages, and so to the main stream of traditional Christian theology.

The Scriptures indeed bear witness to decisive events in the history of the Church and of the world, but considered as historical evidence for these they must inevitably be found inadequate. It is unfortunate that Biblical criticism developed to such an extent in controversy with a particular kind of Protestant fundamentalism that was specially created to refute it, as critical tools began to be applied to the Bible and other ancient literature, in search of historical data. Because an understanding of 'the letter of Scripture' as always and everywhere true to history came to be the 'conservative view' of the inspiration of the Bible in England and Germany, both sides of the controversy came to believe that the Fathers and the schoolmen had always held it. So on the one side we find John Keble defending *The Mysticism attributed to the early Fathers of the Church* against any imputation that any of them disbelieved the history in the Bible, [105] and on the other Frederick Harrison, in an article in the *Westminster Review* for October 1860 on *Essays and Reviews,* a Broad Church symposium, writing of the universities as 'honeycombed with disbelief, running through every phase from mystical interpretation to utter atheism'. Harrison was an agnostic who became a disciple of Comte, the French Positivist philosopher. His reference to mystical interpretation is certainly to Hort and other disciples of Coleridge whom he regarded as moderately Broad, but they were nearer the central tradition than either side in the controversy over *Essays and Reviews.*

A passage in the *Glossa ordinaria,* the standard commentary on the Bible in the schools of the Middle Ages, admits that the Old Testament as we know it was edited from older materials, collected, selected and supplemented by Ezra after the return of the Jews from Babylon to Jerusalem. This point had been made in passing by a number of older writers, Greek and Latin, including St Hilary, St John Chrysostom, and St Isidore of Seville. It was developed by

188

Bede, who had experience in the use of sources for his own historical work, in his allegorical commentary on *Ezra* and *Nehemiah,* and this was quoted in the *Glossa ordinaria,* and summarised in the *Historia Scholastica,* the text-book of Bible history in the schools.[106] But this was not a matter of great interest for those who read the Bible primarily as testimony to the works of God in history, prophetic testimony to be read prophetically. Those accustomed to reading and writing the lives of the saints, themselves testimonies to the work of God in them, saw this in a different light from modern scholars concerned in reconstructing the course of events as it might have been seen by anyone. No doubt some mystical interpretation of Scripture depends on a view of inspiration that cannot be reconciled, as it stands, with attention to literary sources, but to identify all allegory with this is excess, not only because it ignores the measure of attention that was paid to sources in the Old Testament from Bede to Bellarmine, but because it takes no account of the allegorical interpretation of pagan poetry by Christian commentators who found mystical meanings in Virgil and Ovid.

Secular students of the history of literature who take account of 'this medieval practice of allegorical thinking . . .; perhaps the only intellectual technique which men have used extensively and have now completely abandoned', allow that 'if we grant certain presuppositions, and in particular the existence of a Creator who desires to instruct us in theology and morality through the medium of the natural world, we shall not find anything unreasonable or extravagant in methods used by the allegorisers'[107] to interpret not only Biblical and classical texts, but the common habits of beasts and birds.[108] As I see no incompatibility between interest in drafts and cancelled passages for such a modern poem as T. S. Eliot's *The Waste Land,* as lately displayed in Valerie Eliot's critical edition, and the recognition of elements in the poem beyond his knowledge at the time, pointing forward to later developments, so I see nothing to prevent the student of sources in the Old and New Testaments from recognising inspiration in the composition of the books and the collection of the two canons, and multiple meanings in both. The oracular view of inspiration which is incompatible with historical criticism[109] rather belongs to Jewish Rabbis who believe that all prophetic inspiration has ceased, and to Protestant divines who draw a clear line between the Bible and anything else, than to those who expect guidance from the Holy Spirit in the interpretation of

189

Scripture and in their own prophetic inspiration. The two great Alexandrians, Philo the Jew and Origen the Christian, whose methods have been most important for the tradition of allegorical interpretation in Christendom, no doubt believed that the translators of the Old Testament into Greek had been assisted by the Holy Spirit, but this did not prevent Origen from comparing translations in parallel columns or Philo from embellishing the stories of the patriarchs.[110] All through the Middle Ages Bible stories were adapted to the traditions of the nations, so that Noah's ark appears in the genealogy of the Anglo-Saxon kings, and Jacob's stone is the throne of the Scottish kings, while Solomon's ship has a place in Arthurian legend. But the practice of doing sums with Biblical figures is late, as Bishop Colenso found when he tried to calculate the size of the Israelite camp in the wilderness of Sinai, and found that the Levites had to walk six miles to the lavatory.[111] No previous commentator had asked the question or seen the difficulty. But where he saw a priestly imposition, others rushed in to defend the story. So historical critics both imagine and create historical literalism.[112]

7. Testimony and Prophecy today.

The Pentecostal movement in all its aspects cuts across the chasm between fundamentalist and critical approaches to the inspiration of Scripture. It is a great mistake to imagine that belief in the inspiration of prophets, apostles and evangelists, and in the operation of the Holy Spirit in the interpretation of Scripture, must necessarily involve belief in the literal accuracy of every statement in the Old and New Testament that appears to describe a fact. The variety of literatures in the Scriptures[113] has been more precisely observed by scholars in the modern period than ever before, but there is nothing new in the recognition of differences between them, for instance between St Paul's letters and the *Acts of the Apostles*.

In the description of the day of Pentecost in *Acts* 2 'every man heard' the disciples speak 'in his own language'. Clearly all those involved had a different account originally given in different terms of what happened to them. Others not so involved heard a babble of sounds: 'These men are filled with new wine'. St Peter's sermon is addressed to them and seems to suppose that they are the majority. But the story is not told from their point of view, but as an inspired fusion or synthesis of the several testimonies of those who were actually involved.

This is the kind of literature that is understood by those who wrote and read the lives of the saints, and by those who write and read the literature of testimony to experience in the Holy Spirit today. In reading the Biblical accounts of Christ 'alive after his passion', they are not looking for references to an empty tomb that was known to everyone, variously explained, and eventually concealed.[114] This is a matter of historical and archaeological fact, but the Biblical accounts of the resurrection are testimony to the living presence of the risen Christ and of his mysterious identity in soul and body with Jesus of Nazareth. An early stage in the process of gathering testimonies to this can be glimpsed in *1 Corinthians* 15, which is rather like what might be gathered about tongues if all our information was in the chapter before. We have an inspired picture of experience of Pentecost in *Acts* 2, as we have three impressive accounts, not completely consistent, of the Lord after his resurrection in *St Matthew*, *St Luke* and *St John*.

Something analogous to this happens at a prayer meeting. This is not an exercise in group dynamics, an attempt to analyse what is happening to the participants scientifically. Nor is it an attempt to reconstruct what happened in the church of Corinth, although some people think that it should conform with St Paul's directions to Corinthians. In a small book called *Life in a New Dimension*[115] a Cornish evangelist, Don Double, has given an instructive account of how students from a Bible College who 'had been taught that you can only have three messages in tongues at a meeting, and not too much of the gift of prophecy', invaded a lively church, accustomed to prophesying. 'Now nobody knew anything about them at that stage. They came in and sat on the back row ... But it wasn't long before a whole string of prophecies came ... and began to describe the attitude of these young people' before they said anything at all. The point Mr Double is making is that 'If the gift of prophecy is operating properly, people can't come in and ruin the meeting ... Some of the weaker members of the body of Christ should be prophesying. The most elementary Christian can be used in this gift'. He goes on to say: 'Naturally, the deeper we go with God, the deeper the gift of prophecy will become. I am not advocating that it remains on a shallow level'. Clearly he does distinguish levels, if his vocabulary for this is inadequate and might be helped by some term corresponding to 'natural prophecy' in the *De Prophetia* of St Thomas Aquinas. The sense of the situation that enabled people in the meeting to understand the state of mind of the students was certainly aided by the Holy Spirit, probably by extra-sensory perception. But is all extra-sensory perception a gift of the Spirit?

The interpretation of tongues in Pentecostal meetings is generally regarded as a form of prophecy, not as a translation or a paraphrase of a message in an unknown language, but rather as an interpretation or comment through someone who is inspired to understand the impact of the mysterious utterance, which may be much longer or a good deal shorter than the 'interpretation'.[116] The original sense of *1 Corinthians* 14, vv. 6-25, is difficult to determine, perhaps altogether inaccessible in the absence of background information, but the passage can be very useful. Especially the exhortation 'to excel in building up the church', and the commendation of prophecy after and perhaps over tongues helps in a situation where bursts of enthusiastic praise, of singing hymns and singing in tongues, need to be interrupted by a controlled utterance, bringing the group back to the actual situation. This may take the form of a reading, from Scripture or from some spiritual writer, with or without comment, or of a prophetic saying or showing. I have heard prophecies take the form of a picture, a symbolic image described, but not otherwise put into words, that clarifies the position. In the Bible prophets were inspired to perform symbolic actions, Ezekiel to eat a scroll and Agabus to tie himself up.[117] I should not be surprised to hear of something equally bizarre in Puerto Rico, Taiwan or South America, but I have not seen it. I have had some experience of the prophetic actions of 'charismatic communities' in the United States.

All these forms of prophecy have a history in Christian tradition. The common element seems to be an inspired reading of signs, including tongues, music and visual symbols, but also texts from the Scriptures, hymns and other writing in poetry and prose, followed by a word spoken or a deed done that implies a judgement on the situation. This prophetic word or deed may be a good expression of the sense of the meeting, in which case it is not revelation but testimony, inspired extra-sensory perception, on the level of natural prophecy, or it may be so unfamiliar and unexpected that it looks and sounds like a startling innovation, but if it is truly of the Spirit it

192

will contribute to the renewal of tradition. In considering the prophetic actions of Pentecostal and other charismatic prayer groups the foundation of new monastic communities provides useful analogies.

The early Cistercians had prophets, for instance St Bernard and St Aelred, but their prophetic witness to their own age lay in a way of life, a startling interpretation of the rule of St Benedict. In the beginning this was shocking, not only to Benedictine opinion, but to ecclesiastical authority,[118] and where it is unfamiliar it may still shock, as in America, but it made a much larger contribution to the renewal of monastic tradition in the 12th century than the assiduous devotion of others who continued in customary paths.

Charismatic communities like the Community of the Word of God at Ann Arbor owe some of their inspiration to the traditions of monasticism, as transmitted to them by American Cistercians, but they include families, and Protestants. At Ann Arbor Catholics and Evangelicals covenant with one another to support each other materially and spiritually. The common covenant is implemented by particular covenants in households, which may or may not live in one house, but share each other's life. The very existence and composition of this community in a Mid-Western university town, including black and white Americans in the same households, many Lutherans, Protestants of many other denominations, and a majority of Catholics,[119] says something about the prospects for Christian unity in the United States, in its bearings on other problems relating to the place of America in the world. But while the community at Ann Arbor and other charismatic communities pay attention to prophecies in prayer groups (some were founded in consequence of prophecies) I do not think that many of their members have clear ideas of a prophetic significance in the existence of such communities. This is not a criticism; it is a characteristic of prophets that they say and do more than they know.

Some charismatic communities do think of themselves as signs to the Church. The Episcopalian parish of Holy Redeemer, Houston, Texas, which has become the 'Community of Celebration' with offshoots in England and Scotland,[120] regards itself as a model for parish communities, and in an Episcopalian context this makes sense, since most American Episcopal parishes are congregations gathered by spiritual or social motives, and not territorial units. But a territorial parish or diocese must include all sorts and conditions.

In such a context a community that includes families may become a sign to the parish of what parochial life ought to be, as a celibate community is not, but if it were to take over the parochial organisations, so that others who did not belong to the community felt uncomfortable in them, the parish itself might become semi-sectarian. This is much less likely to happen when the community itself has an ecumenical dimension, as at Ann Arbor, and includes members of other parishes and other denominations. Such communities can become spiritual crucibles where disparate elements form new compounds that are real wholes. Catholics whose background has been in an enclosed ethnic group, preserving ancestral culture, learn to love Evangelical hymns and to read unfamiliar parts of the Old Testament, while Evangelicals discover allegory and symbolism, not only in the Bible, but in poetry and fiction. Those who learn from one another that the Bible is inspired literature, and hear Christ speaking to them there and in prayer, are in little danger of falling for a reduced theology, but on the other hand they are open to the best side of American Liberal Protestantism, concern for the oppressed.

Charismatic communities, so far as I can discover, all began with a desire to deepen the bonds of fellowship found in prayer. Then a variety of practical needs compelled them to give this a more concrete form. Generally some of their members are in work that involves them with the needs of others, while all have friends in need. All are also aware of the limitations of the nuclear family in a mobile society, accentuated in America by the sheer size of the country, where grandparents are likely to be thousands of miles away. All charismatic communities share the same basic concerns that have led so many young Americans to experiment in styles of common living based on planned priorities, and intended to provide everyone involved, especially the children with opportunities for physical, mental and spiritual growth, while cutting down on those additional amenities that can so easily become necessities. All such experiments in an alternative way of life are exercises in natural prophecy in St Thomas's sense of the term, in so far as they are based, as they almost always are, on some deep inner conviction that the pursuit of higher and higher standards of material living is making impossible demands on the resources of this world.[121] The evidence for this may be scientifically collected, but it is generally ignored by the scientific community. To act upon it implies vision

194

beyond the usual range of observation, and judgement, the power to decide.

Those who make such judgements may have no conscious religious motivation. They may speak of 'the Christian fallacy'[122] that denies moral significance in our selfish quest for individual and collective gain, and persuades us that we can take what comes to us in the way of income without enquiring into its origin, and save our souls in a world running to ruin. But that is a criticism not of the Christian Church but of personal religion. Where this has become a matter of preserving family tradition, without relation to the life of society, as in America it so often is, religious practice can be a kind of drug, a way of release from the boredom of material advancement. This private religion finds its most extreme expression in the actual use of psychedelic drugs to expose us to every spirit. That this sometimes happens in communities seeking an alternative way of life is to be expected, and is in no way inconsistent with their prophetic character, for indeed it is to be expected that demons and other 'separated substances' in the terms of St Thomas, should haunt those who go out in wilderness in search of another kind of life. Devils have always been troublesome in monasteries, and they are especially dangerous in quasi-monastic communities without religious defences.

But those who are so defended may still be haunted, not only by evil spirits, but by departed souls in need of aid, and always by the problems of the distressed, in body and spirit. I know of a group of Catholic families in the deep South of the United States who sold their homes and bought a block of apartments where they could live together. The block was down town and inhabited by negroes, who did not leave but lived with their new landlords who share their life and their problems. I have read of others who joined those driven by destitution to pick up a scanty living from garbage on a dump in Texas, and helped them to find places to sell it, and so to restore their self-respect that they became a community with leaders of their own who could be helped to help them.[123] These garbage-pickers were probably Mexicans and Puerto-Ricans, part of that great horde of displaced persons from Central and South America, Central and Eastern Europe, and the Middle East, who find it as hard to get a place in the American way of life as the negroes do, perhaps harder. Many of them have Catholic or Eastern Orthodox backgrounds. Into this great underground river drop-outs from respectable middle class families fall and do not return. But I have stayed with another kind of drop-out who jumps into it, and helps to form communities with a style of life that is Christian, Catholic, Evangelical and Pentecostal, but could be open to learn from the wisdom of the East as well.

This underground river is a fact of the situation in every great city today, not only in America, but in Asia, Africa and Europe. Classical Pentecostalists have done more to help people in it than any other Christian group, but often, although not always, they are open to the criticism that they form close-knit communities who escape from their own material problems and neglect those of others, to concentrate entirely on the growth of their own spiritual lives and the propagation of the gospel.[124] But the Catholic charismatic communities are concerned to develop an alternative way of life that does not involve withdrawal from the existing economic structure, but a redirection of expenditure, which does in fact set some of their members free for tasks that would not otherwise be economically viable, and enable others to follow their vocations without regard for financial rewards. This cannot be represented as revolutionary subversion, but it is a powerful witness against the gross and unrealistic materialism that maintains that the world's problems can be solved by raising everyone's standard of material comfort at the expense of our dwindling natural resources, and an acted prophecy of another solution for America and the world through the integration of disparate elements in communion with God, the angels and the saints.

Alternative possibilities can be seen most clearly in parts of Africa where new religions are rising to power. Some of these began as Pentecostal groups, whose prophets made Messianic claims to supersede or to supplement Christ. Independent African churches of various kinds have been examined by missionaries and religious sociologists from a variety of standpoints, theological and social, who generally agree to distinguish the Pentecostal from the pagan, and both from other groups of Christians who want to identify themselves closely with native African traditions, generally associated in their minds with the Ethiopian Church and Empire, however vague and third hand their information may be or have been about this promised land.[125] The position in Latin America has been less thoroughly studied, but may be simpler. Here the indigenous traditions are pagan and Catholic, uneasily mixed, with the Catholic prevailing everywhere over broken fragments of older

196

cults. Protestant and Pentecostal missionary movements tend to divide between those who set their hope in the renewal of the Catholic Church, especially since Vatican II, and those who want a new religion.

The history of Jehovah's Witnesses and of the Seventh Day Adventists, as well as of some African prophetic movements, shows that a new religion can be Biblical without being Christian. In those parts of Asia and Africa, for instance in Korea, where it is traditional to consult the spirits through a diviner about the auspicious time for any enterprise, for instance for a journey or for a wedding, it is hardly surprising that the inspired Pentecostal Christian should be treated as a new kind of spirit-diviner, and should sometimes act according to expectation. The really surprising thing is that this generally does not happen, and that where Pentecostalism might be expected to develop into a new religion, in so many parts of the world Pentecostal Churches have become seed-beds for renewal among Protestants and Catholics, who go to their local Pentecostal Church, and instead of joining it, go back and find themselves moved in the Spirit to do something of the sort in the Church where they are.

That this should develop into a movement or movements, with some structures, is to be expected, but movements need not become sects. It is important to distinguish the role of organised movements, whether they are interdenominational, like the English Fountain Trust, or based in a particular Church, Catholic, Presbyterian, Lutheran or Methodist, from that of prayer groups or of 'covenant communities' like the one at Ann Arbor. That these should provide bases for services available elsewhere is to be expected. But it would be unfortunate if their role in the movement were too much identified with these. I am glad that Cardinal Suenens should recognise their role as 'pilot projects which are a prefiguration of the kind of human community for which the world is searching so painfully'. [126] That is exactly what I mean by calling them acted prophecies, and I hope he would not disagree with me in extending the term in the wider sense of St Thomas's natural prophecy to other experiments in an alternative way of life that are moved by awareness of needs that our modern scientific and technological civilisation refuses to recognise. What his translator calls 'basic communities' translating *Communauté de base,* includes a variety of projects, Catholic and interconfessional, of which some may develop to integrate those who want to be open to the power of the Holy Spirit but do not as yet confess Christ as Lord.

The most important practical difference between Catholic and Protestant approaches to Pentecostal experience is in attitudes to the natural basis of prophetic insight. In our day this is called extra-sensory perception; it operates without regard to space or time, and often involves precognition. But what makes it a natural basis for prophetic gifts of the Holy Spirit is not this precognitive element, but the remoteness from common knowledge of some of the voices heard, the murmurs from labour camps in the Arctic, from the starving poor in Africa and Asia, the praises of the saints, the laments of the dead. To nearly all Protestants and some Catholics inspiration is either of the Holy Spirit or very perilous. Catholics are aware of the perils of the occult, and especially of explorations undertaken out of desire for new and exciting religious experiences, but as they are aware of angels and saints and accustomed to pray for the departed, they are not so startled by appeals for prayer by'those, alive or dead, who do not know where they are. Being more aware of variety in the world of spirits generally, they are less likely to be negative in their attitude to other religions. Discerning studies of Buddhism have been made by Catholics, the best by an Irish Jesuit, Fr William Johnston, who has worked many years as a missionary priest in Japan, and is himself involved in the Catholic charismatic movement.[127]

Discernment of spirits is more than a matter of discerning truth from error and delusion. It is also a matter of distinguishing between the group's common mind and the illumination of the Spirit when he tells us more than we think and more than the prophetic speaker and those who listen to him can immediately understand. He may speak through decisions as well as through speeches and prayers that are not seen as prophetic at the time. The difficult questions connected with exorcism should be seen in this context. In the discernment of spirits, present and absent, good, bad or indifferent, psychology can combine with the science of the saints in a prophetic work where each illuminates the other. St Augustine and St Teresa saw prophetically what Freud analysed and Jung interpreted in a way that throws light on astrology and alchemy. The calm of a brief circulated by the Congregation for the doctrine of the faith (formerly the Holy Office) on the July 11th, 1975,[128] is in welcome contrast with the alarm of some Anglican academic theologians at the idea that the General Synod of the Church of England might say something about devils. The academics seem to imagine that all concern with the subject is due to a literal reading of the New Testament, but even in this field they ignore completely the opposition of the Sadducees to any idea of an angel or a spirit. This seems to have been based on the same narrow concentration on a canonical text that makes it impossible for biblically-based theologians to take account of phenomena familiar to all religious traditions and to most doctors and psychiatrists who have anything at all to do with mental illness. Their protests against demonology should really be directed against scientific institutions, [129] rather than against prayer groups who occasionally encounter demonic activity.

I write as one whose involvement with group prayer began while I belonged to an Anglican religious community and continued in communion with Rome. This was rather the occasion than the cause of my change of allegiance, but it has given me an opportunity to observe differences between faculties of theology in Catholic universities in America and Rome, the seed-beds of Catholic Pentecostalism, and the theological schools of the English universities. Both use much the same methods of historical criticism, but Catholics are less obsessed with insoluble problems about the original meaning of the New Testament. In this they have more in common with conservative Evangelicals emerging from fundamentalism, who have never completely lost interest in the spiritual interpretation of Scripture, than with academic theologians for whom theology has become a specialised branch of historical study, concerned with the Bible and the primitive Church. They are therefore free to pay theological attention to what is happening today, not only in charismatic movements and in the renewed dialogue between Catholics and Protestants begun by Barth, but in the dialogue of religions. They may use contemporary experience of prophecy and tongues in the critical interpretation of the New Testament, but they are no longer obsessed with historical origins as Catholics were at the beginning of the century, and most Anglicans still are.

I see what is actually happening in terms of interpenetration, not only between Christian confessions but also, now as always, between the Church and a diversity of cultures, all having religious aspects. Fr Johnston in *Christian Zen* speaks of his own 'baptism of the Spirit' in a Catholic Pentecostal group as 'a great event'. It gave me some idea of what the early Christians must have experienced. It gave me some inkling of what *satori* must be like.[130] *Satori* is the word used in Japanese Zen Buddhism for 'enlightenment', 'becoming a new man'. That Fr Johnston should associate this 'experience of the unity of all things and the loss of self'[131] with the conversion to single-mindedness that can come to those who wait together for the Spirit, inside and outside the Church, seems to me prophetic. The danger of those who prefer to speak of 'the Catholic charismatic movement',[132] and to play down their debt to classical Pentecostalism, is that they may fall into the sectarian error they seek to avoid. As St Thomas wrote, citing Bede, with direct reference to 'false prophets', 'There is no false doctrine which does not at times mingle truth with falsehood'.[133] It is in the Catholic tradition to learn from heresies and other religions, by prayer and labour to discern truth from error. It is sectarian to make our own corner in charismatic gifts and powers, and to claim to possess the only true interpretation of Scripture. It is the office of the Church to interpret this from age to age in ways that are more diverse than those of any group of scholars, theologians or charismatics.

[1] The *Upanishads* are commentaries on the *Vedas,* corresponding in the Hindu tradition to the Scriptures in Israel and Christendom, but much later poetry is also given the same kind of spiritual interpretation in India as in the West, where Hellenistic and medieval writers interpreted the Greek and Latin classics allegorically, and wrote poetry demanding the same kind of interpretation.

[2] 1:2, 2:15, 17, 23.

[3] See *New Covenant,* 4, no. 8, PO Box 102, Ann Arbor, Michigan 48107, Feb, 1975.

[4] See J. Daniélou, *Origen,* E. T., London 1955, p. 79, citing Fr Prat: 'The literal meaning is not what we understand by the term literal; it is what we call the proper meaning' (*le sens propre* in the original French). 'In Scripture the literal meaning is often figurative'.

[5] The 'Magdeburg Centuriators' published their materials at Basle in 1550-74, to which Baronius replied in his *Annales* in 1588-1607.

[6] Tillemont, Noel Alexander, Dupin and Fleury all published their works on church history between 1676 and 1725.

[7] This trouble came to a head in controversy over the *Syllabus of Errors* issued by Pope Pius IX in September 1864, which included some statements of historical fact, no doubt in slanted forms.

[8] Dollinger, the Professor of Church history at Munich. He was excommunicated, but never actually joined the Old Catholic schism, although he gave advice to those involved.

[9] 1st edition 1886-9, E.T. from 2nd ed. 1893, Edinburgh 1894-9.

[10] His lectures on *What is Christianity?* (1899) are remembered as a summary of Liberal Protestantism, but still important as a picture of the historical Jesus as he appeared to those who did not believe.

[11] Of Ancyra. He agreed with Paul of Samosata, Harnack's hero, that the Word of God of one substance with the Father is not a distinct divine person, and that the centre of Christ's personality is human. He came to Rome with St Athanasius and signed the old Roman creed. He was therefore accepted as orthodox in the West, at least for a time, but not in the East, where St Athanasius was suspected of sharing his heresy.

[12] See F. E. Vokes, *The Riddle of the Didache,* London 1938.

[13] See his *Sources of the Apostolic Canons,* E. T. London, 1895.

[14] Especially in chapters 10 and 13.

[15] And rather more unwilling at the time to allow the possibility of presbyterian ordination at Alexandria and elsewhere. See P. Batiffol, *Etudes d'histoire et de théologie positive* (1902), 7th ed., Paris 1926, pp. 267-80, an excursus added to the later editions, criticising Bishop Gore.

[16] Paris, p. 193.

[17] *op. cit.,* p. 263.

[18] The date of this is in dispute, and so is the date of Pius, but it is evidence of some relationship between the prophet and the Pope.

[19] See A. C. Sundberg, *The Old Testament of the Early Church, Harvard Theological Studies* XX, Cambridge (Mass.) 1964, and 'Towards a revised history of the New Testament Canon', in *Studia Evangelica* IV, ed. F. L. Cross, Berlin 1968, pp. 452-61, a contribution to the Oxford Conference on New Testament Studies in 1965. Sundberg, an American Lutheran, argues that in the early Church 'Scripture' and 'It is written' need not refer to a canon, but to a larger collection, and that the Muratorian fragment belongs to the 4th century. If so there is no evidence of a canon of the New Testament before this. My knowledge of these and of a further paper of his on 'The Biblical canon and the Christian doctrine of inspiration', I owe to Fr Robert Murray, S. J.

[20] In his *Ecclesiastical History* III, 25:4, on the canon, V, 16-9 on Montanism.

[21] See K. Burridge, *New heaven, new earth,* Oxford 1969.

[22] But his writings were preserved by churchmen, especially St Cyprian in the next generation, who according to his secretary, read him every day (quoted by St Jerome in *De viris illustribus* liii, P.L. 23, c. 698. His influence on Western theology may have been exaggerated, but the idea of an 'excessive reaction' against Montanism is an excess.

[23] The Greek is in Harnack,*Sources of the Apostolic Canons.* Ethiopic, Coptic, and Arabic versions, with English translations, are in G. Horner, *The Statutes of the Apostles or Canones Ecclesiastici,* Cambridge 1904, Syriac and English, ed., J. P. Arendzen, in *Journal of theological studies* iii (1901).

[24] *Sources of the Apostolic Canons,* pp. 19-20.

[25] Coptic in Horner, op cit., p. 304, Syriac in J.T.S. iii, pp. 70-1, Latin in *Didascaliae Apostolorum fragmenta Veronensis Latina,* ed. E. Hauler, Leipzig 1900, pp. 95-7.

[26] Horner, *op. cit.,* p. 242.

[27] *Ibid,* p. 136.

[28] *Acts* 5:2, *1 Timothy* 5:16.

[29] See the evidence collected by myself in an essay in *Part-time Priests?,* ed. Robin Denniston, London, 1969, pp. 29-32.

[30] Ed. T. E. Rahmani, Mainz 1899, pp. 27, 83, 163-5, ed. J. Cooper and A. J. MacLean, Edinburgh 1902, pp. 64, 70, 105-8.

[31] P.G. 46, c. 959-99.

[32] P.G. 26, c. 844.

[33] See J. Labourt in *Le Christianisme dans l'empire Perse,* Paris 1904, pp. 28-31.

[34] See F. C. Burkitt, *Early Eastern Christianity,* Cambridge 1904, criticised by Dom R. H. Connolly in J.T.S. vi (1905) pp. 522-9 and viii (1907), pp. 41-5. Contributions to the debate have since been made by the Estonian scholar A. Voobus and by Robert Murray, S.J., in *Symbols of Church and Kingdom,* Cambridge 1975, pp. 11-8.

[35] *Vision* i and passim.

[36] I Corinthians 9:5.

[37] ibid, 4:7, 7:25-34. 9:5.

[38] See M. Wiles, *Making of Christian Doctrine,* Cambridge 1967, pp. 41-61.

[39] See H. Chadwick on 'Eucharist and Christology' in J.T.S. ii (n.s. 1951), pp. 146-64.

[40] M. Wiles op. cit., pp. 84-5 and refs.

[41] *1 Corinthians* 15:29 must refer to some kind of prayer for the dead.

[42] See John Meyendorff, *Byzantine Theology,* New York 1974, p. 96.

[43] See Geoffrey Rowell, *Hell and the Victorians,* Oxford 1974.

[44] *The Passion of St Perpetua* was edited by C.J.M.J. Van Beek, Nijmegen 1936, where the passage (also in P.L. 3, c. 34-9) is on pp. 20-23.

[45] See *The Mystical Element of Religion* by Baron F. von Hügel, London 1908.

[46] Ed. F. Halkin in *Analecta Bollandiana* 77, Brussels 1959, pp. 323-7.

[47] *Eccles. Hist.* III, c. 19.

[48] ibid V. c. 12.

[49] D.T.C. xiii (Paris 1936), c. 1227, 1242-3.

[50] ibid, c. 1225, e.g. the story of the deacon Paschasius whose soul was seen in hot water by Bishop Germanus of Capua in P. L. 77, c. 397-8.

[51] *Treatise on Purgatory,* chapters 1 and 2.

[52] Meyendorff, op. cit., p. 112.

[53] Bishop Forbes of Brechin in his *Explanation of the 39 Articles* (p. 352 in ed. 1881) written in 1867-8 in collaboration with Pusey.

[54] *Dictionnaire d'histoire et de géographie eccles.* xiii (Paris 1949), c. 1513.

[55] Q. xii in vol. iii, Rome 1898, vol ii of E. T. Chicago 1953.

[56] Oxford 1969.

[57] ibid, pp. 6-15, 19-25.

[58] ibid, pp. 56-61, 175-86.

[59] See articles by M Reeves in *Sophia* xix 4 (Padua 1951), in *Medieval and*

Renaissance Studies iii, Warbury Institute, London 1954, and (with Morton W. Blomfield) in *Speculum* xxix (Cambridge, Mass. 1954). I found these together in Dr Williams' Library.

[60] Cited by H. de Lubac in *Exégèse Médiévale* II ii, Paris 1963, pp. 335-6. The text under the title, *De Periculis Ecclesiae* is in *Appendix ad Fasciculum rerum expetendarum et fugiendarum,* ed. E. Brown, London 1690, pp. 18-41.

[61] See H. Rashdall, *Universities of Europe in the Middle Ages,* Oxford ed. 1936, pp. 381-96.

[62] See his *Opus maius,* ed. R. B. Burke, New York 1962, pp. 382, 415 and in *Opera inedita* (Rolls series) ed. J. S. Brewer, London 1859, *Opus tertium* xxiv, p. 86. *Compendium Philosophiae,* p. 402. For his sources of information see Christopher Dawson, *The Mongol Mission,*London, 1955, p. xiv.

[63] Joachim's work, which is the subject of St Thomas Aquinas's *Opusculum* xxiv, is lost, but he probably made the same criticisms that were made with more discretion by Richard of St Victor in his *De Trinitate,* P. L. 196, c. 987.

[64] In William of Tocco's life, c. iv, in *Acts Sanctorum,* March 7. Opinions of his on Joachim are in his commentary on the *Sentences* IV, *dist.* xliii, q. 1, *art,* 3, where he is named as one who predicted some truths about the future, but in some was deceived, and in S. T. I i, q. 106, *art.* 4,, where his views on the *Apocalypse of St John* are contraverted, but he is not named.

[65] *1 Corinthians* 12:10, *De Veritate,* q. xii, *art.* 3.

[66] V. White, *art. cit.,* p. 13.

[67] Q. xii, *art.* 1.

[68] ibid, *art.* 3.

[69] II ii, q. 172, art 4.

[70] *Visions and Prophecies,* E.T. London, 1963, p. 17.

[71] Q. xii, *art.*3..

[72] ibid.

[73] Q. xii, *art.* 9.

[74] William of Tocco, *op. cit.,* c, vii.

[75] Q. xii, art. 9.

[76] *ibid,* art. 12.

[77] ibid, *art.* 9.

[78] S.T. II ii, q. 173, art. 4. See Paul Synave and Pierre Benoit, *Prophecy and Inspiration,* E.T., New York 1961, pp. 72-4 on prophecy in the S.T.

[79] V. White, *art. cit.,* p. 19.

[80] *Epistolae* x, 7, ed. Paget Toynbee, Oxford 1920, pp. 172-3. The genuineness of this is sometimes denied, but it reflects a contemporary view of Dante's poetry.

[81] So Etienne Gilson argues in *Dante the Philosopher,* E.T., London 1948, especially on pp. 251, 263-4, that Siger represents not a person, but a principle. He does not extend this to Joachim, whose presence in Paradise he explains by Dante's approval of some of the prophecies ascribed to him, but he does make the parallel, which is neater if Joachim is prophecy, Siger philosophy, Virgil poetry.

[82] *Paradiso* xxxiii, 86-90.

[83] V. White, *art. cit.,* p. 34.

[83] *Paradiso* xxxiii, 121.

[85] See Keith Thomas, *Religion and the Decline of Magic*, London, 1971, pp. 293-300.

[86] *The Book of Margery Kemp* was edited by W. Butler Bowden in 1936, and is now in the *World's Classics* series.

[87] D. H. G. E. ix (1937), c. 722-8.

[88] As Dr Morton Kelsey does in *Encounter with God*, British ed., London 1972, p. 65.

[98] See especially his *Psychotherapy*, London 1954, pp. 163-321.

[90] Coleridge developed this distinction in *Biographia Literaria* (1817) and *Aids to Reflection* (1825) out of Kant's between speculative and practical reason, but it had other roots in his own distinction between fancy and imagination. Coleridge's reason is more than conscience and near to natural reason and natural prophecy in St Thomas (and his own hero, Hooker).

[91] This misunderstanding in England and America is rooted in the reading of Aristotle after Locke and in his light, but it also colours much scholastic reading of St Thomas in the dark ages of scholasticism after the Enlightenment.

[92] Shakespeare, *Merchant of Venice*, Acts, 5, scene 1.

[93] In controversies on grace in all the confessions between 1584 and 1616.

[94] Devotion to the Sacred Heart began in the circle of St Francis de Sales, but was preached by two of Oliver Cromwell's chaplains, Thomas Godwin and Peter Sterry, before the visions of St Marie Alacoque.

[95] See Morton T. Kelsey, *Tongue Speaking*, Eng. ed., London 1973, pp. 52-5.

[96] For the medieval roots of this see S. T. I i, q. 1, *art.* 8 and 10.

[97] The Dionysian writings declined in prestige when it was discovered that their author was not Dionysius the Areopagite, the companion of St Paul.

[98] See my own *High Church Party, 1688-1718*, London 1956, pp. 136, 169.

[99] See Alexander Dru's introduction to Maurice Blondel, *Letter on Apologetic and History of Dogma*, E.T., London, 1964, pp. 22-4, on Bossuet's influence.

[100] See F. E. Manuel, *The Religion of Isaac Newton*, Oxford 1974.

[101] *Ibid*, p. 101.

[102] That the eclipse was not total appears in a voluminous book on the conditions of canonisation, *De Beatificatione Servorum Dei et de Canonizatione Beatorum* by Prospero Lambertini (1675-1758) who wrote it after 19 years of experience as *promotor fidei* ('the devil's advocate') from 1708-1727, and after it was written was elected Pope Benedict XIV in 1740. In *Lib.* iii he has chapters on prophecy (45-7), and on visions and revelation (50-53). These are 6-8, 11-4, in an abridged English edition, *Heroic Virtue*, London 1850-2, vol. ii, pp. 135-211, 283-408. He does not speak of 'natural prophecy' in his own person, preferring to say 'prophetic insight' which may be wrong (c. 45:6). He does quote with approval an Italian mss by Fr Nicholas Baldelli (1573-1655) who used the term. From St Thomas he cites the S.T., but not the *De Prophetia* which I am sure he had read. In his chapter on revelations (53:2) he says 'those are natural which result from natural causes, from abundance of bile, from bodily weakness, from ... a turbid and over vehement imagination', and cites authorities of his own time or shortly before. Renée Haynes has discussed his book at length in her biography of him, *Philosopher King*, London 1970, and briefly in *The Christian Parapsychologist*,

vol. 1, no. 2, Dec. 1975, where she calls him 'the father of Christian psychical research', He had to deal with the problem of paranormal happenings which in the Middle Ages were regarded as ordinary, and his citations throw much light on the transition to the 'age of reason'.

[103] See *De Verbo Dei* II, c. 1 and IV, c. 4 on Ezra's editing of the O.T.

[104] See Paul Hazard, *The European Mind* 1680-1715, London 1953, pp. 203-16.

[105] In tract 89 of *Tracts for the Times*, London, and Oxford 1841.

[106] Under *Ezra* 7 v. 6, in ed. Cologne 1482, Venice 1495 and other early editions, but not in P. L. 113, from Bede on Ezra in P. L. 91, c. 859. Earlier references to Ezra's editing are in St Irenaeus, P. G. 7, c. 848-9, and Clement of Alexandria, P. G. 8, c. 893. These could refer to an account of his inspiration in *II (IV) Esdras*, c. 14. But St Hilary in P. L 9, c. 238, St John Chrysostom in P. G. 63, c. 74, and St Isidore in P. L. 82, c. 235-6, must refer to intelligent editing from remains. I owe these and other references to Bellarmine.

[107] So R.R. Bolgar *The Classical Heritage and its beneficiaries*, Cambridge 1954, p. 422, in a long note on pp. 217-9.

[108] The wisdom of Solomon described in *1Kings* 4,:32-3 is of this sort.

[109] So Bishop R. P. C. Hanson in *The Attractiveness of God*, London 1973, pp. 10-1.

[110] Bishop Hanson allows this in Origen's *Doctrine of Tradition*, London 1954, pp. 146-8.

[111] *The Pentateuch . . . critically examined*, 2nd ed., London 1862, p. 40.

[112] A doctrine of inerrancy arises when critics say that the Bible lies.

[113] Recognition of this by Pius XII in *Divino afflante Spiritu* (1943), especially in the section *De generibus litterariis in s. Scriptura* (Denzinger-Schonmetzer, *Enchiridion* 3829-30) is called by Hanson in *Attractiveness* 'tortuous, . . . complicated and . . . implausible', but it seems to me in harmony with the traditional evidence summarised by the same author on pp. 37-8 of the same work.

[114] The Jewish tradition as reported in *St Matthew*, 28:11-5, was that the body was stolen. But 27:51, 28:2, *St Mark* 15:38, *St Luke* 23:45, seem to refer to a series of seismic disturbances of which traces found in the 4th century, when the site had been covered for 200 years, are still preserved. Tombs under the Syrian chapel next to the Holy Sepulchre point to the existence of a cemetery closed to discourage pilgrimage or speculation.

[115] *Good News Crusade*, 32a Fore Street, St Austell Cornwall 1974, pp. 44-5.

[116] See Aaron Linford, *Spiritual Gifts*, Nottingham n.d., pp. 21-5. for a classical Pentecostalist comment on this.

[117] *Ezekiel* 3:3, *Acts* 21:11.

[118] Robert of Molesme, the founder of the original monastery of Citeaux, was ordered back to his monastery by his bishop, and told to take the office book with him. His disciples had few or no postulants for some years.

[119] Interesting accounts of beginnings are in *As the Spirit leads us*, ed. Kevin and Dorothy Ranaghan, New York 1971, pp. 179-83 (by Bert Ghezzi) and in *New Covenant* for Feb. 1975. The latest intelligence is that the Protestant proportion is increasing, despite changes of allegiance, generally by

Protestants.

[120] See *Gathered for Power,* by W. Graham Pulkingham, London 1972, The author, founder of the community, is now Provost of the Episcopalian Cathedral at Cumbrae in the Scottish islands.

[121] Peter van Dresser, quoted by Patrick Rivers, in *The Survivalists,* London 1975, p.141, said in 1973: 'I don't think there is a dichotomy between spiritual and material bases. That is a Christian fallacy that has done so much damage'. The book is a collection of testimonies to experiments in alternative ways of living.

[123] Reported by Cindy Conniff in *New Covenant* for April 1974.

[124] This is defended by Peter Wagner in his chapter, 'Are Pentecostals on a "Social Strike"?', in his book on Pentecostalism in South America, *'Look out! the Pentecostals are coming,* London 1974 pp. 137-48. But Walter Hollenweger in *The Pentecostals,* Eng. ed., London 1972, pp. 457-92, has called attention to difference in social stance among Pentecostal denominations, and there is more about this in the essay on pp. 116-7 by John Orme Mills in this book.

[125] See Hollenweger, *op. cit.,* p. 167, citing extensive literature, and *Pentecost between Black and White,* Belfast 1974, pp. 55-75 on the Kimbanguists.

[126] In *A New Pentecost?,* E.T., London 1975, pp.151-2.

[127] His three books, *The Still Point* (1970), *Christian Zen* (1971) and *Silent Music, the Science of Meditation* (1974) are all outstanding.

[128] *Demonology, the Church's Teaching, Infoform* 5, 21, obtainable from the Catholic Information Office at Pinner in Middlesex.

[129] e.g. the Menninger Foundation at Topeka in Kansas, whose publications are considered at length in William Johnston's *Silent Music.*

[130] P. 101, 130 ibid, p. 97.

[131] The use of this term has been severely criticised by among others, Père Yves Congar, and it cannot be said that the answer of Fr Kilian McDonnell in *The Holy Spirit and Power,* New York 1975, pp. 63-73, is wholly satisfactory, though he takes the objection seriously. Pentecostal was a more satisfactory descriptive term for movements influenced by classical Pentecostalism.

[132] S.T. II ii 1. 172, art. 6 from Bede on *St Luke* 7:2 in P. L. 92, c. 542.